D1263742

Dark Hope

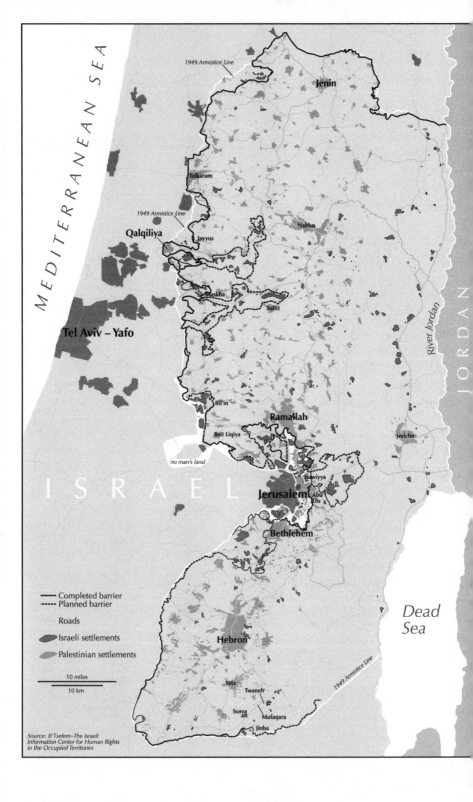

MEDITERRANEAN SEA

1949 Armistice Line

Jenin

Tulkaram

1949 Armistice Line

Qalqiliya

Jayyus

Nablus

Maskha

Salfit

Tel Aviv – Yafo

Bil'in

Ramallah

Beit Liqiya

Jericho

no man's land

I S R A E L

Isawiyya

Jerusalem

Abu Dis

Bethlehem

River Jordan

J O R D A N

Dead Sea

Hebron

Yata

Twaneh

Susya

Mufaqara

Jinba

— Completed barrier
--- Planned barrier

Roads

Israeli settlements

Palestinian settlements

1949 Armistice Line

10 miles
10 km

*Source: B'Tselem–The Israeli
Information Center for Human Rights
in the Occupied Territories*

Dark Hope

Working for Peace in Israel and Palestine

DAVID SHULMAN

The University of Chicago Press ❋ *Chicago and London*

DAVID SHULMAN is the Renée Lang Professor of Humanistic Studies in the Department of Comparative Religion at the Hebrew University of Jerusalem. He is the author or coauthor of many books, including *The Hungry God: Hindu Tales of Filicide and Devotion*, also published by the Press. Originally published as *Ta'ayush: Journal d'un combat pour la paix, Israël Palestine 2002–2005*, © Editions du Seuil, 2006, Collection La Librairie du XXIe siècle, sous la direction de Maurice Olender.

The University of Chicago Press, Chicago 60637
The University of Chicago Press, Ltd., London
© 2007 by The University of Chicago
All rights reserved. Published 2007
Printed in the United States of America
16 15 14 13 12 11 10 09 08 07   1 2 3 4 5
ISBN-13: 978-0-226-75574-8 (cloth)
ISBN-10: 0-226-75574-6 (cloth)

Library of Congress Cataloging-in-Publication Data
Shulman, David.
    Dark Hope: working for peace in Israel and Palestine /
David Shulman.
        p.   cm.
    "Originally published as Ta'ayush: Journal d'un combat
pour la paix, Israël Palestine 2002–2005"—CIP datasheet.
    ISBN-13: 978-0-226-75574-8 (cloth: alk. paper)
    ISBN-10: 0-226-75574-6 (cloth: alk. paper)
    1. Arab-Israeli conflict—1993—Peace.   2. Peace
movements—Israel.   3. Ta'ayush (Organization)—
Political activity.   4. Palestinian Arabs—Government
policy—Israel.   I. Title.
DS119.76.S783   2007
956.9405′4—dc22   2006035630

*For Yigal, Leena, and all the Taʿayushot and Taʿayushim
and in memory of Abbie Ziffren, who would have been with us,
and of Samir Dari, shot by the border police in Isawiyya,
November 9, 2005*

Hell is realizing that one did not help when one could have.
«JAMES MAWDSLEY, *The Heart Must Break*»

Contents

Acknowledgments

I thank Nita Shechet, Adina Hoffman, Peter Cole, Richie Cohen, Shlomit Cohen, Edly Dollar, Gabriel Levin, Yigal Bronner, Charles Malamoud, and Maurice Olender: who brought this book into being.

1

Introduction

I am an Israeli. I live in Jerusalem. I have a story, not yet finished, to tell.

Hence these notes that, however one-sided they may be, speak of my own small slice of the reality in Israel and the occupied territories in the unhappy years 2002–2006. Throughout this period I did as many others did: I went to demonstrations; wrote letters to the minister of defense and the chief prosecutor of the army and the prime minister; went on convoys bringing food and medical supplies to Palestinian villages; was beaten up by settlers— the usual protocol for those active in the Israeli peace camp. I also read newspapers, taught my classes at the university, went to India, listened to music. Life went on as it always does, even in the midst of worsening disaster.

Like the rest of us, I was given a choice, or rather many recurring moments in which choice was possible. I was privileged to serve in the ranks of Taʿayush, Arab-Jewish Partnership, an organization of volunteers set up in the early days of the so-called Al-Aqsa Intifada, in October 2000. As its name implies, Taʿayush (Arabic for "Living together," "Partnership") is a mixed group of Palestinians and Israelis dedicated to the pursuit of peace, to ending the occupation, and to civic equality within Israel proper. Volunteers come from all walks of life and from every corner of

Israel's reality. Most are younger than I (and no doubt more effective). I do not use the word "privilege" lightly; in my eyes, these people tend to be extraordinary. They have emerged, as if from nowhere, out of the terror and cruelty of life in Israel-Palestine during these years. They embody a certain sober hope. Some are mentioned repeatedly by name in the reports that follow.

Many people, it seems, are not aware that an active Israeli peace movement exists. Even in Israel, Ta'ayush and other organizations impinge upon the lives of relatively few Israelis; even those who have heard the names tend to know rather little about what we do. Some Israelis, naturally, hate us. In their eyes, we are aiding and abetting the enemy. The public media sometimes contributes to this distorted vision by creating artificial symmetries: the violent settlers on the extreme right are deliberately paired, especially on the TV news channels, with the so-called extremists of the left. This creates a pleasant sense of balance and positions reporters and editors somewhere safe and comfortable, in the very heart of what they like to describe as "the consensus." In fact, nothing could be more misleading. Most Israeli peace activists— I speak from long experience—are moderate, sensible people who abhor violence of any kind. Perhaps they are extreme in their gentle moderation. They have nothing whatsoever in common with the fanatics among the settlers and the politicians who support them.

Make no mistake: Israel, like any society, has violent, sociopathic elements. What is unusual about the last four decades in Israel is that many destructive individuals have found a haven, complete with ideological legitimation, within the settlement enterprise. Here, in places like Chavat Maon, Itamar, Tapuach, and Hebron, they have, in effect, unfettered freedom to terrorize the local Palestinian population; to attack, shoot, injure, sometimes kill—all in the name of the alleged sanctity of the land and of the Jews' exclusive right to it.

There is a mystery, a historical conundrum, embedded in the fact that Israel, once a home to utopian idealists and humanists, should have engendered and given free rein to a murderous, also ultimately suicidal, messianism. Did our deepest values, the humane heart of the Jewish tradition, always contain with them these seeds of self-righteous terror? Do these two modes inevitably intersect? If I look deeply into myself, I can identify—side by side with hope, faith, and a certain embryonic capacity for empathy—the same dark forces that are active among the most predatory of the settlers. I, too, am capable of hate and of polarizing the world. Perhaps the balance, individual or collective, is always precarious. Here is a reason to act.

In the absence of other recourse, Ta'ayush and many like-minded organizations—Gush Shalom, Bat Shalom, Machsom Watch, HaMoked, B'Tselem, the Rabbis for Human Rights, the Israeli Committee Against House Demolitions, Yesh Gvul, and many others—have tried to step into the gap, to both protect innocent Palestinian populations and keep the hope of peace alive in the Israeli public arena. This book aims at showing something of the Israeli peace movement in action, on the basis of one individual's very limited experience, in the hope of reaching out both to other Israelis and to wider circles within the international community. It is not a history of the search for peace in Israel-Palestine nor a systematic description of our work during the Al-Aqsa Intifada. Someday, I am sure, a historian will tell the larger story. That is not my task. I want to give you some sense of what it feels like to be a part of this struggle and of why we do it. I hope my grandchildren will be proud of me. More important, I hope and believe that we can still effect a real change.

>>><<<

I suppose I should tell you something, at least, of my idiosyncratic history and my politics; perhaps I can string together a story about my slow and rather reluctant move toward political involvement. It was not really part of my makeup. I write poetry, teach Sanskrit at university, read texts in various other exotic languages; in general, I need large open spaces and plentiful time to think. I'm a slow reader. I have a family—my wife, Eileen, three grown sons, and two grandsons. Political work takes time (ask Eileen).

It also tends to force one into open conflict with a recalcitrant, opaque, and ambiguous reality that, at best, as Rilke said, "coolly disdains to destroy us."

Politics, in short, is not my métier. So for many years I, like many of my colleagues, went into a kind of internal exile, becoming more and more alienated from wider Israeli society. The rise of the Israeli right, from 1977 on, shocked me, infuriated me, and undermined my faith in the world I lived in. A raucous, viciously self-righteous tone came to dominate public life; Menachem Begin was its first prophet or, better, demagogue. His actions followed his words—in this sense, Begin was an honest man. The results, in my view, were catastrophic; I watched in horror as Israel rapidly transformed itself into a paranoid, smug, and rather violent ghetto. But let me go back to the beginning.

I was not born here. Like my parents before me, I was born in the tranquil flatlands of Iowa, a land of cornfields and the vast, open sky. My grandparents came to America before the First World War, from small towns in the Ukraine and Belarus. My father was a doctor and the most decent human being I have known—one of those doctors who can truly heal, a man of elemental honesty and moderation. I came to Israel in 1967, aged eighteen, mostly because I had fallen in love with the Hebrew language. At the Hebrew University, I studied Arabic and Islam but eventually drifted eastwards into Indian studies. My real passion is for classical Hindustani music. I was trained as a combat medic in the Israeli army and went to war in Lebanon in 1982 in a medical unit attached to a tank brigade. I was against that war, convinced that it was at best an arrogant folly, at worst a crime. I saw men die.

Still, it was only in the late 1980s that I first became truly active, at the time of the first Intifada. (I don't count the ten years before that of standing in demonstrations, listening to speeches, feeling foolish.) It wasn't really a conscious decision. I have seen how, at times, a seemingly trivial event can trigger a powerful response, can galvanize a person into action. More often, however, the process is slow, cumulative, and uneven, as it was for me. When I

returned from sabbatical in 1988, a grassroots dialogue group—
one of the first of many—was forming among friends of mine
in West Jerusalem and Palestinian activists from the village of
Beit Sahour, near Bethlehem. Although the political situation
was dreadful, in terms relative to that period—much worse was,
as we now know, in store—those were also heady times. A new
landscape was rapidly emerging. To go to Beit Sahour, sometimes circumventing the army roadblocks, to speak candidly with
Palestinian friends, to begin to internalize something of their vision, to imagine, with them, the contours of peace, an available,
attainable peace—all this was exhilarating. Among others, I met
Ghassan Andoni, a physicist fresh from Israeli prison, formerly
linked with the Popular Front, now fully committed to a peaceful
solution.

I went often to Beit Sahour, and our Palestinian friends also
came to meet us in our houses in the southern quarters of
Jerusalem. Not all our experiences were positive. I remember,
for example, one Sunday gathering in the church—Beit Sahour
is mostly Christian—when my close friend Yaron Ezrahi made
a passionate speech about human freedom, citing Jean-Jacques
Rousseau and other Western icons. As he spoke, a growing chorus from the back rows nearly overpowered his voice: "In blood
and fire / we will liberate Palestine." The elders of the village tried,
mostly unsuccessfully, to hush these younger hotheads. We took
the point.

The dialogue sessions, though intoxicating in their own way,
soon came to feel insufficient. I tired of the endless words. I
wanted to do something more tangible: the reports of terrible
suffering, of brutal treatment of innocent Palestinians by soldiers
in the territories, were driving me mad. So I began to volunteer, one day a week, in the East Jerusalem offices of HaMoked:
Center for the Defence of the Individual, a private organization founded by Lote Salzberger and Yossi Schwartz in response
to the worsening situation. HaMoked offered practical help to
the Palestinian distressed: legal recourse for civilians who had
been mistreated by the army or the authorities, civil rights work

of many kinds, and help for families whose sons or fathers or brothers had been arrested and disappeared, sometimes for many days, into army jails and detention camps. My most vivid memories are of Palestinian mothers who would sit before me in their flowing black dresses, their eyes filling and refilling with tears, as I telephoned the jails, one by one, trying to locate a lost son—usually, I might add, successfully, though often the task was long, frustrating, and exhausting.

I used to think of HaMoked as one of a series of Israeli organizations that, together, were weaving a fine gossamer web around a raging tiger—the Shamir government in its various public guises and institutional mechanisms. We could never actually stop the tiger or change its nature, but occasionally we could hold it back briefly, perhaps only for a second, just long enough to alleviate someone's personal pain or to produce a slight respite. These were also the years in which B'Tselem, the Israeli Information Center for Human Rights in the Occupied Territories (founded 1989), came into its own. Often HaMoked and B'Tselem worked together in cases of gross violation of human rights. Along with a dedicated core of lawyers and activists, who were achieving more and more international attention, such groups did come to constitute a subtle restraint upon the government and the Civil Administration in the territories. A few years later, Yitzhak Rabin paid a backhanded compliment to the human rights' organizations when he explained why he expected the PLO, newly restored to Palestine under the Oslo Accords, to be effective in imposing its will on the inhabitants of the territories: "They can rule without Bagatz [the Israeli Supreme Court] and without B'Tselem."

The first Intifada ended, but the gross abuse of human rights in the territories continued apace, as did the cruel Israeli settlement enterprise, right through the Oslo years. Nonetheless, with the Oslo process, a certain optimism began to filter down to the Israeli peace organizations. Contacts with the Palestinians were now intense and wide-ranging; gone were the days of the first tentative probings, as in Beit Sahour. Some of us came to feel that, fundamentally, we were "winning" the struggle for peace. First, the question of the partner had been resolved: Israel clearly had to come to terms with the Palestinian national movement (remember that in the '70s Golda Meir, speaking for many Israelis, had denied the very existence of the Palestinians as a living collective entity). Second, the principle of partitioning the land was, it seemed, becoming almost universally accepted; the mad dream of a "greater Israel" in the whole of Palestine was relegated to the margins of Israeli society. Or so we hoped. What remained at issue was the question of precisely where the border would run. I, for one, did not foresee the day when the two sides would be fighting ruthlessly over every olive tree.

This introduction should suffice. You can see where my sympathies lie. I believe that Israel's occupation of Palestinian territory is unacceptable, illegal, and ultimately self-destructive. Yet I am not one of those who think that what has happened here is entirely our fault. The "other side," as it is called, is also staggering under a burden of folly and crime. Neither side has a monopoly on right or, for that matter, wrong. There is much harshness and suffering everywhere. By temperament and belief, I am a moderate, committed to a notion, or perhaps a fantasy, of basic decency. I can even remember feeling patriotic (occasionally), though in general modern nationalism of all sorts seems ugly to me. I don't much like the idea of killing other human beings so you can have your own postage stamps. I am against killing altogether, but I am not a pacifist across the board. I recognize that sometimes one has to fight.

There is, however, a particular perception at the heart of my assessment of our situation that has moved me to act. No one can understand what has happened here unless he or she sees how Palestinian terrorism is systematically exploited by the Israeli right to further its own far-reaching, brutal program. In this sense, the Palestinians themselves have supplied the Israeli hyper-nationalists with everything they could ever want or need. The threat of terrorism is a fact that cannot be denied. However, its exploitation and cynical manipulation to further a policy of land-grab, domination, and the creation of an inhuman regime in the occupied territories—all this, which is of our own doing, must be clearly seen. It is, in many ways, a key to the current impasse.

And there is something more, a rather simple principle. Crime has its own deadly integrity. A second crime will not balance or redress the first. Violent resistance by some Palestinians to the Jews' presence in this land goes back to the very beginning, if there was a beginning, as does the Israeli illusion that sheer violent coercion is an adequate—indeed the only adequate—answer. I am not interested in who "started" the fight. I want to end it. I care about human lives, none worth more than any other. By the same token, each act of cruelty is entirely and irreducibly singular in conception and execution. The victim is always one or more irreplaceable human beings. Ethnic conflict habitually sets up a false equation, as if violence or wrongdoing on *our* part were somehow commensurate with an alleged cause or, more often, excuse supplied by the enemy. In reality, no such commensurability is ever possible. Nothing done by one side, however terrible, can mitigate or rationalize the crimes of the other. What Israel has done and is doing, on a large scale, to civilian Palestinian populations in the territories, in Jinba, Yanun, Bil'in, and dozens of other places, is *singularly* cruel.

Our failure to acknowledge this truth, our passionate delight in—indeed continuous reinvention of—our victimhood, our persistent tendency to blame the other, our enduring fearfulness and moral cowardice, our betrayal of our own once-cherished values and of our wider humanity—all these are symptoms of a pervasive cultural illness that serves to perpetuate and deepen the war. This illness has its natural, inverted counterpart among many who live in Ramallah, Gaza, and Jenin.

But perhaps "illness" is the wrong word. I believe that the set of features just outlined constitutes a clear collective choice.

We should also bear in mind the vast disparity in power between the two sides. Israel has the potential to change reality, to make peace. Were she genuinely to want to do this, and were her

American backer and banker to want it, Israel could, I am certain, create the conditions for breakthrough. Anyone who knows the Palestinian reality, in all its complexity, on the ground knows the powerful forces there that are ready and eager to move toward peace. I am not claiming that they are the only forces in the field; I have seen something of the others as well, and I am not given to underestimating them. In this matter of the partner—for peace or war—Israel, again, has a choice. She can attempt to move toward an agreement with those Palestinian actors who are committed to a peaceful solution and capable of effecting it (not least among them, senior figures among Palestinian prisoners currently held in Israeli jails); or she can continue to humiliate and undermine such people and thus hasten the outbreak of the next round of bloodshed, which is likely to be worse than the last one. But it is perhaps too much to hope that a community, a modern state—or, for that matter, even an isolated individual—can admit to being wrong.

Beyond this, I have no special wisdom or vision, only a profound feeling that the conflict raging in this tormented country is not a zero-sum game in which only one side can win. The transparent truth is that either both sides win or both sides lose. Most people here probably recognize this on some level. Meanwhile, innocents are dying. Anyway, for what it is worth, I support a negotiated two-state solution, with Israel's permanent borders established more or less along the pre-1967 Green Line, with suitable security arrangements for both parties, and so on. In this, I apparently belong with the overwhelming majority of people on both sides of the conflict. Whether our leaders want this solution is another matter.

Someday the conflict will be resolved, but for now there is much to be done. Daily reality is mostly unbearable. I could bear it no longer, sitting in my study. I feel responsible for the atrocities committed in my name, by the Israeli half of the story. Let the Palestinians take responsibility for those committed in their name. On our side, there is the ongoing story of the settlements, established on plundered land with the apparent aim of making any eventual compromise impossible. And along with that kind of violence, which has wrought havoc throughout the territories—so that we are now facing something like a crazed, predatory state of armed settlers and soldiers across the Green Line in the territories occupied by Israel—along with such violence, there is the equally unacceptable violence of heart and mind, the self-righteous narrowness and egoism of the modern nationalist. In Israel, it is this strident voice that is more and more heard.

A last word to the reader: Many of the following entries were written in anger. I cannot apologize for this anger; I believe that if you were to come with me to Jinba or Nu'aman or Bil'in or Salfit, were you to see what happens daily in such places, you, too, would feel enraged. Perhaps the words I have chosen will seem, at times, excessive. Human suffering is, in itself, mostly excessive—and it is all the worse when it derives from indifference, cowardice, or outright malice. I am profoundly aware of the immense suffering on the Israeli side as well; I, too, lived through these years of terror in fear and strain. There were several terrorist explosions not far from my home. A good friend of mine was killed by a bomb while riding home on the bus. I cannot forgive such evil. Nothing could justify any of it. But that is not the story I want to tell here.

>>><<<

Note: Ta'ayush came into being in the autumn of 2000, during the first weeks of the Al-Aqsa Intifada. In November 2000, activists from Tel Aviv and from Kafr Qasem paid a solidarity visit to the Arab town of Umm al-Fahem in the wake of the October riots and the violent response of army and police forces. What was needed at this point? Surely more than yet another manifesto or futile demonstration. Someone brought up the idea of sending food convoys into the occupied territories—direct, concrete, nonviolent action in a situation of severe crisis. That was the beginning. Soon there were branches of volunteers, Israelis and Palestinians together, in Tel Aviv, Jerusalem, and the north. Throughout that autumn and winter, Ta'ayush organized convoys bringing food and medical supplies to Palestinian villages under siege at various points in the occupied territories. The army and police found it difficult to turn back these humanitarian missions. Close ties were forged between Ta'ayush and Palestinian grassroots organizations in places such as Hawara, Salfit, Bethlehem, and Nablus. Soon the missions ramified and diversified, in ways documented in the following pages. Positive action within Israel, aimed at overcoming discrimination against Arab citizens and decades of neglect in building the infrastructure of many Arab communities, became a central part of the Ta'ayush vision.

Ta'ayush is not affiliated with any political party or organization. There is no formal process for joining and no declared ideological program. One becomes part of the movement by taking part in its activities and becoming involved in the process of decision. Activists—female and male, young and old, Israeli and Palestinian—come from all walks of life and hold diverse views and opinions, though all abhor the Israeli occupation of Palestinian territories and believe in the urgency, and the possibility, of reaching a peaceful solution. We follow the classical tradition of civil disobedience, in the footsteps of Gandhi, Thoreau, and Martin Luther King. From the beginning there has been a consistent emphasis on action, in real time, on the ground. The goal: to construct a true Arab-Jewish partnership. "A future of equality, justice, and peace begins today, between us, through concrete, daily actions of solidarity to end the Israeli occupation of the Palestinian territories and to achieve full civil equality for all Israeli citizens."

2

Jinba, Twaneh,
the South Hebron Hills

Political activism, in general, is riddled with the ambiguous. Hence the fanaticism that sometimes characterizes die-hard activists. It is not so easy to contain the nagging sense that dependably arises from this kind of work, that we are reducing complexity to some kind of manageable, operative slice of reality; that our ideas and plans impinge, at best, rather obliquely on that reality; and that tremendous displacements and surreal reconfigurations are taking place at every moment. Everyone brings his or her own world to politics, and we inevitably project our own cosmology onto the shadowy externalities with which we are engaged. Some choices are unconscious. We all have a tendency to polarize, making our declared opponents the embodiment of dark forces and our chosen friends the messengers of light. Sometimes we may end up doing more harm than good. We read the world as best we can, and we are often wrong.

Occasionally, however, things can be remarkably straightforward. Such is the case in Jinba and Twaneh and the dozens of other small *khirbehs* in the hills south of Hebron, where a population of several thousand Palestinian herders and farmers lives, for the most part, in natural rock caves. They have been there at least since the 1830s. The region is dry and stony, and agriculture is possible only in relatively restricted patches spread over the hills; nonetheless, the cave dwellers grow annual crops of wheat and barley—when they are not prevented from reaching their fields by Israeli settlers.

There are several hard-core settlements in this area—Susya, Maon, Carmel, and others—along with a satellite population of even more predatory, mostly younger fanatics living in sites such as Chavat Maon, Chavat David, and other illegal (or perhaps one should say, more illegal) "outposts." These settlements have all been established on Palestinian land, which the government declared to be "*miri,*" or state lands—a term taken from the Ottoman land-tenure system and cynically appropriated by Israel in order to rationalize the settlement enterprise. Aerial photographs from the early 1980s clearly show the areas that were subsequently taken over to build the settlements still under Palestinian cultivation.[*]

There are also military camps in the region, and the army has been trying to get large parts of the area declared out of bounds for the alleged purpose of creating firing ranges. So far the Israeli courts have not allowed this. But there is no doubt whatsoever that Israeli governments, from both sides of the political spectrum, have been attempting to evict the Palestinian cave dwellers from their lands and their homes in the interests of annexing the territory to Israel—free from any Palestinian population. It should be stressed that the cave dwellers have never been involved in hostile activities; they are an innocent population with a unique mode of life, biblical in color, which they are determined to preserve in the face of the threat from the settlers, the army, the Civil Administration, and successive Israeli governments.

A campaign aimed at driving these people out began with sporadic cases of harassment and expulsion in the late 1970s and early 1980s and gathered force in 1999, under the Barak government,

---

[*]See Yigal Bronner, *The Eviction of the Palestinian Population of the Southern Hebron Hills* (Jerusalem, 2001), p. 6.

which attempted a mass eviction from the caves: army bulldozers tore down many of the Palestinian tents and temporary shelters and also blocked the entrance to their cave homes with earth and boulders. The residents hung on; and in the spring of 2000, the Israeli Supreme Court, responding to a public campaign within Israel and an appeal submitted by the Association for Civil Rights and attorney Shlomo Lecker, theoretically restored the status quo ante. Attacks by the army continued, nonetheless. Between July 3 and July 5, 2001, a particularly vicious military action resulted in the actual destruction of many of the caves, the stopping up of wells (the key to survival in this arid region), the liquidation of flocks and herds, and the physical expulsion of hundreds of families. In the days immediately following this attack, the army also prevented the Red Cross from supplying the population with basic humanitarian aid (food, tents, blankets). Many have somehow survived, living in temporary structures near their old homes. The legal campaign has gone on, by now, for seven years, so far without resolution: the army and the Civil Administration, driven by the settlers, are still trying to empty the region of its Palestinian inhabitants, who are appealing to the court for protection.

Harassment, intimidation, and violence against the cave dwellers on the part of the settlers and, sometimes, Israeli soldiers have not abated. Quite the contrary: the Palestinians of South Hebron are surviving a reign of terror, innocent victims of powerful forces relentlessly pressing up against them. Ta'ayush has maintained a long-term presence in the region and has mounted mass protests, run media campaigns and international petitions, and taken part in the legal battle. The threat of transfer—the forcible expulsion of the entire cave-dwelling population—is still very grave.

January 11, 2002   Blankets

We gather at the Shoket Junction, near the old-new Green Line, the pre-1967 border. It is sunny, the height of winter, the desert and the hills limned in green, the land itself like a living presence, so beautiful that it hurts to look.

There are some fifty cars, some 250 to 300 volunteers. Each car tapes a number on the windshield; we will go as a convoy. Many have signs saying, "End the Occupation." There is a briefing in Hebrew, Arabic, English. The good news is that the legal battle against the government and the army seems to have achieved a momentary victory; so far the cave dwellers are still in place, though most of their homes have been wrecked, sometimes repeatedly wrecked. The court has put off the next hearing for three months. This is time gained and a sign that the government lawyers are facing stiff opposition and are unsure of the outcome.

The public campaign is bearing fruit, but, as Hillel reminds me, we cannot deal with every such situation; and there are hundreds like this, in various modes and intensities, all over the territories. We are facing an ongoing policy of criminal violence aimed at civilians. There is a logic to it, too, that of transfer. If their lives are miserable enough, the Arabs will leave, or at least submit.

We set off around 10:30, in the sunshine. Within five minutes we hit the first roadblock. They are waiting for us. The area has been declared a closed military zone. Meanwhile, police escorts, including the settler police, have joined us. I am with Yigal, Yasir, and Manal in the last car in the convoy, the police flashing their blue lights behind us.

For some reason—is it the luminous winter morning?—we are optimistic, and indeed we go fairly quickly through the first blockade. Have the soldiers been told to let us through? Supposedly, we have received firm promises from nameless men of influence in the army and the government. We are only delivering blankets, after all. Maybe this explains our initial progress.

Ten minutes later, already beyond the Green Line, we are stopped again. I stare at the hills. It is a hard landscape: rocks, more rocks, a few trees, a wadi between us and the small town of Yata in the distance. The settlements are by now coming into view, red-tiled roofs scattered over the hilltops. You can also see, in the distance, the first signs of devastation, the blasted huts and blocked wells of the Palestinians, clustered in small nuclei, still far away.

We wait. Warm in the sun. I realize there is no place in the world I would rather be at this moment. I am glad to be with these people. I feel free: the essay I am working on at home doesn't matter, and my classes require little attention. It is a Friday morning in midwinter, two days before my birthday, Eileen is visiting our new grandson, our son Edani is at school, and my heart is free. Almost singing. A certain heaviness has been burned away by the sun. Two days ago there was snow. Yigal and I speak of Sanskrit poems.

Once again, the police or the army give way, for whatever reason, and we proceed.

It is perhaps twenty minutes, perhaps less, until the next roadblock, and this one is serious. We are on the outskirts of Susya, a large settlement, not the most fanatic in this region, but definitely deeply implicated in the dispossession of the cave dwellers. The police and the army are well represented; there are many jeeps and cars, many soldiers behind us and before us, perhaps twenty-five to thirty policemen, everyone armed. The settlers have blocked the road with their cars to keep us from passing; the police and the army are either unable or, more likely, unwilling to clear the way. We park on the side of the road and gather before the roadblock. By now my eyes are beginning to recognize faces I have seen before in demonstrations or at the university; there are many young people, also some gray-haired ladies, the well-meaning and the innocent who will shortly have to walk through the human barrier of the police, though so far they do not realize this. French television has sent a camera crew. Many photographers are at work on both sides of the barrier, the police videotaping the faces of all these dangerous peace fanatics and the license plates of all the cars, the journalists scanning the crowd, the landscape, and the "enemy."

Somewhere in the hills beyond the settlement are, we are told, the cave dwellers, waiting for our blankets.

Negotiations begin with the police, this time in earnest. We get occasional briefings by loudspeaker; in between, Yigal lectures

the volunteers on the history of the cave dwellers and their eviction from their homes. By now there is no doubt that the whole
cruel process has been carefully premeditated. Behind the onslaught stand the settlers and, one can only suppose, right-wing
officers in the army command and, very likely, gray "banal" bureaucrats in government ministries, of the same persuasion. Behind them, the politicians of the right, all the way up to the prime
minister.

Eventually it becomes clear that we will have to act in the face
of opposition by the police. The negotiations break down. We file
to the truck loaded with blankets; everyone gets a blanket encased
in fragile plastic. The handle on mine tears within seconds, so
from this point on I will be clutching the blanket either under
my arm or to my chest. It is thick, heavy, folded somewhat awkwardly, and not easy to carry. This, however, is the only weapon
I will have.

We stand unevenly, huddled together, in the face of a human wall of soldiers and police. Gadi Algazi—a charismatic figure, medieval historian, and one of the founders of Taʿayush—is
pressed up against the barrier, waiting to give the sign. I wonder
what he is thinking. Will anyone be hurt? Is there a chance still
to avoid a head-on collision with the soldiers? Is there no choice?
When is the right moment? I admire, from afar, his ability to
shoulder this burden, to take responsibility for endangering some
of us, for making the calculation of risk and need and right and
loss. He seems to know. I wonder if I, in that position, would
have the courage to make the decision, knowing what it might
mean. And would I have the faith? I can see his face, and I see
he has chosen. "Do you have a song?" he calls out to us, turning back to the ragged line of volunteers hugging their blankets.
We start to sing. There are, at first, incongruous tunes from
the '60s, which some of us remember from other contexts. "We
Shall Overcome." Also "Heveinu Shalom Aleichem" ("We bring
peace to you"—a staple of Zionist youth movements) and "Hinei
ma tov u-ma naim shevet achim gam yachad" ("How good and

pleasant it is when brothers dwell together in unity," Psalms 133).
The singing ebbs and swells, by no means a mighty chorus, since
by now many are afraid of what is certain to come.

We move forward. We have come to deliver blankets to the
dispossessed; it is cold. We will not be violent, but we will also
not be deterred. However, in my mind, this "heroic" thought
seems no less absurd, at this moment, than all the rest of the
situation at noon in the Hebron Hills. The police, the soldiers—
what kind of an enemy are they, anyway? Their hearts cannot be
in this. As for the settlers, that is another matter.

There is rather a lot of noise. I hear residual shreds of the
singing; the police are yelling through their megaphones that we
are breaking the law, that we will all be arrested; the police and
army jeeps behind us are blaring their horns continuously; some
people cry out when the policemen jump at them and drag them
out of the line, and some are arrested; there are shouts from up
front to keep on walking, to stick together, to hold hands tightly.
We break through the first line of police, but they quickly regroup
ahead of us, while their vehicles are prodding us from behind.
One of the settlers' cars accidentally runs over the foot of one of
the policemen, who falls to the ground; a demonstrator pounds
on the hood and screams at the driver, "You idiot, look who
you've run down!"

Gadi and other leaders among the peace marchers have by now
been arrested and disappeared. Orphaned, we march on, flowing
like broken drops of mercury around the clusters of soldiers and
police. Our ranks thin as the police pull more and more out of the
line. I glance back at the motley, irregular, disoriented human
mass behind me. Some have draped the blankets around their
shoulders, perhaps as a cushion against the blows they anticipate
from the soldiers. Configurations shift—at one point my arm is
tightly clutched by a dark Palestinian woman, at another by a
blond Israeli; at other moments I am walking free, clutching my
blanket, expecting at any moment to be pulled aside and arrested.
I am in some unfamiliar internal space, a limbo in which there
is no sense of future and also very little past, but I don't much

care. Foolishly, I have left my thick winter coat in the car, since
it is noon and relatively warm outside, but I can vaguely imagine
spending the evening in some jail in Hebron or Beersheba. It
will be cold and, worse, the book that I brought along for just
such an emergency is in the pocket of my coat, locked in the car.
Such matters flit through my mind as I keep walking through
the strangely structure-less, labile space. The noise intensifies;
the marchers are now scattered in small patches along the road
and also in the mud on either side, moving forward as the soldiers
and the police scramble and scream. We have walked perhaps
two hundred meters. I see my friend and colleague Yuri in the
grip of a policeman, who pulls him off the road; they tussle. I
am carried forward by the stream, surprised still to be walking
without harm. Later Yuri tells me that he struggled for some
time with the policeman while the action continued moving past
them, until at one point Yuri said to his opponent, "Look, we're
here all alone, why stay behind?" At which point the policeman
released him and they both rushed forward, back to the fray.

I lose track of time; there is a somewhat delicious, but also
unnerving, sense of no-space through which I and the blanket
are sleepwalking. My confreres present varying visages: there
is the fanatic, best avoided; there are many who are obviously
frightened; there are older people who stumble and sometimes
fall; and there are a few who seem to be enjoying the spectacle,
in all its clumsy, chaotic reality. The TV crew is filming without
pause, and the police videographer has his hands full too. The
police have more or less lost control by now; the top officer
turns to the army commander and says to him, desperately, "It's
your duty to arrest all these people." The army man—obviously a
reservist, hardly committed to this folly—answers the policeman,
"Can't you see they're making a fool out of you?"

We are directed by someone amongst us to the side of the
road, a mud-soaked hill. The limbo state is over, the parts of my
mind that had shut down suddenly come to life, and I am happy,
a simple, straightforward happiness, no doubt entirely dependent on having gone through that limbo. There is no happiness

quite like that which spontaneously rises up out of destructured space. Negotiations briefly resume. I am not the only one to have been mildly transformed. It rapidly transpires that the police and the soldiers have turned benign. The police officer announces through the megaphone that we will be allowed to deliver the blankets, that those arrested will be released, that the army will now protect us as we march the remaining four kilometers to the caves. He wishes us a pleasant afternoon. The condition is that we follow orders and remain nonviolent, avoiding any friction and even verbal exchanges with the settlers. From this point the soldiers are with us; conversations develop. The high officer, overheard as he speaks into his cell phone, makes a bitter joke: "Everything is OK, except that I'll never be able to go to any European country again." War criminal: he has been filmed repeatedly by the French TV crew.

We start off over the hills, our shoes sinking into the mud at every step. But it is not over. The settlers have their turn. A young woman, her hair hidden under a kerchief, emerges from the settlement and begins to scream at us with a truly amazing richness of sordid language. Where did these religious Jews learn to speak? Curses soar like arias in a high soprano. She is not alone. One of the men shouts that we are on the side of Bin Laden. Perhaps we are Bin Laden. We ignore all this and keep walking, but the settlers have allies among the policemen. Another bout of blocking and resistance is inevitable; they are determined to keep these blankets away from the cave dwellers. It is quite cold in the Hebron Hills, but the blankets will apparently leave indelible scars of ignominy on the history of the Jews. Who knows, this is probably a matter of life and death, since the Jews' survival is so fragile a business; delivery of a single blanket could be fatal. This moment is the ugliest of the day, made still worse by the fact that Yasir, walking beside me, is suddenly attacked by a policeman who hits him hard and continuously, screaming at him as he does so, "You're attacking me!" Do they teach them this useful phrase in the police academy?

They put Yasir in the police jeep. He is under arrest and will be taken to the police station in one of the nearby settlements, to be charged. He has done nothing but walk along with the rest of us, with his blanket; his mistake was to wear a keffiyeh around his neck. The policeman, in need of a victim, picked out a Palestinian. There is some confusion, but a determined group of marchers surrounds the jeep and refuses to let it move; some lie on the ground around it. Eventually, the police give in yet again, and Yasir is released.

We are stuck on the road, which is now blocked by settlers' vehicles, from which a steady river of vituperation is flowing fast; the police, at least some of them, are showing solidarity with their settler allies. It is getting late, past 3:00; soon it will be dark, also very cold. The Palestinians are still at least a kilometer away. Somehow we have to get them the blankets, connect with them, and still get back. A few religious members of our group, who have to be in Jerusalem or Tel Aviv before Shabbat begins at around 4:00, have very reluctantly turned back toward the cars. The rest of us have to decide what to do next. The police offer a compromise: they will send someone to deliver the blankets, but we are to leave the area immediately. We reject this offer and prepare to walk through yet another blockade; we want to reach the living human beings who are waiting for us on the other side.

Determination works. The police and the settlers give way. I wonder, as I walk, whether there are soldiers there who see the whole lunatic scenario—this straggling army of blanket holders stumbling through the mud over the hills—and for a moment, at least, see through the veil: see the misery, the occupation, the human evil, the coercion and cruelty, the pointlessness, the falseness, our own deep and enduring foolishness. Is there one of them who would resist an order to demolish an innocent Palestinian's home? Does what we are doing have any meaning? Evil is rampant on both sides in this conflict, and perhaps we are caught up in a gesture of quixotic futility. What difference does it make? On the other hand, surely one must act from precisely this point, only this point, which is the steady, recurrent, dependable matrix, a place of utmost ambiguity. There is work to be done within, through, and beyond the confusion; because of the confusion.

By 4:00 we have reached them: a lone tractor, a smiling young Palestinian man at the wheel. Very cognizant of the moment, I toss my blanket into the container attached to the tractor. We climb the hill toward their tiny cluster of shacks, sheep pens, and caves. They are waiting for us. Some embrace us. Many of the volunteers have been to this area before, in the course of the campaign; I see one of the Palestinians, a tall, sturdy man, kiss the cheeks of his Israeli friend four times, with a kind of fierceness. The old men—fathers of large households, heavy in their robes—watch us with eyes that seem to see back many years, perhaps centuries. This moment is hardly more than a flicker. Ragged children run among us. Some of them are chasing after the lambs. It is high in the hills; we can see, in the distance, the lights of Arad—also, of course, the lights of the nearest settlement. Someone has a fire ready and is making tea, the thick, sweet tea with *marwa* that has come when most needed, just as we are beginning to suffer the cold. It is a heady moment: there are short speeches, and the leader of the cave dwellers speaks, in Hebrew, of a real, not a false, peace—the peace that must someday come, though so far we cannot see it. I believe him. He thanks us from the heart for coming today, for not giving in, for being friends.

I have time, before we leave, to go into one of the caves. This family has been living here since the 1830s. There is a father, a self-possessed mother, and thirteen children; also several sheep. The cave is surprisingly warm, well-appointed; copper vessels line a long shelf. I observe a raised level where you can sit comfortably, and behind and below it, a long section set apart for sleeping. It is clean, lived-in, inviting; I would happily stay the night if invited. The French cameraman is talking, through an interpreter, with the mother. Would she like to move into a nice house, a villa, somewhere else? She listens and laughs. She is perhaps uneducated, but she knows where he is from: "Even if you offer me a villa in Paris, I want to be here in my home. This cave is where we were born and where we grew up. We prefer to die here rather than leave our land."

May 4, 2002   Wheat Harvest, Jinba

I have never held a sickle before, and it is different from what I imagined. Compact, handy, light, and sharp enough so that with a simple, quick circular movement the blade can cut through the relatively fragile, dry stalks of wheat. It is two weeks before Shavuot and, as for Ruth and Boaz in the Bible, the wheat harvest is overdue. The Palestinians of the caves have given us a short lesson in harvesting. The left hand grabs the top of the sheaves, the right cuts through the bottom, close to the earth; you cast your cumulating handfuls onto neat yellow piles as you proceed through the field. Leftover sheaves remain standing, here and there, prickly reminders of the fate of foreigners, the after-gleaners, then and now.

It is hot, early afternoon, by the time we begin. The world is yellow—the bleached white-yellow-green of the ripe sheaves, the deeper semi-gold of the field seen as a whole, the molten gold pouring out of the sky, the brown-yellow of the rocky hills. City dweller that I am, I have never stood so close to the mystery of wheat. How did they ever learn that from the forked, crisscrossing tip of the sheaf, enclosed in russet-gold chaff, you could end up with a loaf of bread? Human beings are infinitely inventive. We are entering the cycle as the grain has reached its fullness; next will come the business of threshing, then sifting, grinding—if, that is, the High Court does not cut the cycle short and order these farmers evicted from their lands, as the government demands. The court is due to sit on Thursday. Shlomo Lecker, the eloquent lawyer in charge of their case, is with us today, and he is, as usual, pessimistic. In the current atmosphere in Israel of sinister nationalist hysteria, the cave dwellers may not stand a chance.

A lone bird of prey circles overhead as we approach the meeting point, traveling down a bumpy dirt road, since the army has turned us away from the main road (which serves the settlers, and only the settlers). The Palestinians are waiting for us with four tractors harnessed to big wagons. We clamber on. The ride over the trails—through the hills, into the almost eerie openness of this space—is somewhat traumatic: we jostle and bounce and crumple into one another. The tractor drivers are uncommunicative, and our Ta'ayush contact driving with them, orange bandanna on his head, knows no Arabic and not much Hebrew—he is French, very keen, jocular, energetic, and ineffectual. He has only a rudimentary idea of where we are going or how long it will take, and so, therefore, do we. Meanwhile, the tractors climb, twist, and descend like roller coasters under the thick midday sun.

A young Palestinian boy with astonishing eyes sits on the back of the tractor, staring back at us, this odd collection of several hundred Jews and Arabs of all ages who have fetched up near his home, who have come to help with the wheat harvest. Does he connect us in any way with the Jews of Susya just over the hill, who have been terrorizing his people, poisoning their wells? Can he imagine what it means for a community to be so divided? The army is present in our honor, one lonely tank stationed on top of a ridge with another jeep full of soldiers beside it, watching us through binoculars as we crawl along the paths.

We have been assigned various patches and fields, some downhill, some on the other side of the small set of caves and tents and goat pens. Some of us set to work on the barley, others on the wheat, a somewhat stumpy variety that will go, in part, for fodder. Relieved that none of the tractors overturned (after all) and that I was not called upon to set bones or give infusions, I leave the medic's pouch behind a stone and begin to work my way through the clumps of wheat. Sweat floods my body; I am thirsty, also happy in another of those unpredictable bursts that have been happening these last days. The stalks are home to the brilliant red-black ladybirds that are called in Hebrew *parat moshe rabbeinu*, "Moses' cow," and, as we now learn from one of the locals, *umm sulaiman*, "Solomon's mother," in Arabic. Working side by side like this makes even monotheism seem almost bearable, not wholly lacking in playful variation.

An older woman borrows my sickle, and I am left to work, like many of the others, with bare hands (they quickly become scratched and rough). I am tempted to ask for it back, but she is, she says, getting into the rhythm of it, exploring its possibilities; married to a movement therapist, who am I to interrupt this experiment? I go back to breaking the stalks at their base with my fingers. After a while she straightens up and surveys the odd scene with satisfaction—dozens of us bending over the wheat at many points in this field—and says, fully aware of the resonant irony, "*Avoda ivrit*," "Hebrew labor"—the slogan of the Jewish pioneers of the Third Aliyah.*

Something in me remains skeptical. Can anything worthy really grow out of this parched, brown, meager soil? What kind of a crop can this be? I come from Iowa. Real soil is black and soggy or oily, dripping with dark nutrients, and also deep, nothing like this crumbly desiccated cake of clods. Near me a Palestinian man in his twenties is deep in conversation with a stunning young girl from Tel Aviv, both immersed in harvesting the sheaves, edging deeper into the field. I overhear brief fragments of their conversation. "Where do you live? How many brothers and sisters? What is your name?" I can almost overhear their mute fantasies. There is something natural and right. The whole life of these cave dwellers has this quality. With Maya I steal away after lunch, while the usual Ta'ayush speeches are droning on, for a quick home visit. We meet Suwad, a young woman happy to show us around. We speak in short bursts of language, half Arabic, half English. We introduce ourselves. "How long have you been living in this cave?" Seven years, since her marriage. She smiles. The cave is far less inviting than the one I saw in January; chaotic, the level set apart for the goats encroaching on the living

*The Third Aliyah, in the 1920s, made "Hebrew labor"—especially manual labor in the fields, in paving roads, and so on—a central value in the attempt to reinvent a modern, full-blooded Jewish person. The stress was on Jews' performing such tasks themselves, without middlemen or employed workers—a striking departure from the Eastern European Jewish ethos. The ideal of "Hebrew labor" drew its legitimacy from a Tolstoyan utopian socialism and the writings of the Second Aliyah ideologue, A. D. Gordon.

space for people, the kitchen unappealing, tight. We continue to another cave, this one much better; there is an "annex" slightly up the hill, for cooking. In the afternoon heat, the caves are cool and gray and dusty. A young man takes over the tour and leads us up to the well, fed only by rainwater. Each tanker of water they bring here from outside costs eighty shekels—a fortune for these people. He takes us into the sheepfold, divided into two parts. In one, young animals cluster around the water trough; in the second is the postnatal ward, with tiny goats and sheep, some born this same day, still clumsy as they try to stand or walk. We take turns cradling one brown baby goat with a tiny white flourish at the tip of his tail.

We make our way back via a row of young mothers standing, babies in their arms, clearly wanting to greet us, perhaps curious: who are these strangers who have come to help in the fields? More names. We can offer little more than this exchange of names, the simplest, perhaps also the deepest, form of language. Boxes of powdered milk, Materna for babies, have been unloaded and will go to Yata, not far away. In the distance, wheat fields sprawl over the stubborn hills. There are many more fields than I would have guessed, separated from one another by stony, infertile plots. The young men, unemployed since the Intifada began, have spent the morning hours harvesting. There is little else to do, and no money comes in. I ask if they know about Thursday's pending court decision. They know.

It is like India, like a village anywhere: rooted, continuous, fluid with the stuff of life, work, food, marriage, babies, water, milk, fields, flocks. Who could have the temerity, let alone the right, to tell these families to leave this place? This is their home, has always been their home. One cave has a television set. There is no kindergarten here, no school. The children walk several kilometers over the hills each day. Someday there should be a school. During our visit, the army calls the Ta'ayush team: some officer is angry because we have, they think, set in place a wooden pike somewhere in one of the fields. It isn't true, but you can follow the bitter, impudent logic. No one is to build anything here, to strengthen a home, a fence, a goat pen. It is forbidden. No one, that is, other than the settlers, who have already taken most of the land.

The usual speeches over at last, we begin the jolting ride back to the cars. I stand beside Ehud, a mathematician; he tries to explain to me the meaning of combinatorics, the mathematical play with riddles. He was interviewed on TV this week, defending our letter in support of the soldiers who refuse to serve in the territories. He was clear and humane, but his voice was drowned out by the strident, self-righteous fury of the nationalists who had been invited for the sake of "balance." He left the studio remembering all he might have said—*l'esprit de l'escalier*, unavoidable at such moments. All of us are tongue-tied against this enormity, the pain of the earth itself, now gulping in vast measures of the liquid late-afternoon light. The hills have become stark, preternaturally lucid, dark as one looks west. One could go mad in this delicious light; mad with beauty, mad with pain. I listen to the wind in the sheaves standing in the fields we didn't touch, a subtle symphony, beyond human music, beyond the mind.

But the mind is awake and working now, even as I dream, in and out of consciousness, while Iva drives a full car home to Jerusalem. It is Motzei Shabbat, the birth of a new week. The young couple we took down and back in the car wish us a good week when we pull up at Binyanei Hauma—a week, they say, in which, let us hope, justice will win. Jerusalem is cool. I unlock the door and wash the chaff and mud from my hands. By the time Eileen comes home, I am, I suddenly realize, possessed with a fury I rarely know. What we are fighting in the South Hebron Hills is pure, rarefied, unadulterated, unreasoning, uncontainable human evil. Nothing but malice drives this campaign to uproot the few thousand cave dwellers with their babies and lambs. They have hurt nobody. They were never a security threat. They led peaceful, if somewhat impoverished lives until the settlers came. Since then, there has been no peace. They are tormented, terrified, incredulous. As am I. What black greed, what unwitting hatred, has turned Israeli Jews into torturers of the innocent? The settlers come first, violent and cruel—but above them is a vast, ramified system, official Israel, that sustains them and protects them, that corrupts our minds and our language, God's language, with vile rationalizations. I rage in my well-appointed kitchen; I am inflamed, crushed, mad with pain.

If the court decides against them, if the army comes to evict them, I will be there beside them; I will try to stop them with my body.

May 12, 2002   The Court

On Thursday to the Supreme Court with Sanjay, visiting from Paris. We arrive at 10:30, just as the case is being tried. The state's attorney is addressing the court, wildly distorting the facts. There must be a name for this kind of impudent twisting of reality, but I can't think of it as I listen, angry, unbelieving. The Palestinians in question, he says, belong to the town of Yata; only by some fluke are they now in the caves. Let the court appoint a committee to investigate, headed by someone from the Civil Administration, of course—the enemy of the local population. And they can't really need all those wells, can they—why not let the army stop them up with sand?

The cave dwellers were given permission to come to the court to hear their case, but the permission was recorded in a document in some army camp miles away, and the roads are closed; so they couldn't take advantage of the army's gracious indulgence of their curiosity as to their fate.

There are some twenty of us in the back benches; a large group from Ta'ayush was kept waiting for over an hour outside, probably on purpose ("for security reasons," they were told). Shlomo Lecker and Manal, for our side, are on the left, draped in lawyer's robes. Manal is crisp, confident, and eloquent, in her Nazarene Hebrew with its mellifluous Arabic *r*'s, defending these people, literally well by well. It is hot in the hills, and they have fields to harvest. The atmosphere turns in our favor. Justices Matza, Levi, and Procaccia are sitting in judgment; Matza is impatient but trying, it appears, to be fair.

The room is at once harsh and elegant, with traces of wooden paneling along with the ubiquitous Jerusalem stone. The settlers are there in the front benches, skullcaps blazing. I will have to learn to overcome the anger I feel.

Most of all, as the proceedings drone on in incomprehensible legal language, I am struck by the absurdity. Kafka knew it well. A few days ago I stood in the caves; I worked in the field; I held the baby goat and spoke with the young mothers. Only a madman could consider judging these people's right to be at home: it is like appointing a triumvirate of solemn judges to decide if a tree can stand beside a pool, a cloud drift across the sky. What possible jurisdiction do these dignified and powerful judges have over the goats, the wheat, the wells? (Debate flows back and forth about the wells, ending finally on a positive note: if the army intends to destroy yet another one, they will have to give seventy-two hours' notice—long enough for us to garner support to prevent this.) The land in question is not in Israel, does not belong to Israel, not even in the most right-wing reading of the legal reality, but Israel is nevertheless sitting in judgment, with ceremony and seriousness and pretense, in the harsh and elegant chamber, over those who have lived on this piece of land for centuries. The whole affair is absurd. A protest rises to my throat, and I gag.

It ends, or peters out, in another delay, which is what we want: two more months on the land. The court will reconvene at the end of June. Each deferral is a victory. Perhaps things will go on like this until the end of the occupation, which can't, after all, be that long away—another couple of years, five, ten? We will draw it out until one day the army is gone, the settlers go home to the old Israel (how will we live with them so close?), and the cave dwellers will have to fend for themselves in some Palestinian state perhaps more threatening, in its own way, to their lives. Maya reminds me that their world is, in any case, doomed; the new always sweeps away the old, as the poet Bialik says, speaking of loneliness, and of love.

Matters of ceremony are matters of substance: behind the ritual lies a vicious threat. The settlers are waiting; not biding their time, for there are daily pressures on the cave people, attacks, humiliations, threats. They are waiting for the end they believe they can engineer. Justice Procaccia, they say, has no patience for these settlers, and I cannot believe that Chief Justice Aharon Barak would allow the cave people to be evicted. All in all, there is a good chance we will keep this one small patch of the Palestinian world alive, for the moment.

Twaneh, January 18, 2003   Tu B'shvat, the New Year for Trees

The first shots seem somehow innocuous. In the vastness of the hills, the desert, the rain, they are little more than thin, sharp cracks, whiplike, distant. It is surprising how long it takes to notice that someone is shooting at you.

We are in Twaneh in the South Hebron Hills, something between a village and another set of caves. The seasons change as the earth turns; it is eight months since May, the wheat harvest. Then in the autumn there was the olive harvest. Now it is time to plow and to sow. The earth is soft, soggy with rain, ready to receive the seeds. But for the last two weeks or so, settlers have been terrorizing the farmers; they run riot over the fields, chase the farmers off with guns. In some cases over the last few days, settlers have taken possession at gunpoint of Palestinian fields and begun to plow them themselves. So Ta'ayush sends us here to stand beside our friends from the caves, to plow with them, to protect them, bodily, from the settlers.

I drive down with Ezra, Efrat, and Natasha. Ezra knows these roads and the villagers well; he speaks fluent (Iraqi) Arabic from home (he is also, as it happens, our plumber). Over the years he has helped the villagers endlessly, in many practical ways. He is fearless, committed, a true friend. Natasha is Czech, eight years in Israel, a photographer preparing a feature film on Ta'ayush. Efrat works in the office of Shlomo Lecker, the cave dwellers' attorney. We set off through mist and fog, driving south past Bethlehem and Hebron. The hills are wet, muted by rain; the mist weaves across the road in thick, menacing swirls. A good day, Ezra says, for an ambush.

But we arrive early and safely, before 10:00. The villagers are waiting for us with their tractors. They tell us that last night the settlers came, shooting their rifles, into the village. Nights are especially nerve-racking, the villagers utterly alone to face the terror. Now, in the daylight, there are some fifteen of us here to help. We greet our friends, shake hands, talk a bit about the plowing. Soon we are walking over the muddy hills toward the chosen field. With us are elders in a dark swirl of robes, their heads hidden by the black fabric; they have long beards and gnarled hands, like figures from a distant past. This impression gains power as they begin to work. A bag of barley seed is opened. They scoop up big fistfuls of seeds and begin to walk the field in the wake of the crisscrossing tractors; they cast the seeds in a wide arc through the air, an elegant and ancient movement, dipping their hands deep into their robes, then dispersing a parabola of barley over the fresh furrows. It is cold and gray and we are high in the hills, with astonishing vistas of the frozen desert to the east and south. There is the delicious smell of upturned soil and the sweet cold of rain and wind.

Suddenly, shots. On the hill above us, some two hundred meters away, sit the caravans of Chavat Maon, inhabited mostly by the dregs of the settler movement; even Maon, one of the hardcore settlements in this area, is said to have no patience for the wild ways of its daughter colony. These are young men who have found a way, and a reason, to unleash their hatred without check or restraint. They come pouring down the hillside, screaming furiously, some of them shooting short bursts in our direction. One of the Ta'ayush men hears a bullet fly over his head. It is like a nightmare sickeningly familiar, expected, recurrent. They are hurling rocks at us—they have learned something, these young settlers, from the Intifada—and one of them has perfected a sling, again resonantly biblical. Repeatedly he lets heavy rocks fly from the sling; they are terrifying, obviously lethal, whistling past like missiles, and they are getting closer every second.

Ezra, who seems almost to relish this moment, cries out to us: "Don't be afraid. Stand your ground." But already the Palestinians are giving way, retreating before the onslaught of shots and stones. By now the settlers are upon us, all in their twenties or so, with long embroidered skullcaps and tzitzit fringes and guns: "You should be ashamed," they scream at us. "What kind of Jews are you?" Helpless, angry, I yell back: "I am a Jew. That's why I am here." And so on, pitting my useless, wishful words against their stones. They seem to hear me and to become yet more enraged, and now one of them hits out at me suddenly, hard, hurls me to the ground. Brown soggy soil covers my fingers, my knees, my right eyebrow; my right hand is badly scraped and bleeding. He punches me a few more times before moving on to his next target, before I can respond. I feel pain, surprise, fear, rage. What is worse, I have seen their faces up close, and it is perhaps the most unsettling vision I have ever taken in, one I will later try to blot out, for these are not the faces of the usual human mix of good and evil, of confusion and clarity, of love and hate; the eyes are mad, killers' eyes—it is like looking at something utterly demonic, something from the world of myth. We are staring not into an abyss—for all is here on the surface, present, evident, and horrible—but into a volatile vortex of pure hate. I have no doubt they will kill us if they can. They seem to hate us, the leftist traitors, even more than they hate their Palestinian victims.

I pull myself up, brush off the mud as best I can, survey the battlefield. Much has happened in the minutes I was busy with my own attacker. Lawrence, a tall, bearded, somewhat older Canadian volunteer from the Christian Peacemaker Team in Hebron, has been fiercely attacked, his camera torn from his grip and smashed. Liora has been pummeled and thrown, her glasses destroyed. Ezra is bleeding from his cheek. Another young Ta'ayush man has been savagely kicked in the groin. One of the Palestinian tractors has been tumbled down the hill, overturned. The settlers loathe cameras above all—the dangerous recording of their crimes—and they yell out to one another whenever they catch sight of another one; now they move in on Natasha, who has been heroically filming throughout, from the moment the first shots rang out and the settlers came pouring down the hill. She is small and agile, and as they strike out at her, trying to wrest away the camera, she screams and circles in a rush to escape, her throat producing an unearthly, high-pitched eerie warble. For some unknown reason, this seems to deter them, and she manages, miraculously, to reach safety on the higher ground toward which our group is slowly, confusedly, retreating.

The newly plowed field is behind us and below; Twaneh village is perhaps two kilometers away across the hills. It suddenly occurs to me that we are deeply and dangerously alone. There is no one we can call for help, no emergency number, no force that could stand up to the settlers and their guns. This, of course, is no more than what the Palestinians face daily; they are without succor or recourse, at the mercy of the settlers' marauding bands. They watch their homes, their fields, their possessions being remorselessly stripped from them at their enemies' whim. The army will not protect them; the police turn a blind eye. Their blood is permitted, their hands tied. For the moment, for these people from the South Hebron Hills, the Supreme Court has ordered that the status quo be preserved—that they be allowed to till their fields, harvest their olives, draw water from their wells—pending a final decision in their case. In practice, on the spot, nothing, no one, stands between them and the settlers. No one but us, and we have been shattered by the first violent onslaught.

One of the Palestinians can take it no longer—perhaps it is being driven off his own field that drives him mad; perhaps it is the long accumulation of misery, week after week and year after year. In any case, he reaches for a rock and prepares to hurl it at the invaders. I cry out to him: "Don't throw!" Suddenly I am truly, consciously afraid, for the first time today: this will be all they have been waiting for. They will open fire indiscriminately;

someone is about to be killed. One of the foreign CPTs joins me in the bitter business of persuasion, and the villager reluctantly drops his stone. I can see him still, outlined against the gray sky, standing erect on the hilltop with the rock in his hand—the only emblem of defiance this wet wintry morning. Did we save his life by stopping him?

Time is passing, rocks still flying at our heads; Greg, another volunteer, is hit in the thigh. At least the shooting seems to have stopped. A small gap has opened up between us and the attacking settlers. Most of the Palestinians have fled up the hills with their tractors; we stand, bedraggled but on our feet, between them and the settlers. Perhaps fifteen minutes have passed since the shooting started. Now, belatedly, the army turns up. First there is the security officer of the settlement, not in uniform, heavily armed, skullcap on his head. He begins by shouting at us, livid with rage: "This is a closed military area. You have broken the law by coming here. You will all be arrested." He tries to arrest Ezra and push him into his jeep, unsuccessfully. He seizes the identity card of one of the villagers. There is a nasty, pinched, scornful quality to this man—he is, after all, a settler. But his presence is the first sign that we are entering a new phase. Another jeep arrives, then another; the soldiers climb out into the cold and rain. The settlers, their rampage over for the moment, slowly begin to turn away.

A young officer, also religious, takes charge. To my surprise, he is clear-headed, authoritative, and humane. He gives no hint of being outraged at what the settlers have done; he listens impassively to our reports—Liora floods him with a furious harangue—and makes no attempt to find those who shot at us. This, apparently, is not his job. He doesn't care. He seems familiar with the scenario, unmoved, but at least not hostile to the villagers or to us. He consults with his superiors by field radio, then draws a line: the field, our field, is beyond it, out of bounds, a closed military area. However, if we want to plow and sow farther west, over the hill, that is permitted. He will leave a small body of soldiers to guard us this time. Most of these soldiers are huddling around the jeeps, obviously frozen, wet, and bored.

But our Palestinian friends are too frightened to go on with the plowing. They sit, hunched, on the wet ground, in small groups; they look sick at heart, or perhaps it is only I, the observer, who feels this sickness spreading in me. I feel horror at the whole sordid business, this grasping and tugging over every centimeter of rocky soil. For a moment my love of the Mediterranean landscapes abandons me, I want only to go far away, far from the Jews and their furies, far from the Palestinians and their darkness. All is ugly here, and to make it worse, it is now raining hard, soaking all of us as we stand miserably waiting—as always, in such matters, one waits—for some temporary resolution, something that will allow us to leave. We cannot go, of course, until the farmer gets back his identity card, that much is clear. The army is taking its inexorable time; meanwhile, the Hebron police have arrived.

With the soldiers behind us, we slip and stagger through the mud to where the tractor lies, its wheels in the sky like Kafka's bewildered beetle. The rain is slashing at us, I can barely see, but somehow, together, we manage to tie the tractor to another one—brought down from the hill—and to set it right. The cable keeps snapping, but the salvaged tractor slowly hobbles back toward the village. One object has been saved.

Finally, mysteriously, it is all over, and we begin the long walk back to Twaneh. A few more Ta'ayush volunteers have arrived from Tel Aviv, including Itai, the brave one-legged student, on crutches, whom I often see in these circumstances. Anwar, one of our lawyers, is also with us now, and he instructs us in the futile but ineluctable procedure of submitting a complaint to the police against our attackers. We know they will do nothing; settlers always go scot-free. Still, we will go to the Russian Compound in Jerusalem and file our report, and there is Natasha's video footage to back it up. If the police wanted to—but they won't—they could easily identify each of the faces of the stone throwers and of those who shot.

In Twaneh they insist on giving us tea. We sit for half an hour in the school building, in the principal's office, under a large picture of Arafat smiling in his cunning, abhorrent way. Aviad sums up what we have experienced, why we came, what comes

next. Did we achieve anything? Yes: no one was badly hurt. We
will be back; we must come back if the plowing is to happen—
we cannot abandon these people. Perhaps we can get the army
to protect us next time. One of the villagers, clearly a man well
versed in the ways of the peace organizations, gets up to thank
us. For once, the speech is short, lucid, and focused. He thanks
us for coming to Twaneh. He thanks us for caring and taking the
time. He thanks us for taking the blows that are usually reserved
for them.

As we leave, fresh bread appears in huge flat loaves and, fam-
ished, we tear off huge chunks of it. It is better than any bread I
have tasted in all the years of my life, this simple, unsalted, un-
garnished meal. It has the taste of these hills, this sharp gray sky.
Our hosts utter the simple and lyrical blessings of good-bye. In an
hour, as we approach Jerusalem, there is a telephone call for Ezra
from our friend in Twaneh. "Where are you?" "On our way to the
Moskubiyya, the police compound, to fill in the forms." "Good
luck," says the voice from the village, "and Shabbat Shalom to all
the Jews, *jami' al-yahud.*"

February 1, 2003   Susya: Plowing

In Sanskrit they would say: It is like trying to bind a rampaging
elephant with a lotus stalk.

The Palestinian farmer wants to plow and sow his land. This
is the season; the soil is soft and ready. No rational person dis-
putes that it's his land, but the settlers will do everything possible
to drive him off it; in their eyes, God has given the entire Land
of Israel to the Jews and only to the Jews. The Civil Administration of the territories—that is, the occupation, still in place—
recognizes the peasant's right to plow. But will they protect him
from the settlers? In theory, they recognize that this, too, is
their responsibility. They have thus reached an agreement with
Ta'ayush for today's plowing in the South Hebron Hills, after
the debacle of two weeks ago: they will send Lieutenant Colonel
Tarik, their man in charge, to see to it that no one disturbs the

cave-dwelling farmers; this on condition that the "leftists"—that is us, Ta'ayush—don't turn up.

The plowing is what matters, and of course we accept the condition; but we have to be sure the army/Civil Administration keeps their side of the bargain. So we meet, once again, at Shoket Junction on a sun-swept winter morning. There are perhaps forty of us, double our strength two weeks ago when the settlers attacked us, and this time we have the full complement of veteran leaders of Ta'ayush, with rich experience in these matters. Things should, in theory, go smoothly.

At first that seems to be the case. We hear by phone that the farmers are on their way to the fields. Everything is calm. They begin to plow. We wait, chat aimlessly in the sun. After a couple of hours, it seems clear that today our presence is not needed. We decide to picnic together in a forest along the old Green Line. There are days when the activists can rest, perhaps even forget.

It is nearly noon as we drive up to the forest, alight with pines, not far from the caves, and now word reaches us: settlers have, again, attacked our friends as they began to plow. A Palestinian woman has been badly beaten—a blow to the head from a rifle butt. Others are also hurt. The settlers also appropriated several of the Palestinian tractors, worth many thousands of shekels. Eight Palestinians have been arrested for the crime of plowing their lands. Not only did Tarik fail to intervene or protect, but the paramilitary security officers of Susya, the nearby settlement, were themselves active in the violence.

The deal is off. We rush toward Susya.

Perhaps two or three kilometers from the Palestinian tents— most of the caves have been destroyed—the inevitable police barricade is waiting for us, several police cars blocking the road, also soldiers in one or two jeeps. We clamber out of the minibuses, and negotiations begin. We explain that a promise has been broken, the farmers brutally attacked, and we have to see them. Below us, very near, are the red-roofed cottages of well-to-do Susya, full of settlers, sitting astride Palestinian lands. The attackers came from there.

The police are far from receptive to our pleas. As usual, they produce a sheet of paper that declares the whole area a closed military zone. We are violating a military ordinance and can be arrested. We consult among ourselves in the limpid sun. We will have to walk through this barrier at whatever cost.

Both sides brace for the moment of ungovernable chaos. Suddenly we are off, moving rapidly to the right of the road, past the police cars and the soldiers. The soil is soaked with rain, spongy, and sinks under my feet; there are also cracks and holes, often hidden by thorns, so you have to pay attention to your feet while trying to evade the police, who are grabbing as many of us as they can. Amiel, only three months ago shot by a settler during the olive picking, leads the way briskly. One of the soldiers scuffles with a young volunteer, who tries to shake him off; Udi, walking beside me, serenely says to the soldier, "You cannot arrest him; you are breaking the law." The soldier drops behind. Ahead of me, incredibly keeping pace with the fastest of us, is Itai, on crutches, with his single leg. He has done this kind of thing many times in the past; perhaps he is immune to police persecution, or feels himself to be.

It is hot, now, as I walk, unhappy that it has, again, come to this, a little uneasy but determined to go on. Natasha is filming furiously, forward and backward; we will have plenty of video documentation this time. The soldiers, laden with their belts and rifles, are having a hard time keeping up with us. Still, little by little our ranks are thinning. Amnon and Neve have driven ahead by some mysterious route to the Palestinians; Yigal has been arrested; Aviad has disappeared. We are leaderless, decapitated, not even sure where the cave dwellers' encampment is and how to get there.

Long minutes pass in movement. I look back. Perhaps only twelve or fifteen of us are still walking. Karen, another veteran, takes charge. It is time, she says to me, to negotiate again. We will offer to withdraw from the area if they release everyone they have arrested, including the eight Palestinian farmers with their tractors. At her orders, we stop and sit down in the middle of the road around a jeep that is holding some of our people prisoner. Karen sends word down the road that we are willing to talk to the commander of the police.

I am suddenly seized by a terrible thirst. We have walked perhaps a kilometer over the caked mud of the hill. We are too few, the soldiers too many; there is no way to keep going forward. They can very easily arrest us all. Even if we reach the tents, now clearly visible beneath us, there is little we can do there; our goal now is to ensure that the farmers are released. To this end, Karen engages the officer in a tedious discussion. Peace work is like this—mostly boring, mostly waiting, punctuated with intense, short bursts of movement or action or fear, like in war.

Louise, who grew up in South Africa, has much to say to me as we sit on the road. Did the white peace movement—the counterpart to Ta'ayush—make a difference there? Yes, it made a difference. The turning point was when the leftists unionized the masses of black workers, and South African industry could no longer function with autocratic and arbitrary cruelty. An alliance was forged. It is something like that—not with workers, but perhaps with the grassroots social organizations of protest that are cropping up all over Israel—that Ta'ayush must achieve if it is to turn itself from a small spearhead of hard-core activists into a popular movement that can change this reality. And this is the moment when it should happen, the moment when a beginning can be made. She can sense it, smell it; sitting on the road beside her, so can I.

At Karen's signal, we begin to withdraw. Some of our people are released. Still there is one sitting handcuffed in the main police van. We are now back at the original barricade, but they are not keeping their word. Anyway, we will not leave until the fate of the arrested Palestinians has been resolved. We mill around, cell phones buzzing. We call our lawyers in Jerusalem; we call Neve and Amnon. A vast flock of white birds settles like swirling snow, wave after wave, like the sowing of seeds, on the rocky hill. We sit on the road, the vast green-brown vista of the hills unrolling in waves before us, and wait.

Like evil omens, a flock of settlers from Susya descends upon us; they have come to gape at and to curse these misguided
Jews who are defending the Arabs. Luckily, they have left their
guns at home. They stand at the roadside, hurling taunts and
insults but nothing worse; content, perhaps, to let the army take
care of this unwelcome intrusion. Indeed, an enormous armored
vehicle packed with soldiers soon arrives, closing off the road
from the other end. We are hemmed in by army and police on
all sides; they could easily cart us all off to some police post,
probably in Hebron. Yigal, free again, is bemused at the new
arrivals. "Look at all those soldiers. There are very dangerous
people here." "Who?" I ask. "You and me."

One of the settlers is smugly yelling: "In a few years there will
be a city of Jews on this spot. Like Tel Aviv." He is very sure, yet
for some reason today, in the midst of the foolishness and the
cruelty, the fierce and desperate ambiguity of all human things, I
think, again, that we will win this struggle—not alone, of course,
but with reality and some factor of recalcitrant, residual decency
on our side.

3:00 P.M.: another deal is struck. They will release the last
Taʿayush prisoner, and Tarik, from the Civil Administration,
will himself come to the Palestinian encampment and see to the
release of the Palestinians and their tractors. We, in turn, will go
back to the Green Line. Can we trust them? Uncertain, we climb
back into the minibuses. A small detachment—Neve, Amnon,
Natasha, Anwar—stay behind at the barricade to make certain
we are not being fooled. The rest of us drive back to the forest on
the Green Line, where, as the afternoon deepens and the air turns
cold, we eat the picnic food we have brought. Leena—lithe and
restless, from a small village in Galilee, as always searching for the
mysterious herbs that only Palestinians know and use—initiates
me into the mysteries of the prickly, onion-like *aqub*.

It is getting late. A large detachment, nearly half of us, heads
back in two cars to Tel Aviv. Our work, however, is not finished,
for the police and Tarik and the army have all lied to us, as

suddenly becomes clear. The Palestinians are still being held in an army camp nearby; the Civil Administration has gone home, washing their hands of this affair. The police have no particular interest in us anymore, but they cannot let us stay much longer in the area as night approaches. Angry, we turn back toward Susya, toward the barricade.

Again we wait. More negotiations. Suddenly the news spreads that the *Columbia* space shuttle has exploded on reentry with the Israeli astronaut Ilan Ramon on board—and that its pieces have fallen on the town of Palestine, Texas. In the surreal world of the territories, the occupation, the unplowed fields, playacting police, marauding settlers, and Ta'ayush volunteers hobbling over the hills, this tragedy seems only too much in place, an almost predictable part of the sun's sudden plunge beyond sight. It is cold. Leena cites a Palestinian proverb: *Allah ma 'indosh hajara le-irjit*; Allah has no stones to throw. (Hence, she explains, he resorts to causing random calamities.)

Another tedious and tenuous compromise is hammered out, and this time we can truly leave, winding our way back down the hills and through the forest to Shoket Junction. "Have we achieved anything today?" I ask Yigal. "I don't know," he says. "Tomorrow will tell. We acted correctly, in real time. Perhaps tomorrow they will plow. And there is the matter of the record, doing what is right for the sake of the record." "I am not interested in the record," I reply. "I want to stop this nightmare." The cell phone rings in the dark minibus, and we hear good news: the Palestinians have been released. We confirm this directly with them. They were kept handcuffed and blindfolded for eight hours in the army camp, their reward for wanting to plow their own fields.

Such was today's infinitesimal kindness, for the record. We forced them to release our friends. We did not give up. For a few hours, there was someone to stand between these cave dwellers and the settlers. Our friends knew this. They may have felt, momentarily, not quite so dreadfully alone. We won't desert them. It isn't much, it may not matter, and Allah has no stones.

May 31, 2003   Mufaqara and Twaneh

Dissonance, disjuncture, despair—these are the stuff of our experience, though these days the despair is punctuated by sudden bursts of irrational hope, since the American pressure has begun to be felt. This was the week Sharon used the word "occupation." One can assume he didn't mean it, yet for all that, something has now shifted, perhaps irrevocably. At the very least, we have the engaging spectacle of the extremist right squirming and sweating. I feel this is, perhaps, the beginning of the preliminaries to the opening of the prelude to the end.

But in Mufaqara and Twaneh, it is business as usual. The wheat and barley are ripe, waiting for the harvesters, but every single patch of earth that our friends manage to harvest is a near miracle, a victory over the settlers, the army, the government, the Civil Administration, and the distorting weight of Jewish history. Last week when Ta'ayush volunteers went down to South Hebron and were stopped by the army, the soldiers said to them: "*Yesh lanu atraot al katzir*"—"We have had intelligence warnings about a harvest"—as if working the land were something like a terrorist attack, something to be prevented at any price. As we drive down today in a minibus full of artists and actors from Tel Aviv, as well as the benign and lively presence of my anthropologist colleague from Columbia University, Val Daniel, I feel in my fingers the sheaves I picked last year at this time and place. Shavuot, Ruth and Boaz, the yellow wheat, the rocky hills, the tractors, the sinister tank on the hilltop—all are close to the surface of memory. A year has passed, and what has changed?

For Mahmud and Sabr, nothing. We crowd into the cave— the very first cave I visited in South Hebron, in the winter of 2002. It is as it was then: smoky, cool, dark, well-appointed, domestic, inviting. We listen once again to the terrible story. They tell it as the Jews tell the Passover story, but for the cave dwellers there is no one to divide the sea, to lead them to freedom. There is only a continuously shrinking world in which settlers and soldiers intrude, encroach, steal, push them closer and closer to the breaking point. The only light in the cave is the human link that Ta'ayush has created; they speak of this again and again. They tell the stories of our visits—I hear a straight, epic-style version of my own moment last winter of facing the marauding settlers from Chavat Maon; I hear how we were beaten and attacked and how the settlers pushed the tractor down the hill. . . . There is no doubt about one thing: for these people, Ta'ayush matters, like oxygen to the drowning.

Mahmud wants nothing more than to work his fields and come home peacefully to his cave. He used to work in Tel Aviv, but he could not understand how human beings could live in a place so full of glass and metal. "How can you sleep there?" He needs the open spaces, which are even more spectacular than usual this morning—a clear sweep across the horizon past the yellow-brown hills into the desert. In the old days, the time of his grandfather, these people owned and farmed lands all the way up to Tel Arad, today deep inside Israel. Nearly all this land is lost, of course, most of it swallowed up by the settlers. What is left is in constant danger.

We walk over the hill toward Twaneh, stopping across from Chavat Maon—where the settlers (conspicuously but only very briefly cleared away four years ago by the Barak government) are expanding their holdings, their ugly trailers staining the landscape. A long new building—a chicken coop?—sprawls over the hill beneath the pines. As we walk down into the village, the army seems to wake up; jeeps drive past, studying us, perhaps warning us, before continuing up the hill toward the settlement. We have tea as the narration continues: most families in Twaneh live in overcrowded homes, often with thirteen to fifteen family members in a single small space, but the villagers are not allowed to build—not even allowed to put in a modern bathroom in their courtyard (most of the houses have no modern plumbing), since that would constitute "expansion." The settlers, of course, are building steadily all the time, no problem there. The Palestinian schoolchildren now have to walk over ten kilometers to get to school instead of taking the direct route (two kilometers) past

Maon—because the settlers harass them, even shoot at them, beat them. When Sabr's eighty-two-year-old mother was out herding sheep last month, a settler arrived and began beating her. Ta'ayush members, who were in the village, rushed to her aid, and the settler started shooting; Salomke was hit by a ricochet (fortunately, nothing serious). A young settler boy, maybe thirteen years old, a Jewish child-turning-man, having learned the rules of life from his father, started beating Sabr's screaming mother on the head with a rock. So it goes. They tell these stories as if reality naturally held within it this dimension of normative cruelty, also as if they had hidden their selves somewhere deep enough to be at least partly immune to the continuous state of humiliation and attack. They can, however, continue the narrative indefinitely—it has endless chapters and illustrations; the suffering is great and the list very long. They are hurt; they are afraid. From their vantage point, George Bush's "road map" is so ethereal and abstract as to be wholly without meaning.

I do not think it is without meaning, but I am certain that the reality on the ground—in village after village, *khirbeh* after *khirbeh*, cave after cave—is desperate and will continue to be so. It is as if there were vast forces at work that will soon begin to mark boundaries, push people this way and that, ride roughshod over the wounded countryside, inexpressibly sad and beautiful as the light begins to change. Within this vortex, there are certain stable features: the murderous greed of the settlers, the cramped meanness of spirit that has infected so many of the Jews and nearly all their leaders, the deep loneliness of these simple farmers and herders still clinging, barely, almost hopelessly, to their homes. I do not think their loneliness will go away.

We are back in Jerusalem by 4:30, via the short road over the hills, via Zif, where settlers bombed the Palestinians' school, via the roadblocks and ever more settlements and the tunnels. From Jerusalem south to Hebron, the road runs past continuous settlement blocks, one large semi-urban sprawl. Will any of it ever go away? Is it too late? At home I turn on the news, and I hear, happily, that the Americans are preparing a list of sanctions against Israel if she drags her feet on implementing their road map. Something is changing here, yet plus ça change. . . .

April 24, 2004   *Jinba: Excavating Home*

It has been a hard winter, and the struggle is intensifying as conditions worsen on the ground. Now the great wall or fence threatens to slice off all this territory, adding it to Israel; Jinba, Twaneh, al-Mirkez, and other *khirbehs* belonging to the cave dwellers may be caught between the wall and the Green Line. More precisely, Jinba, Twaneh, al-Mirkez, and the other *khirbehs* are meant to disappear. Recently the Civil Administration has been trying to "persuade" the cave dwellers to move out of the caves, away from their fields and pasturelands, to the city of Yata, north of this area.

It is time, again, for the wheat harvest; a sunny spring day. Some two hundred of us have come to help with the harvest, as in previous years, and also to build a road (since all the roads here are forbidden to Palestinians) and to try to dig out the cave homes that the army destroyed from under heavy mounds of rock and dirt. By midmorning we are there. No army roadblocks await us this time; perhaps they have decided that a Ta'ayush workday in Jinba is of little consequence in light of their long-range plans. As the buses painfully climb the hill, I notice that I am very happy to be back, almost like coming home. Our friends—Muhammad, Jum'a, and the rest—are waiting. Charles M., my dear Parisian colleague, has joined us; part of me is seeing this scene through his eyes.

We quickly organize into work details. I start off, with fifteen others, harvesting the ripe wheat, first with my bare hands, later with a blunt, primitive, black sickle. It takes some minutes before I feel the rhythm of it working for me or through me. I start to feel the sun burning into me as I work. Unlike the last time, our Jinba hosts seem to feel a sense of real urgency; they need our help and want to use it to the utmost—perhaps they fear that the settlers will force them away from the fields and the wheat will rot or dry up. Their women are active beside us, managing their husbands and sons, rushing up and down the hill from field to goat pen to home. Within half an hour or so, we have cleared a small patch. The sheaves lie in large piles on the hill; a tractor arrives, and we lift the sheaves to our chests and load them onto the huge container it is pulling—a surprising plenty. It is so rare in political activity that one feels anything remotely like this kind of direct fulfillment. Harvesting wheat is like baking bread: an elemental instinct. A few hands—by now heavily scratched and pricked by thorns and already callused from the sickles—have done something real, made a small difference.

I look over the hills: there is the breathtaking view of the open desert below us, stretching to Arad on the horizon; Moab, in Jordan, is also visible to the east. All over the slopes, groups of Israeli activists are hard at work in little bunches, some in the wheat, others clearing stones or paving the road through the wadi. The happiness inside me surges upward, into my eyes: the mere sight of these friends, working side by side under the sun, conjures up a buried, stubborn sense of hope. The Israelis—some very young, some aging veterans of the peace movements—have all taken a day out of their lives to come to Jinba. Charles, who last harvested wheat as a boy of ten while hiding in the countryside during the war in France—sixty years ago—is working his way silently and skillfully through another field.

As always, I am on duty as the medic, with the medic's pouch beside me, and for once I am needed: Ezra, the true, tireless hero of South Hebron, comes looking for me. A young boy has fallen, earlier in the day, and opened a large gash over his left eye. I take the pouch and pick my way through the rocks uphill to a large goat pen, where several Palestinians are busy shearing sheep. "Here is the doctor," Ezra says to them, a little playfully, teasing them and me. They bring the boy, maybe four years old, maybe five. I spread out my simple tools beside a large rock; Ezra sits on it, the child on his lap. "What is your name?" I ask, and he answers, very softly, almost a whisper, "Issam." I wash my hands and unwind the dirty bandage they have wound around

his head. The gash is not too deep—it would be better if he could
be taken to a clinic or a hospital, where they might want to stitch
it together, but there is no way for this to happen; I am on my
own. I pour disinfectant on a gauze pad; I tell him it will sting
a little. Issam accepts this without complaint. I clean the wound
as best I can while Ezra holds the boy close to him, murmuring
to him, calming him with a gentleness beyond anything I have
ever seen in a man. This same Ezra who stood his ground with
me over a year ago in Twaneh when the settlers attacked us,
who fought back fearlessly—perhaps even relishing the fight—is
suddenly revealed to me in his deeper self. He seems to have
absorbed Issam's pain into himself in a matter-of-fact empathy,
without sentimentality, that lets him speak to the boy in very
simple, melodious Arabic: "Soon it will stop hurting. It's OK,
Issam. He's almost finished. One minute more." And to the
parents: "He will have a tiny scar, so you can remember this day."
I bandage the wound with a little antibiotic and give the tube
to the parents with several clean pads, I tell them to change the
bandage twice a day, to watch out for fever. Issam climbs down
from Ezra's lap and runs off. A sheep bleats plaintively as the
scissors cut through its curls.

I return to the wheat but soon am shifted uphill to one of
the cave brigades. There is a large group of foreign volunteers—
a Japanese girl, several middle-aged Swiss men, some younger
women—straining to excavate the entrance to one of the caves.
They are already tired; it is hard work, filling plastic buckets with
earth and stones and carrying them up and away from the buried
entrance to the cave. We have to break up some of the heavier
rocks with a pickax. A chain is formed to pass the heavy, full
buckets from hand to hand. Down below some workers are inside
the cave itself, sending up buckets filled with rocks. Somewhere,
beneath the thick layers of dirt, are buried the original stone steps
leading down to this home—destroyed, the owner tells us, by the
army in 1984 or 1985. By now it is noon, hot and heavy; soon I am
covered in dust. I am not so adept with the hoe and the pickax,
but after a while I get the hang of it. Ezra is working with us

here, with astonishing, impatient energy; eventually I am able to follow his method, quickly filling the buckets and passing them upward. But we seem to be making no progress at all, even after an hour or more; the entranceway is still buried, and there is no end to the earth and the buckets and the rocks.

Muhammad, watching us, is full of stories. There is the recent example of the armed settler who arrived here just after a ewe had given birth; the settler shot the mother in the head and also killed the baby lamb—just like that. Or the two shepherds who were abducted by settlers one morning, not far from Jinba, while their herds were out on the hills. When they were finally released hours later, the sheep and goats were, of course, gone—lost beyond recovery. In March 2003 an army patrol together with representatives of the Ministry of Agriculture and the Nature Reserves Authority confiscated the herd of Muhammad Mahmud Jabarin on the excuse that it had crossed the Green Line and entered a nature reserve. The patrol quickly brought the herd to an abattoir, where they ordered it to be slaughtered, claiming they feared that hoof-and-mouth disease would enter Israel. After that Mr. Jabarin had to pay the state the sum of NIS 64,000 for services rendered—the slaughtering of more than two hundred goats and sheep, some of them pregnant, that comprised all of his property, the earnings of twenty-five years' work.* And so on: there are many such stories, always of being attacked, and again attacked, and again, of hurt and insult and humiliation and dispossession and unfairness and straightforward malice and hate. I listen, I think I should try to remember all of it, to record it so that someone, somewhere, someday will know what we Israelis have done to these people; but there are too many wounds, the details run together, and these stories are anyway but a variation on the endless theme of human cruelty from all over the

*In the spring of 2005, a Jerusalem court awarded Muhammad Mahmud Jabarin NIS 250,000 in damages for his losses; the court also severely reprimanded the Ministry of Agriculture and the Ministry of the Environment for this arbitrary act of confiscation and destruction.

territories, in shockingly consistent repetition. What can we do? I return to the buckets, but I overhear an older activist say to Muhammad: "If they try to drive you away, we will stand beside you." Muhammad says without bitterness: "The only way they will get us to leave is if they shoot us and carry us away dead."

Never before have I dug up a buried home. How can a soldier bury a home? Did it mean nothing to him to run his bulldozer up to the entrance, to gouge out chunks of earth and rock and pour them over it, sealing it for years? Did he not think about the children born in that cave and about the old people who had died in it, about the fireplace with its pots and pans and coffee *finjan*, the skins and rugs and beds, the tools that generations had made and treasured, the shoes and clothes and ornaments? How could he bury a family's entire memory under the ground? And now, years later, we are slowly, heavily, awkwardly unveiling it, bucket by bucket, stone by stone. We work steadily for some three hours, and gradually the mound of earth we have displaced becomes bigger as we dump the buckets at the edge of the hill until, amazingly, at last, around 2:30, the first buried stone step appears. This family will soon reenter its home. Will the army, or the settlers, come back to undo all our work, perhaps in a single half-hour? Will we have to return to excavate it again?

They bring us the sweet, strong tea of these hills. I listen for a moment to the sounds of the desert, the music of Jinba. Roosters crow. Lambs bleat. Camels groan. Children run, fall, cry. Mothers call them. The wind. And for some reason, there flashes through my mind the text of the afternoon prayer, Minchah, for Shabbat, the poignant hope for this sweet moment in the week when the Jews are meant to rest: "May Your children recognize and know that their rest comes from You, and may they bless Your name for their rest." I hear the words in my mind, like a mantra, and though I am busy with the buckets and the stones, though I am tired, thirsty, blistered, baked in sun and dust, I think: This is my Shabbat rest, and I am truly at rest. For a brief second I wonder, amused, if the Jewish God would be capable of recognizing it and blessing his name.

April 2, 2005   Poisoned Fields, Mufaqara

It began some two weeks ago when Palestinians from Twaneh noticed a settler—almost certainly from Chavat Maon, the most virulent of the settlements in the area—walking deliberately through their fields in the early morning. Shortly afterward the animals got sick and the first sheep died. Then the shepherds found the poison scattered over the hills, tiny blue-green pellets of barley coated with what we later discovered was 10,080, or Rosh 80, as it is known in Israel—deadly rat poison from the fluoroacetate family. The quantities were large, and clearly more than one settler was involved; most likely it was a team of at least three or four who took the trouble to soak the barley in the poison and then spread it through the Palestinian fields, often carefully hiding it behind rocks or the thorny shrubs that dot these hills. The aim was clear: to kill the herds of goats and sheep, the backbone of the cave dwellers' subsistence economy in this harsh terrain, and thus to force them off the land.

Soon wild animals, too, started to die, including four deer and a *samur* weasel, an endangered species. Ezra found one of the dead deer and loaded it onto his truck; he left it at the entrance to the settlement of Maon, where it was photographed against the pastoral roofs of the settlers' homes. *Haaretz* published the color photo on page 2 of the news section; after that, the country seems to have lost interest. The Nature Reserves Authority sent someone down with a team to check out the situation and to start cleaning up the poison. They hardly made a dent. Last weekend Ta'ayush brought thirty volunteers to work all day in the fields, picking up the pellets with their hands. Today a second wave of volunteers will continue the task.

We are about twenty, including Eileen, for the first time on such a mission, and her cousin Judy from San Francisco, a veteran activist who is visiting Israel with a group from her synagogue; Judy has brought along another member of the tour, Ken, a longshoreman with a record of political engagement stretching back to the anti-segregation struggle in the 1960s. We hesitated about putting these guests from abroad at risk; there is always the danger of a clash with the settlers or the soldiers. But Judy insisted, citing the old civil rights ethic: "You have to talk the talk, and you have to walk the walk." Today she and Ken will walk and work beside us and our friends from the caves. Then there is Hagai, our seventeen-year-old neighbor, his long hair flowing over eyes and shoulders, who is studying the secrets of the soil; gentle Yael, a student at the university, one of our campus activists; a poet, Hamutal; Raanan, lucid and decisive; Amiel, who was on last week's expedition and has since acquired an amazingly precise knowledge of toxins; Anat, who has taken the cave people into her heart and put them at the center of her life; Isadora, from Ta'ayush Tel Aviv—in short, the usual happy cross-section of those who refuse to be silent, who need to act.

By a little after 10:00 we are passing the gates of Maon. Suddenly Anat, who is leading us together with Aviad, sees from the window of the Transit that Palestinian shepherds, some two hundred meters away, are in trouble. She stops and rushes off to help. From a distance we can see the shepherds and their flocks, and to their right a group of settlers, one of them armed; there are army jeeps and reserve soldiers and a few policemen as well, some standing between the two hostile camps, some parked at the edge of the highway. Amiel has already followed after Anat, and I follow him; Judy, Ken, and Eileen join me as we set off through the muddy fields. It is cold, windy, with light rain, but I assume this is just a quick stop to check things out, and we are in a hurry—so I foolishly leave my coat behind in the van. When will I ever learn? By the time we reach the shepherds, the rain has intensified, and soon we are drenched, frozen, and mired in mud. We hear the story, first from a shepherd draped in red keffiyeh, who is furious, spitting out the words: this field belongs to the shepherds, like all the rest, but the settlers have taken it for themselves; the herds can't graze now in the poisoned fields, so they had to come here; but the settlers tried to drive them off with a hail of stones. Luckily, no one was hurt before the soldiers arrived. "Why is there no boundary between us and them?" he is screaming. "Why do they attack us wherever we go? I am tired of this, day after day, tired of being stoned and poisoned and shot at." The soldiers, who are relatively relaxed and in good humor, calm him down. But the settlers are still there, only a few yards away, and full of hate—especially for us, the Jewish traitors who have come to stand behind our Palestinian friends. "You fuck Goyot, non-Jewish women!" they yell at us, their faces contorted with hate—apparently they think this is a terrible insult, though many of us would no doubt cheerfully accept the notion in principle. The rain continues lashing at us, whipped by a freezing wind.

Suddenly, a familiar face: bearded, lightly wrinkled, eyes glowing inside the hood of his red windbreaker. I can't quite remember him; he introduces himself as Lawrence, from the Christian Peacemaker Team (CPT). He has been living for the last weeks in Twaneh; he comes from a small town south of Winnipeg in Canada. Something about him, standing in the mud under the cold rain in South Hebron, open to the sky and the hills, uncannily tugs at my memory; and as we talk we both suddenly realize that we have been through this before, together, under worse conditions—that rainy day in January of 2003 (Lawrence remembers exactly) when the settlers from Chavat Maon came charging at us down the hill, shooting and hurling stones. "I'm the one," he reminds me, "whose camera they smashed. I still feel sore about that." Lawrence left the country after that, but something— the eerie magic of these landscapes? the innocence of the cave people?—has drawn him back here, into the danger and the anger and the cold. In life, everything repeats. We are standing here again, outside of Twaneh, wet to the skin, beside the shepherds from the caves, and our enemies, too, are here, unchanged.

Shivering, we wait for some decision on the part of the soldiers; we are afraid to leave the shepherds to face this alone. But we have work to do. After an hour or so, as the stalemate seems more or less stable, both sides standing their ground until the higher officer turns up, we slog back to the Transits through the mud. Anat stays behind to be sure the shepherds are not harmed. To my relief, the sun suddenly emerges, and I can begin to dry out.

Just before I leave, one of the Palestinians rushes over to offer me an umbrella. "It's for you, keep it," he says to me, smiling. "You deserve it."

The sun gathers courage; we move on to Mufaqara, a ramshackle set of tents, goat pens, and caves under the dark shadow of Chavat Maon. Children are playing on the stony hill; one of them cries out to his mother as we approach, "Al-Yahud! Al-Yahud!" ("The Jews!") We walk past the decaying carcass of a goat, not long dead. There are international volunteers here, waiting for us, some from the CPT, others from the Italian Dove group; they have plastic gloves ready for us and face masks for those who want them. We walk down the long path to the poisoned fields. There is a short briefing, and Amiel shows us a specimen of the pellets we will be looking for. We are off.

At first, nothing. We scour the nearest hill, poking at the shrubs, trying hard to see the turquoise glint of poison. This field was worked over by last week's volunteers—did they get it all? After half an hour I start to wonder if we have come here for nothing. I stare hard at the rocky ground, the purple wildflowers, the thorns, the fresh sheep droppings. Still no poison. Then a surprise: bending low, with my face nearly touching the soil, I see two—no, three—of the blue-green grains of poisoned barley. I scrape them up into the bag. Five minutes later Judy strikes gold—a huge cache of them. One of the shepherds had marked the spot with stones piled on stones; he points, Judy tries to see, at first sees nothing, looks again—suddenly her eyes take them in. It requires a certain kind of sensitized scanning. I rush over in answer to her cry, and we gather up many dozens of poison pellets with the help of the old spoons we brought with us from Jerusalem.

The real art of this grotesque treasure hunt is to retrace the vanished footsteps of the poisoner; one pile of pellets should, in theory, lead to another. And so, indeed, it goes. I find a large cache, Yael, working not far from me, another. Soon our sacks are filling up with poison mingled with earth and pebbles. The rain and wind have scattered the pellets or driven them deeper into the soil; each time we find another dumping place, we have to dig deep, well past the surface, to be sure we have got them all. This is another devilish aspect of the whole sordid business: the poisoner clearly thought it through and took pains to conceal the deadly barley from everyone except the hapless sheep and other animals grazing amidst these rocks. He left large enough quantities at each spot to ensure a kill. It takes 0.4 milligrams of active poison per kilo of sheep to kill—Amiel gives me the figures, the fruit of his toxicological studies all week long—which means consuming something like 300 milligrams altogether, with the barley. Several dozen pellets will do it. The poison acts on the heart, the brain, and the kidneys, blocking the production of two critical enzymes. The shepherds working alongside us tell us that they found many dead rodents, and there is also a dead black snake that seems to have swallowed a poisoned weasel.

They tell me that another six or seven sheep are dead, after the first eleven, and about seventy sick. I ask about other animals, and they mention the *samur* and the four dead deer—*ghazal*, that exquisite Arabic word. They say it with the easy familiarity of men who live outside, close to other creatures, and the syllables at once conjure up an image from one of the wine songs of the classical poet Abu Nuwwas:

> *wa-ghazālin min banī al-aṣ / fari maṣūbin bi-tāji*
> and a saffron fawn circled by a crown

And the poem's hopeful conclusion:

> *yā abā 'l-qāsimi ṣabran / kullu hammin li'nfirāji*
> Patience, Abu 'l-Qasim: every sorrow will be dispelled!

Maybe, after all, the poet was right and will be proven right again. But this comforting thought is at once replaced by a sad memory from the time of my last active reserve duty, in 1994, patrolling near Beit Guvrin. One of the army jeeps hit a wild deer on the highway after dark. The soldiers picked up the injured animal and brought it back to our base, where it lay dying over two or three days. There was nothing to be done to save it, but we could see it was in terrible pain. Above all, I remember its staring, tortured eyes, which seemed to me to be appealing for help. When it died, the Bedouin came to take the body. I suppose the magnificent deer of South Hebron also lay crumpled like that amidst the stones and thorns, dying alone under the open sky.

All the while, on the hill across from us, directly under Chavat Maon, one of these settlers, with his gun, is watching us, advancing in tandem as we move; he is dressed in black, an ominous presence, an Israeli Darth Vader. Farther up, a set of army jeeps is also in place. Maybe this time, at least, they'll keep the settlers from attacking us. By now the sun is warm and my clothes have mostly dried out, though a harsh wind is still slicing through us as we bend, scrape at the earth, occasionally excavate a horde of pellets. It is hard work, but above all it is baffling and agonizing, something beyond belief, this attempt to clean the desecrated land. As Eileen remarks, there is also something strangely intimate about the process of creeping over the soil, taking it in our fingers, sifting, examining, pressing, caressing, cleansing. From time to time, I straighten up and glance back over the wide, steep field, with twenty volunteers crouching at various points and angles in the utterly surreal choreography of rock and sun and slope; in the distance, the desert stretches away, covered at first, closer to us, in a thin spring coat of green. Wind stirs the grasses like the touch of some ironic, playful god.

Crossing the wadi, we climb up to the next field, and suddenly there are huge piles of poison clearly evident at many points, some marked by the sharp-eyed shepherds with "*rujumim*," as Hagai calls them—three balanced rocks. Our sacks are filling up with poisoned pellets. We tug at the roots of the weeds, claw at the soil. The blue-green grains are maddeningly elusive, and there seems to be no end to them; as we dig down, more and more come into view. The sense deepens of a well-thought-out, highly systematic scheme; this is not an act of random terror but a calculated plan with far-reaching consequences. The poison, decomposing, seeps into the soil and enters the food cycle. Perhaps it is already in the milk from these herds that the cave people are drinking every day. If we can bring back a sample, Dudy has offered to have it analyzed. It would be good to know. But already Birzeit University has studied the poison and identified it. The real mystery is not in these details, crucial as they are.

I have always hated the symbolic. It is the cheapest, most meretricious act of the mind, and the furthest away from anything real. But today, as I sift through the brown, moist soil under the eyes of the settlers, even I cannot resist the sense of something horribly symbolic. They claim to feel something for this land, yet they treat it—her—with contempt. It, she, interests them mostly as an object to be raped, despoiled, and above all stolen by brute force from its rightful owners. It belongs, in this wild, ravished, ravishing landscape, to the people of the caves. This is not merely a matter of injustice, though flagrant injustice screams out, unmistakably, at every point. Nor is it a matter of madness, though the settlers here are truly demented. It is, in the most serious, most atrocious sense of the word, a crime—a crime against the land the settlers glibly call holy, against life itself. Who, what human individual, would deliberately poison a wild deer? What kind of man would poison a whole herd and, through this, the community of human beings who live off this herd? But then the settlers have poisoned far more than a few rocky fields.

They are not, of course, alone. The intricate machine that put them there and kept them there for decades is still in place. The land is alive, a living being, worthy of nurture and love, but it is not a person like these shepherds whom the settlers and the government are trying to destroy. They are the true miracle, each one of them a world in his or her own right. Each one of them is more important, more worthy of nurture, than any piece of land, any field or terraced hill, any state or flag. It is they who are threatened now, and if we fail to protect them, it is our own selves that we fail. I will do what little I can, taking any risk.

It is getting late, and the wind has become fiercer, the light thinner, etching the surface of the hills, accentuating the rich play of green and brown. There is still a large amount of poison hidden in the field. We are tired after hours of combing the ground. We will have to return. The shepherds call us to eat. We peel off the plastic gloves, rinse the last traces of poison from our fingers. We are hungry; there is bread—the rough, fresh pita of the caves; also hummus mixed liberally with olive oil, tomatoes, tuna, tea—all spread before us on the ground with the astonishing simplicity and goodness of these people. "Eat," Hafiz urges us, one word saying it all, the sharing, the thanks, the hopelessness, the dignity and need. Bread tastes better out here in the fields. Just above us, on the hilltop, the soldiers watch, waiting for us to leave.

September 24, 2005   Susya, Settlers' Attack

It was, at first, a perfect autumn day in South Hebron. The light is changed, the hills more starkly outlined now. Birds are already flying south; white flocks of doves swirl upward, a grand gesture, from the caked, brown surface of thorn and rock and soil into a sapphire sky. As we walk from *khirbeh* to *khirbeh*, tracing the new map that is rapidly coming into existence here, a solemn illusion of serenity descends upon us; the slopes are mostly silent except for the occasional barking of a dog or braying of a donkey. We know it is an illusion. The new map, if we cannot stop it from turning into reality, will devastate still further the lives of our friends, Palestinian farmers and herders in the Susya encampment and the surrounding hills.

First there is the Separation Wall, which dips deep into Palestine in order to incorporate Beit Yatir and a string of new settlements (or so-called "illegal outposts") into Israel. Our old friend Muhammad Nwajeh points to a wide sweep of scraggly hill and field: "All this is my land—my grandfather purchased it himself in the time of the Turks; all of it will be lost." No one, needless to say, speaks of compensating Palestinian landowners for what the wall is swallowing up. But that is only the beginning. For the government planners have recently informed the Palestinians that thousands of *dunams* will also be seized to create a so-called "security zone" around the Jewish settlement of Susya, thereby impoverishing still further veteran families like Haraini, Umm Hubeitah, and, again, Nwajeh. The losses are immense—and utterly unjustified and cruel; the sole purpose guiding the planners is to take over reserves of land for the future expansion of Jewish settlement. Here is the one hope for action: the High Court of Justice might still force the government to back down, if our friends can organize themselves effectively for the legal battle.

We are here, seven Taʿayush volunteers, to help them. We have the latest maps, the boundaries adjusted to the confiscation orders that were posted two weeks ago; we walk in the afternoon sun over the hills, correlating map to field, photographing, recording, learning the land. At each one of the *khirbehs*—usually home to one or two families, with their children and sheep and goats—we are warmly greeted, offered cold well water or tea. Each family has its own story to tell. On one high hilltop, we meet the shepherd who was assaulted by settlers three weeks ago, then immediately charged by the army, in good Orwellian style, with having attacked his attackers; he spent these weeks in prison, and the case against him is still pending. Chances are he will be sentenced to a long term. He knows no Hebrew and cannot follow the court proceedings. We try to persuade him to file his own complaint against the settlers, the true villains, but he is uncertain, afraid of any further contact with the soldiers or the Civil Administration. This is the situation everywhere in these hills, Muhammad Nwajeh says to me afterward as we are walking. The people are exhausted, tormented, traumatized; they lose, over and over, to the settlers; they lose also in the Israeli courts; they are succumbing to despair. He has spent ten years of his life (and been arrested ten times) trying to galvanize the cave dwellers to action. It is a lonely business.

He is a good and gentle man, and he, too, knows the taste of despair. The system, the occupation, is killing him. Still, I say to him, trying to be hopeful, we may be able to save most of this newly confiscated land, and someday there will surely be peace; most Israelis do want peace. "What does it mean to want peace?" he says to me, the bitterness suddenly spilling over. "It means nothing, nothing at all, if you are not prepared to act in order to make peace happen. Everyone wants peace in theory. Where are the hundreds of thousands of Israelis who should be demonstrating in the streets, demanding an end to these endless crimes? Why do they sit silently at home?"

Why, indeed? Israel has left Gaza only to strangle Palestinian life on the West Bank. If you live in Twaneh or Jinba or Palestinian Susya, you know what it feels like to be helpless in the face of continuous predatory attack, wanton destruction, shots, blows, attempts to kill—all this with the connivance of the heartless machine of occupation. We are about to experience it again ourselves. At the last encampment we visit, Maya and I chat with a Palestinian mother, three children clustering at her feet. She points to the well that serves this family, some one hundred meters away. Yesterday they had just drawn water from the well for the flock of sheep when settlers from Susya descended upon them and spilled out the water on the ground. It happens almost every day. They come with guns; they threaten; they beat whoever is there. As we are listening, we see a small group of settlers approaching the well. Perhaps they are the teenagers we saw walking in the wadi just a few minutes before. Perhaps they will go away. It looks, at first, like that is what is happening. So we say good-bye to this articulate, good-natured woman and head for Ezra's truck, parked below the encampment. It is 4:30—we have been here all day—and it is time to head back to Jerusalem.

We are already seated in the back of the truck when I hear the first cries: our friend, the mother, is running over the hill, frantically waving her arms, screaming, clutching at her children. It takes a few seconds to take in what has happened. I see the settlers in a mad sprint into the middle of the Palestinian homes and sheep pens, I hear them yelling, and suddenly I see Raanan, one of our volunteers—we hadn't realized he was still uphill—struggling with a tall, heavyset settler who has masked his face with a shirt. We leap out of the truck and rush toward Raanan, and now I can see he is bleeding profusely from a head wound, his neck a brilliant, sticky mass of red, his gray T-shirt soaked in blood. The settlers, we learn later, saw him photographing them as they threw something into the Palestinian well; his attacker then rushed at him, threw him to the ground, and smashed at his skull with the barrel of his M16 rifle, opening a deep gash. In accordance with the dependable laws of God's orderly universe, my medic's kit is locked in the trunk of Anat's car, miles away over the hills—it seemed superfluous to drag it around through the long, tranquil hours of our visit; we kept carefully away from the lands the settlers have blocked off, and we weren't expecting any confrontation. I will have to improvise some way to treat Raanan. But first things first; another batch of settlers, most of them in their white Shabbat clothes, has suddenly appeared and is closing in on the rest of us. Two of them are carrying long clubs; another starts hurling rocks at us from close quarters. Ezra, well versed in moments like these, strides directly toward them, his rather fierce-looking black dog beside him. They seem to be afraid of the dog—our only means of deterrence—but by now they have circled us and are lashing out with clubs and fists.

An indescribable choreography enacts itself on the rocky slope. Raanan, remarkably, is still on his feet, camera in hand—he is a gifted film director and he wants to record this attack; Nissim, also a professional filmmaker, has managed to videotape everything up to this moment and is still working the camera valiantly as the settlers try to snatch it from his hands. I try to keep them away from Raanan. I yell to them, over and over, that he is badly wounded, that I'm a medic and need to attend to him; this, of course, makes no impression. They chase him up the hill. I take a few blows myself, nothing terrible. They lash out at Raanan's camera, and he fights them off. One of the settlers breaks a club on Ezra's head, while another one manages to grab Nissim's video camera, which he smashes immediately against a rock—but with incredible presence of mind, Nissim has already extracted the cassette and hidden it in his pocket, so, with luck, we will yet have clear documentation to show the police and the press. Minutes pass; we scramble over the rocks, with the settlers snapping at us, hitting out. Anat shouts a timely reminder not to respond to violence with violence—another miraculous moment of awareness in the midst of the noise, confusion, and pain. One of the settlers reaches for my shoulder bag and tears out the map we have so carefully outlined and corrected throughout the day. A steady stream of invective, some of it rather inventive, envelops us: "You drive on Shabbat. You take pictures. You are aiding the enemies of the Jews—they want to kill us and you help them; you should be ashamed. You are our worst enemies; you are worse than them. It's because of you that there is terror." Some of these fine sayings come from the mouths of young settler women, who have joined their men on this pleasant Shabbat afternoon outing; with them is the notorious Black Widow, the wife of Yair Har-Sinai, who terrorized the Palestinians of South Hebron until he was killed in a brawl some years ago. These women seem to relish the sight of blood. As for the men, the faces of those closest to me—religious Jews with skullcaps, most with beards—are disfigured by the chilling presence of undiluted hate.

The rest of the rite is more familiar. Soldiers eventually arrive—they were not, in fact, so far away; an army patrol had stopped to question us only some ten minutes before the settlers attacked. They shout orders and separate us from the settlers, who huddle together a few meters away, toward the well. In charge is an officer named Tzuri. He orders us to leave this place, which is, as of this moment, a closed military zone. If we stay a moment longer, so he says, he'll arrest us. We show him the settlers who attacked us, including the one who wounded Raanan; we beg him to arrest *them*, but he is utterly indifferent to this idea. "They don't interest me," he says coolly. As a result, the attackers quickly slip away to safety. An opportunity lost. The soldiers are more concerned with getting rid of us, the troublesome peace activists, but at least now there is time to clean Raanan's wound; I soak up some of the blood with an army bandage, and one of the soldiers expertly dresses the deep gash.

Suddenly the police are also there, and there is another surprise in store. The first officer is gruff, angry, hostile; he, too, makes no move to detain any of the remaining settlers, despite our urgings. But a young, apparently higher-ranking policeman takes over, and he is everything one could want at such a moment. He is a mensch. He understands; he is here to help us; he will do whatever he can to find the culprits. He is at once serious, self-assured, somehow cheerful, and profoundly humane. He tells us later that settlers in Hebron have taken out a "contract" on his name—they of course see a man like him, honest and aware, as their enemy. I don't know what the Israeli police department has done to deserve having this officer in its ranks. I, in any case, won't forget him. One of the incalculable benefits of days like today is the occasional chance meeting with such a person.

Whatever plans we might have had for this Saturday night are put aside. We spend the next six hours in the police station in Hebron, submitting our complaint and being questioned by the investigators. It is cold, we are hungry and tired, but the company is good and there is much to talk about and remember. I think back to our lunch—was it only a few hours ago?—in the tent at Susya; the trays of heavy, coarse pita and salads; the strangely bitter, delicious tea, bitter and sweet like the breath of life itself in these harsh hills. I remember how Raanan spoke to our hosts of the need to organize now, without delay, to bring their case to court; how he reassured them that we would be there to help at every stage; and how, when they thanked him, he brushed it aside and said, "You don't say thank you to someone who is just doing his duty." Now his head is hurting; he and Ezra will go straight from the police station to the emergency room in Jerusalem. First, however, they will testify, before any detail is forgotten. Maybe there is some slight chance that this time, for once, the settlers will not get off scot-free.

But probably not.

Still, we laugh, we were lucky today. There is the closeness we share, even if we were wrong to trust, even for a passing moment, that autumn facade of serenity. Nissim, who lost his expensive video camera—it is not the first one he has seen destroyed in the

South Hebron Hills—smiles ruefully at himself. "I sometimes think how boring my life was," he says, "until I met Ezra."

Sometime after midnight I reach home. All is quiet, but I cannot sleep. I am haunted by the vision of that Palestinian mother trying to shield her children from the marauders. I can hear her cries. I cannot comfort her. She and her family are alone, tonight, like all other nights, in the *khirbeh*, in the vast solitude of the desert and the hills. Alone but for her Jewish neighbors, who will stop at nothing in their attempt to destroy her.

3

Jerusalem: Isawiyya, Mount Scopus, 'Anata, Silwan

I teach at the Hebrew University. My office and most of my classes are on Mount Scopus, the original home of the university. From my window I can see the Mount of Olives, a slice of Abu Dis (and Al-Quds University), and the Old City, including Al-Haram al-Sharif—a good view, I usually tell visitors, of the capital of the Palestinian state-to-be.

Right next door to the university is the large village of Isawiyya, with some eight thousand residents. Isawiyya is, by Israeli law, part of the city of Jerusalem (it was annexed in 1967 after the Six-Day War); its citizens are Jerusalemites and should, in theory, enjoy the rights and privileges of all the rest of us. In practice, they do not. They cannot vote in national elections. They are subject to ongoing harassment by the police, the border police, and the Jerusalem municipality (which has a particular fondness for demolishing houses in Isawiyya that were built without official permits—such permits being almost impossible to obtain). Occasionally the village has been blocked off temporarily, and raids by the border police are not unusual. For most of the last three years, the main access road from the village into town, via Mount Scopus, has been cut off by a large barrier. In extenuation of these practices, the police will no doubt claim that shots have been fired from the direction of Isawiyya toward the campus or toward the road leading to the large settlement/suburb Maaleh Adumim, in the Judaean desert; or that stones are sometimes thrown by children of the village at traffic on this road or in the direction of the Hadassah Hospital. Even if these arguments are true, we are left with the fact that a neighborhood of Jerusalem is being systematically and collectively punished over long periods of time. There is no precedent for such collective punishment being directed at any Jewish neighborhood, nor would the Jewish residents of such a neighborhood accept anything remotely like what happens routinely in Isawiyya.

I do not want to give the wrong impression. The case of Isawiyya is not, by a long shot, one of the most painful. The residents are managing; at least one of the three roads to the village is usually open, and they have some access to the responsible officers in the police, who sometimes pay attention to what is happening in the village. None of this is comparable to what happens only a few kilometers north, in West Bank villages encircled by the army. Nonetheless, what passes for "normal" in Isawiyya, these last years of the Intifada, is clearly a situation of ongoing discrimination and humiliation—and that is how the villagers themselves perceive it. They are bitter and angry. To make matters worse— much worse—much of Isawiyya's traditional land (once covering a large area up to the borders of Al-Za'im to the southeast) has, over the years, been appropriated by the state. Recently a military camp was built on Isawiyya's property, and a serious threat of massive expropriation, in the interests of building the new settlement of Mevo Adumim, now hovers over the heads of the villagers.

Many of us at the Hebrew University, professors and students, feel a need to act. We cannot be indifferent to the fate of our closest neighbors. We see recurrent acts of oppression and injustice taking place no more than a few hundred meters from where we work, and we share our friends' sense of outrage. That is why, again and again, we have done what we could to lift the blockade,

acting in concert with Ta'ayush, which has long-standing ties
with the village.

January 29, 2002   House Demolitions, Isawiyya

To watch the destruction—self-destruction—of an entire world,
you need only ordinary eyes and the gift of not looking away.
A sickness sinks into the minds of many. Those who speak on
television, who read the news; those in the army who select and
organize their world according to some working idea, perhaps
a primitive one, in any case without the minimal empathy that
alone attaches us to reality and to each other; those who walk
the streets and ride the buses and close inward to shut out the
truth—all of these are infected without knowing it, and they pass
the infection on with a light, unconscious touch.

It is cold in the university, like the cold in the skin and what
lies under the skin. Heart of winter, a winter's heart. The air has
the sweetness of the rain and pines; there would be a great beauty
in the sky—a rainbow today as we set out for Isawiyya—but even
to see this beauty is now difficult, for the human ugliness in us
and around us blinds us all. Students wrapped in coats and scarves
glide darkly through the dismal corridors.

At 2:00, after my seminar, I rush to meet the Ta'ayush group at
the outer gate. I am wondering whether I will be back in time for
my 4:00 class. The forecast was for dry, cold hours in the afternoon, but it is wet still at 2:00 and soon gets worse. We notice
the rainbow. Yuri kindly gives me his umbrella; I have left mine
in the car this morning because I believed the forecast.

There are perhaps sixty or seventy of us, many Palestinians,
a few lecturers, mostly students. We are not expecting trouble.
This is a visit to the village—we are guests; we are not here to
demonstrate. Still, there are signs: "Destroying houses is a war
crime," in various languages. Yuri briefs us: We have come to
learn about the municipality's campaign of house demolitions in
Isawiyya. Three houses were demolished last week, and another
thirteen are in line—no Jewish neighborhood is ever targeted like
this. We set off. The police have a car in place to watch us, and

soon the border police appear in their jeep; but this is a minimal presence today—we are not worth more attention.

It is raining harder and harder as we walk down into the village, down and farther down, a long descent past the shops and houses of the main street that twists over the hill. It could be anywhere in the Mediterranean world in winter, the stone pink-gray-beige, rain-soaked under dark clouds. "This is their Rehov Yafo,"* someone beside me remarks. "But safer than ours," I say. Two days ago there was another suicide bomb, this time a woman; my colleague Vardit's father-in-law was killed. The heart of Jerusalem is becoming a ghost town, and the people of Jerusalem are afraid.

Catherine introduces herself, an image from the cinema, a born revolutionary in her brown beret, clear features, lucid presence. I had seen her in the Hebron Hills; today she is relaxed and speaks of her Ph.D. work in the English department. Maya, too, has a hat hiding her long hair; her umbrella has moved along to someone else, so I shield her with Yuri's as the rain intensifies. It is cold. The border police jeep has halted down below us in a field and is observing us, but we make no contact.

Darwish, one of the leaders of the Isawiyya community, guides us to the site of the latest house demolition. Just like on television, so it must be real: the twisted metal and jagged blocks of blown-up houses. We clamber down the lane to the three main demolition sites. Across from us there is a wadi and, just beyond it, many more houses, all scheduled to be destroyed. In the now-driving rain, the very idea of "house" assumes a certain salience: what does it mean to destroy a home, to destroy nine homes, to choose them because they are Palestinian, for no other reason, to punish the innocent, then to send the mayor's minion to lie about this to the owners? Ethnic war is a battle of lies, its very brittleness a sign of the brittle surface of the lie itself. The sheer transparency of the subterfuge makes the liar more brazen and more fanatical. Standing in semi-shelter on the steps of another house, Maya and I discuss the origin of the

---

*The main street of downtown West Jerusalem.

feeling. What comes first, the obscure urge to destroy and the rooted hate, or the ideation that identifies "them"—the despised other—and then "us"? I argue that the fundamental movement, given a priori, carries hatred without rationale. It is simply there, part of being human. Nationalism merely provides the super-structure. Maya is, I think, not convinced. She is probably right and wiser than me, yet is it not always more appealing to imagine people as moved to wreck or kill by an idea? Some tattered wisp of a romantic humanism makes us cling even to this negative of a richer rationality, Max Weber's belief that human beings are meaning-making animals, given to spinning words.

A few words at this point too: they thank us; we tell them we are with them. There are flags of Palestine being waved, noth-ing novel here. As usual, the sense of futility overwhelms me, ex-acerbated this time by the weather and the true pointlessness of going to look at the ruins. Maybe somewhere, along one of the streets, someone is touched by the fact that we came to witness and comfort.

Minibuses drive some of us up the hill. I am back in the uni-versity, in the backyard of the village, within a few minutes. On the way up, the minibus stops to pick up two Arab schoolgirls in bright red, soaked to the skin.

Tonight the news is mostly about the wall they plan to build. Sharon, true to character, changed the original suggestion so that the wall will include Abu Dis. The Sharon principle: When it is possible to humiliate them, do not miss an opportunity. And is the wall feasible at all? That the grim vision of this division seems to offer some dim promise, some semi-separation, a movement back from the settler state, is a clear sign of how low we have sunk. Are all walls made, first, of irony and only afterward of stones and wire?

Tuesday, February 19, 2002   *Dismantling the Barricade*

At first glance, it is clear: there are far too few of us. We stand in the bright afternoon light—maybe ninety, maybe a hundred activists—at the entrance to Isawiyya, near the new barrier. The police are, of course, waiting, with horses—a bad sign.

Isawiyya has now been partially cut off, the road blocked by the usual confabulation of mud and heavy rocks, piled up to a height of two to three meters. The holiday of 'Id al-Adha is approaching, always a time for family visits; the road that remains open, in French Hill, is steep and largely inadequate for the expected volume of traffic. Hence the timing of today's action, which would otherwise have been postponed in order to garner more supporters. Perhaps it would have been wiser to wait. But Isawiyya is not in the territories; after all, these people are part of Jerusalem and, literally, our next-door neighbors. There is something infuriating about the notion that we go on as usual, teaching our irrelevancies, drinking coffee in the faculty club, reading Telugu poetry, sitting on committees, whatever, and next door to us is a Palestinian ghetto of our own—that is, the army's—making.

On the way here, Galit tells me that the Knesset presidency has, this morning, agreed to open debate on Michael Kleiner's proposed legislation: economic incentives are to be offered to any Palestinian who will emigrate from Israel. The vote was five to three, with Naomi Chazan of Meretz opposing. Another sign of the times, another jolt. The legal adviser to the Knesset wanted the bill barred as racist, but she was overruled.

Not that things are clear-cut at the barricade, despite the limpid late-afternoon sunlight, the crystal pink of desert and hills. Last night my son Edan, hearing I was going on this action, gently asked if the barrier didn't, after all, fulfill some purpose. Maybe it would stop or slow down a terrorist? What gives me the right to remove it? I contemplate his doubt through the day (he is also afraid for me, I think, correctly sensing that this time there might be danger). The present misery was in some measure precipitated, at least in its most recent phases, by violent decisions of the Palestinian leadership. It would have been possible, in the foolish fantasy of the virtual, to have solved it all without this. Not everything is our fault.

Still, I am looking forward to removing that blockade.

Darwish is waiting for us as we climb down to the road, carrying shovels and plastic buckets. He embodies a certain old-fashioned dignity, and his face lights up when he sees me; apparently he remembers me from last time, though we didn't speak. Am I doing this for him, for the more or less innocent who live beside him, beside us? It must mean something to him, to them, that a group of Israelis and Palestinians comes together to rid him of one locked and bolted door. It means something to me.

The briefing is longer than usual, as we anticipate that there will be arrests. If the first line is arrested, there is a fallback leadership that will show us what to do. If arrested, we have the right to remain silent, as is strongly advised. Those not eager to reach this point are instructed, gently and with understanding, to stand in the outer periphery, away from the diggers.

As we hit the road, the police announce clearly over their loudspeakers that we have the right to visit the village of Isawiyya, but anyone who touches the roadblock is breaking the law and will be arrested. They say this with a certain panache, a Wonderland-like certainty that sounds absurd in the shadowless light. Absurdity is, in my experience, the primary texture of all such moments. Most of the policemen—there may be twenty or thirty—are, it turns out, Arabs. One of our group calls out to them, as things heat up: "What would you do if this were your own village?"

We lock into physical labor on top of the roadblock. I find swinging the pickax a little frustrating. There are too many people, several men above me on the heavy mound, all working rapidly but without coordination; rocks get hurled dangerously close to our heads, toward the wadi. Eventually I abandon the pickax and dig into the wet dirt with my hands. This is much better, both more satisfying and more effective. So far the police are making various loud noises but doing nothing serious, and the roadblock is shrinking visibly. The heavy rocks on the top can't be moved by one man alone (not in this generation, probably our grandfathers could have done it); but this gives rise to the even deeper satisfaction of working together. With a young

Palestinian from the village, tugging hard and scraping, I pry one of them loose and somehow push it to the edge of the chasm and down. This moment is probably the best of the afternoon for me.

Feeling somewhat superfluous, a geared-up, aging professor, I putter around the mound, filling baskets of earth and emptying them, pushing at the rocks, making a dent, my very own dent, though all of it, we know, is entirely futile—even if they let us demolish this roadblock, within an hour or two the army will have built a bigger, less vulnerable one. Usually under such circumstances, they return to sink concrete blocks into the pavement. It is not in our power to keep this road open. What, then, is the point? Doing it is the point.

The serious workers are mostly young men from the village, who seem to be enjoying this opportunity to use their muscles in the open air. They laugh a bit, despite ominous, restive movements in the police line just a few meters away. I enjoy seeing these village boys released into activity, protected as best we can by the Ta'ayush envelope around them. I cast my glance around, hoping Galit is OK, also Maya, who has never been through this before; who was until recently not the activist type at all, as she tells me later. She is by no means the only one to have been traumatized and galvanized by recent events, the steady ascent of the blind and strident fanatics who rule us and claim to speak for us. But now there is fear in the air—I feel it in me as well, though less than in the past; one gets used to these mini-confrontations after a while, and it is even possible to enjoy—yes, enjoy—the limbo of uncertainty before the tide turns.

Of course the police charge finally comes. We have been working perhaps fifteen minutes; it is hard to guess the time. They come right through us, some swinging clubs—these police-issue clubs have a nasty crook built into them and can cause real damage. Worse than the rampaging policemen on foot are the horsemen. A horse is truly astonishing in its size and weight when it comes at you—there is no way you can face it down—and the police riders are hitting out hard with their whips. Several of our people are hurt at this stage, including women who take whip blows on the head. The horses plow right through the roadblock, in a way furthering our attempt to destroy it; in any case, by now the big rocks are gone and much of the earth has been removed. We are fast approaching ground level, so the road could even be said to be precariously open again, for these minutes. We have lifted the siege.

Surprisingly, the policemen and border police retreat and regroup. Now they stand across from us in a surly, uncertain line, the commanders on horseback before them. We resume our work. I think the worst is certainly over now and take a moment to comfort Maya, who is clearly shaken. I then return to the line facing the policemen; we link arms, while behind us the village boys are still digging briskly. We sing a bit, and there are rounds of shouting: "This roadblock is illegal!" "Peace, yes; roadblocks, no." Despite our instructions—to remain nonviolent and nonconfrontational at all times, verbally as well as physically—some of the front line are shouting at the policemen: "Aren't you ashamed of yourselves? Haven't you ever heard of democracy? What are you doing beating up women and civilians? You are responsible for your actions, and it is your duty to refuse to carry out an illegal order. You may be guilty of war crimes. Think it over. Don't act blindly just because they tell you to." And so on. Do any of them hear any of this? Probably not. Meanwhile, reinforcements have arrived; we can see other police cars pulling up beside the university entrance.

The second charge is much more devastating than the first. Something has changed in their assessment: we are, no doubt, too few; were there only another thirty or forty of us, they might have hesitated. This time there are no holds barred as they attack, whipping, lashing out with the sticks, targeting some of us whom they seem to know from previous encounters. I can see clearly the sadistic pleasure one of the riders is taking as he lashes out at us. He has been waiting for this moment. Worse still, they start throwing stun grenades and tear gas; there are loud explosions. One gets used to even this noise, but the stun grenades can hurt if they go off too close to you. Some of the villagers are now running down the hill back to the village; meanwhile, we have some casualties, including Chana Keller, in her seventies, one of those tough Israeli women who have been through it all many times, too many times. Gadi wonderfully pilots her out of the main area of confrontation and sits her down on the curb. Blood is pouring from her head. Belatedly, but not too late, I remember that I am a medic; I am supposed to know what to do. I inspect the wound, wash it with mineral water and clean tissues. It looks superficial to me, though the blood is impressive, and she is cut in various places on her face. She is, however, much more collected than all of us hovering around her (Galit is crying); she reassures us and only with some difficulty can she be persuaded to be sent off with one of our cars to the emergency room at Hadassah, not far away. Gadi, holding her, says: "Chana, this is the second time in the last few months. I know it is now 2002, but still I think this is too much." He, too, has tears in his eyes.

She is not the only one to be hurt. Someone's arm has been broken. Others have minor cuts. Meanwhile, the police have deliberately started throwing stones—to make it look as if they were coming from the Palestinians. This makes good sense: they know very well how to handle flying stones, much prefer this to having to deal with nonviolent, principled protest. The world reverts to its sensible, if deadly, logic: *they* are attacking *us*. What they cannot understand, what baffles and enrages them, is the sight of a Jewish grandmother dismantling with her own hands a barricade they themselves have built against their proclaimed enemy. As one of the horsemen tells us later, with real venom: "I cannot forgive you for helping *them*."

I wander back toward the half-open space at the front, where a policeman is poking and pulling at Catherine and a Palestinian man, who lie prostrate on the ground, shielding themselves with their arms from the attack; Galit has rushed in to protect them, and I arrive a second later, to shield Catherine; the police give up, scornfully yelling, in their retreat, "Let them finish fucking one another." The implication is miscegenation, another unthinkable perversion. I lift Catherine to her feet; she is caked with mud, but otherwise unhurt. A few minutes later, another policeman grabs her by her long hair and drags her some distance before Yigal comes to her rescue.

Yasir, my friend of the Hebron Hills, is mistaken by a policeman for one of his own (he looks a bit like the border police). In the noise and confusion, the policeman urges him, "Throw a few rocks; get them going." Eventually some rocks do come hurling up from down below, from the direction of the village, and everyone is satisfied. Now things can wind down to an appropriate end. Neve, meanwhile, has been arrested. On the six o'clock news they will announce that Palestinians from Isawiyya threw rocks at the police, who then quelled their demonstration. It is good to inhabit an orderly world.

We relinquish the site and take up positions on the road leading into the university. The principle is: If Isawiyya cannot move about freely, neither can the university. Traffic begins to pile up behind us, buses, cars. An ambulance, apparently sent in by the police to pick up Chana, who is no longer there, is stuck and blares its siren; we clear a path immediately. A driver gets out of another car and comes toward us: "I have to deliver some books to the university, otherwise I would join you." Strangely, there seems to be no irritation among these drivers—they wait patiently; some probably support us. But the police want one last sweet revenge: they come in again, swinging clubs. This time Yigal is pounded in the leg and arrested to boot, along with two others. This is the moment of diminishing returns: if it goes on any longer, there is a real danger the police will head down into the village and start making arbitrary arrests. We reconvene in the parking lot to debrief, to hear a few words of thanks. Darwish stands, entirely unbewildered, in the midst of the motley army that came to his aid.

It is 5:30: two hours have passed. The roadblock is gone, for now. We will stand for three more hours in the Russian Compound, across from police headquarters, where our four captives have been taken. At 8:30 the arrested are released. Yigal emerges limping, in some pain. They have spent hours filling out forms; it is worse than India, this lunatic bureaucracy of the police station, perhaps still crazier than the rocks and mud and stun grenades, to say nothing of the words. It is quite cold in the Russian Compound, but the mood is easier now, and we are confident that all will be released. The Isawiyya contingent that has joined us, an entire bus-full, brings us fresh pita, falafel, *za'atar*, water. Lea Tzemel, inside the station, will handle the legal side of matters. This is the first action of Ta'ayush Jerusalem to produce arrests, not merely the *ikuv*, detention, that sometimes precedes arrest. No one seems unduly perturbed. People are chatting in Arabic and Hebrew, holding up Ta'ayush signs. A woman walks by and screams at us in hate, her voice sharp like the obsidian clarity of the night: we are the spoiled children of the ice-cream parlors, she says. Indeed.

At home, trying again to make sense, I open my e-mail. My mother has sent a note: "As for the Jews, we will get past this period, and we shall revert to *tzedek tzedek tirdof*—Justice, Justice, shalt thou follow*... I am sure of it." This in response, no doubt, to one of my querulous statements of despair about the Jews, who, en masse, like any mass, by and large disappoint. I should refrain from complaining like this to her; it hurts her. She is, I remember clearly, the one who taught me decades ago that because we were slaves in Egypt, we understand, we feel, we imagine, we will never hurt those who are oppressed.

November 14, 2002   Voluntary Transfer

It is Mario the Magician all over again. In any large-scale human conflict, we will find the slick jugglers who are able to mesmerize and delude, who can move a crowd to unconscious cruelty, against their own better judgment; who offer simple, stark solutions to a murky, ambiguous world.

Beni Elon has come to speak at the Hebrew University about "transfer," the forcible exile of the entire Palestinian population

*Deuteronomy 16:20.

of Israel and the territories, which he cheerfully advocates. The lecture is titled "All the Questions You Were Afraid to Ask About..." We gather in front of the auditorium, a large group of the left peace bloc, many new faces, a new batch of students. This is encouraging—at first it seems Elon will have no audience other than us. We laugh and relax; a breath of the old, sane Israel blows through the rain and the trees on Mount Scopus. It is not, after all, Italy of the 1920s. This is a struggle we will yet win.

But we are wrong. By the time we enter the hall, it is full. Elon himself will come in through the underground parking lot, so there is no point in draping our eloquent posters outside. "Zionism has no room for racism," and so on. There are several dozen of us milling around, including some young, obviously energetic men, who would be quite happy, I think, to get into a scrape with the thugs of Moledet, Elon's political party. We discuss strategy: should we sit through the sickening lecture and heckle the speaker, disrupt the event from within? I am firmly against this—it is *their* standard strategy; I have no wish to descend to this level, though, as one of the young peaceniks points out, it has worked wonders for the right. Look where they are today, and where we are. Still, I am opposed. Should we then stand silently in protest as the Moledet supporters walk into the hall? Eventually we decide we will enter, take our seats, and make a demonstrative mass exit as Elon begins to speak.

We go through the body search, empty our pockets. Going anywhere in Israel is now like getting on a plane. The security personnel seem taut; there are many on duty. We sit in the front rows and wait. He is, of course, late; let the audience warm up with anticipation. Many are holding *sforim*, old Jewish books that have been recruited to the struggle, that now seem naturally to belong to this atmosphere of genteel hate. Yet not so long ago these same books were, for me, the treasures of *humanitas*, guarantors of the values I thought were "Jewish," my mother's notions of kindness, the deep decency and moderation of my father, my grandfather's socialist convictions. I wonder what would happen if these books could vote.

I am sitting beside Louise, who came to Israel from South Africa in the mid-'80s. She had to make a choice—either to stay in South Africa and dedicate herself to the struggle against apartheid, or to adopt the Zionist-socialist option and come here. She chose the latter, her sister the former. Today her sister lives happily in South Africa, which crossed over the Styx. Miracles do happen. Louise is stuck, twenty years later, with the struggle against some Middle Eastern mutation of apartheid. The irony is not lost on her. The South Africans, she says, were lucky; the blacks had a worthy leader, and they were committed in a real way to democratic values—so when the moment of decision came, the whites were able to summon up some minimal trust. The Palestinians, I say, fail on both these counts. So much the worse for us, she says.

Meanwhile, Elon has come. He is heavy, bearded, capped with a huge white *kippa*. Viscous self-satisfaction oozes from every pore. He smiles, scanning his large audience. He fully embodies the settlers' ethos: self-righteous, fanatical, infatuated with brute power, contemptuous of the Arabs. He is introduced by the soft-spoken leader of the Moledet cell on campus, who says he knows not everyone in the hall is of their persuasion; but, he promises, by the end of the evening there will be many new members. Elon stands and takes the microphone. Yuri is ready first. Standing in the first row, he says, rather gently, overriding the protest from the podium: "We believe that this meeting is not appropriate, *lo ra'ui*, and we will now show you what 'voluntary transfer' looks like. We are leaving this room in protest." The Moledet audience claps as we get up and walk up the steps; they are happy to see us go. "I would not clap if I were you," Elon says from the podium. "Let them stay and hear the truth." I look back; the huge auditorium is still half full.

One of the security guards employed by the university seizes his opportunity. He was a former Likud activist on campus, and apparently he hates Arabs. Earlier, as we entered, he eyed a Palestinian man in our group and said to him, "I want to do something to you, but I can't right now." At this moment, as he sees us leaving, the urge must be too strong; he strikes out hard at the Palestinian, pushing and shoving and pounding him at the entrance to the hall and beyond, into the foyer. Violence unfurls like a flag, from the epicenter where these two men struggle and scream at one another. It is like watching a wave curl and spread. People fold around the two who are pummeling one another. Currents eddy and whirl; there is a rush of noise and fists and a riptide of fear. How far will it go? I can see Moledet toughs rushing up from inside the hall, eager to join the fray. Yet somehow the two are separated, though the screaming continues. Chana Rahmimov, dean of students, wisely and calmly intervenes; she is a full-bodied, authoritative presence, and slowly she talks the Palestinian man back to normal. She knows the name of the security guard who started the fight; very likely, she says to us, he will be dismissed.

We walk the black paths of Scopus toward the Humanities Building, where we are parked. Amiel, still recovering from the gunshot wound he got from a settler at the olive picking, is tired, too tired to speak; at night he feels the pain. The campus is eerie in the winter darkness, and naturally we get lost. We have been living in this labyrinth for twenty years, and—such is the nature of the buildings, the tortuous plan with which we have disfigured this mountain—we are still constantly getting lost. It doesn't surprise us. The one surprise tonight was the appearance of these young, sane, good-natured students, hungry for peace, ready for battle. They are tough and smart and lovable, like no others in the world. I see them in my classes, year after year. We are no longer the mainstream or the majority, we are no longer "Israel," but I would go with these people to the ends of the earth.

June 17, 2002   Sheikh Jarrah

The octopus seems inexhaustible; one turns momentarily away from one tentacle and another reaches out for you. The faces of suffering are also inexhaustible. Today we meet Mahir, who has been evicted from his home in Sheikh Jarrah, in East Jerusalem, in the wake of the settlers' campaign (led by Beni Elon and his cohorts). How many decades has Mahir lived in this house? The legal niceties are in dispute, have been since the 1970s; the Sephardic Council claims they owned this land from before 1948. In the meantime there was war, and the Jordanians took over and allowed building nearby. Mahir's family, refugees from some-where near Tulkaram, gave up their refugee cards and received this plot. After the 1967 war, the old claims came to haunt them, but only recently has the court allowed the government to evict these people. Previously, Israeli law protected them as *dayyarim muganim*, that is, tenants safe from eviction, whatever the precise legal status of their ownership. Now this has changed and the courts seem to be going along with the drive to take over lands in the eastern part of the city, closing off any gaps, encircling Arab neighborhoods, driving Palestinians from their homes, perhaps in the hope that thousands will leave. Transfer, in short: slowly, house by house.

It is hot, a dry summer afternoon. We meet Mahir outside his house, as he is now forbidden from entering it. We sit on a veranda next door; the lawyer explains to us the emerging night-mare. A young man makes the rounds offering cold juice or Coke, and later tiny plastic cups of Turkish coffee. Ta'ayush activists who have accompanied these families during the April week of threats and, eventually, the violent eviction (by vast forces that the army/police allocated for this heroic task) speak with the passion of friendship. Point by point, the houses are falling, and each one hurts.

Nasir is in the next street, also dispossessed. He is now living in a tent in the street right beside his own house, which he is not allowed to enter. Palestinian women with babies emerge from the tent to stare at us, the odd Jews who seem to care. The TV team is filming, the reporters taking notes; yet who will believe them? The whole scene is barely credible, the normative surreal-ism of our life: you inhabit a black tent outside your own locked front door. Nasir is determined; he will not leave: "The air of Jerusalem is good, unique. We will not exchange it for anywhere." For decades this has been home.

It is, in a way, a simple principle, common to ethnic war: what is mine is mine and what is yours is mine. If you object, I will kill you, quickly or slowly. The only bit that is out of place and unreasonable is our presence here, in between the lines. Can we help? What can we possibly do to strangle the octopus? These little outposts of settlement are springing up everywhere, to say nothing of the grandiose plan at Jabal Mukabbar, a big link in the chain. Middlemen, straw land-dealers, are buying up houses like these for the settlers; many Palestinians are now so desperate that they are prepared to sell anything they have. This is an old story around here. Those who won't sell are thrown out of their houses by the army, court orders in hand.

The afternoon is golden, sandy, rife with sadness. Were someone to apply the judicial principle of restoring some lost status quo ante, then my house too—which we purchased from Jews who had bought it from other Jews, settled there by the government after the War of Independence—would be given back to its original Palestinian owners. Much of West Jerusalem would be restored to Arabs. But of course the courts are uninterested in this symmetry; they are quite prepared to let the system serve the government and the settlers. It is all legal, and foolish, and wrong, unbearably wrong.

We climb up the hill to the settlers, smugly ensconced above a cave they have recently declared to be that of Shimon the Righteous, a Second Temple–period rabbi. Wherever you go in Israel-Palestine, there are rocks, caves, springs, trees, that must be holy to someone, therefore a reason or excuse to steal. So this dusty, foul-smelling cave is invested with the mystery of invented memory, and this is reason enough to drive out any innocent Palestinians who happen to live nearby. A heavy religious woman asks who we are, and we explain. "Are you not ashamed," Emanuel asks her, "to be living here after evicting the owners?" No, she is not ashamed. These were Jewish homes before 1948 and the

Arabs chased out the Jews, so now she is chasing them out. Thick Jewish books—Gemara, Shulchan Aruch—are piled on shelves in the dark room. She doesn't care about Arabs; the notion they might have rights of any kind is ludicrous. Besides, she proudly tells us, holding her child on her lap, relations with her Palestinian neighbors here are excellent. "Indeed," replies Emanuel, "that is how people speak about their dogs, their cats, their mules; they have excellent relations with them, and the animals have no rights." The woman is untroubled by the analogy. However, seeing her up close, my urge to scream and claw and hit is suddenly gone. I am tired, mired in grief. I have no energy to begin to argue and explain. That is why, for now at least, she will win. She sits doggedly at peace inside her sick inner world, as all of us inhabit our worlds. I can see she is human, can even imagine something of the childhood that produced this opacity of spirit, this blindness—this fear and hate. Still, I cannot forgive it, not for anything in the world.

It is hopeless; anyone can see it. Two ruthless national movements are locked in conflict, street by street, house by house. One side is infinitely stronger than the other, but no more generous; it repeatedly uses, or misuses, its power—the vast apparatus of state and army and court—to dispossess, to threaten, to appropriate, to dominate, to destroy. In this it is perhaps not very different from most modern states. Its citizens, for the most part, are silently complicit. The losers put up tents in the streets, trudge off to court to lose again, go mad with hurt. Nothing will heal it.

On the way back, the Transit takes a few of us to see the new expropriation of lands from Isawiyya, just past the highway going south to the Dead Sea. The army has already marked off the land. Isawiyya had twelve thousand *dunams* of land once, not so long ago; farmland, for the most part, theirs since long before the Turks came here, since the Mamluks, maybe before the Mamluks. Land that was home. Today they are left with some six hundred *dunams*, and I am not sure if this includes the latest slice of thirty *dunams* expropriated for the new army base. The army turned up two weeks ago and left a written announcement of the

impending action lying on the ground. They didn't even bother
to tell the people of Isawiyya, their victims, directly. Muhammad,
standing on the hill in the vastness, shows us the plan, entirely
transparent even to my unpracticed eyes. A line of settlements
will link up Anatot to the north with Kfar Adumim to the south,
effectively blocking off the Palestinian neighborhoods, cutting
any contiguity. They are being hemmed into tiny, stifling prisons,
stripped of what was theirs and of the future that should have
been theirs.

A blue jeep of border police, perhaps Mukhabbarat—Shin
Bet—is in the village as we drive back toward the university.
We decide not to stop. Muhammad is clear and articulate and
impassioned at the latest outrage, consistent with all the others.
We will try to stop this act of cruelty—one more—but I am far
from sanguine about the outcome. I drink in the afternoon light,
the breathtaking shift in vantage point; another piece of this
tortured country has now come into focus for me as I look back
toward the university from the other side of the big road south.
In the distance, Al-Zaʿim, then Al-ʿAyzarīyah, then Abu Dis.
Heartrending beauty once linked these villages together with
invisible threads. The threads are being cut day by day, one by
one, wantonly, willfully, relentlessly.

As for me, I feel rather like the simple Jew who went every
day to the Western Wall to pray for peace. Years passed, and he
never missed a day. Still no peace. After twenty-five years they
sent an angel from heaven to talk to him. "Very impressive," said
the angel, "coming every day for twenty-five years. What does it
feel like?" Said the Jew, "It's like talking to a wall."

February 20, 2003   The Campus Will Not Be Silent

Some thirty of us, professors and students, gather tonight in the
Geology Building on the Givat Ram campus to found yet another
peace organization. It has been raining hard all day in this soaked
and windy Mediterranean winter, the "limitless rain," *athesfatos
ombros*, that Homer speaks of. Nights are fragrant and cold. The

almond trees have blossomed; silken bursts of white punctuate
the gray-green of the hills; spring will come.

We sit around a long rectangle of tables under Dudy's gentle
command. There are dozens of leftover fragments of the Israeli
left, still active or newly active, some highly effective (Ta'ayush
more than most); but, in general, the academic community committed to peace has yet to make its voice heard either within
or beyond the university ramparts. Tel Aviv University has one
organization, HaKampus Lo Shotek, "The Campus Will Not
Be Silent." Now we in Jerusalem will set up our own parallel
group under the same name. (Some, like Galit, want to include
Brit Shalom in our title—a deliberate echo of the legendary organization of Gershom Scholem, Shmuel Hugo Bergman, Ernst
Simon, and others, from 1925; Martin Buber and Jehudah Lieb
Magnes, first president of the Hebrew University, supported it
from afar. Old Jewish revolutions, however doomed or ineffectual, never die.)

There is much that requires immediate action. Take the case
of the Israeli Arab student from Haifa repeatedly denied entry
to the Mount Scopus Library, which he needs for his research—
even after the police issued him a security clearance. Amiel will
pursue this one. There is the unconscionable treatment of the
Palestinian janitors who work for a pittance cleaning the university buildings. We need to strengthen ties and express solidarity
with the (usually closed-down) Palestinian universities. There is
the matter of the refuseniks, recruits and reservists who refuse
to serve in the occupied territories, including Yoni Ben-Artzi
(well on his way, I think, to becoming a folk hero—now over the
200-day mark in jail). But beyond these immediate, mostly practical matters is the need to reclaim our patrimony. Once we—
professors, students—held in our hands the keys to the symbolic
resources of this society. We have let them slip.

Our medium is words, so it is with words we must begin. I
am in charge of organizing the first teach-in, in two weeks' time.
Shades of Vietnam, or of Paris during the Algerian war. There is
no dearth of topics: the ongoing appropriations in East Jerusalem,

Gandhi and nonviolent resistance, the occupation as an idea, the silence of the intellectuals. I personally favor focusing on war crimes, in particular expulsion. We hear tonight that many Palestinians from Hebron have, in recent weeks, been driven from their homes and concentrated in temporary camps. I want to make this visible and knowable and to link it with the long list of Jewish communities in Europe exiled repeatedly, over centuries, from their homes. A pointed lesson in the common history of the Semitic peoples.

It is a beginning, no more, yet I am heady with hope as I drive home. Something is ripening here under the last weeks' cold rain. Perhaps—no, almost certainly—we will fail. Yet tonight I see the resilience of human decency in hard times, and I am glad to have some small part in this story, the story of my generation and its choices. I am even oddly grateful. Eileen tells me when I come home: "You've become an activist." I wonder how, or why. I'm not much good at it. I can barely explain it. And what of my motives—the restlessness, the rage? Is it the same with the others? Still, I can't look away. Few of us, it seems to me, thinking back over tonight's discussions, nurture operative illusions. As in the *Bhagavad Gita*, action is not about results, not about "having" or even "winning." It is, surprisingly, about "being," or about not deadening ourselves to the cruelty all around us. Thus, being alive, one takes a stand. It is not for us, now or ever, to complete the task, but, like the almond, we need to ripen, burst open, bloom.

May 23, 2004   Police Headquarters, Russian Compound

Zion Shai is chief operations officer in the Jerusalem Police. We file in—Yuri, Alon, Galit, and I together with Darwish Darwish, our old friend and one of the elders of Isawiyya, and two members of the village council, Daud and Muhammad Abu Hummus. Darwish is decked in white keffiyeh, rosary, gray robes—a massive presence. Our object is to get the police to reopen the road from Isawiyya to the university.

The barrier we took apart with our bare hands on that winter afternoon two years ago, when we faced the horses and the whips and the stun grenades, has been replaced by a more serious obstacle made of immovable concrete blocks; even pedestrians can only barely squeeze past. The village is left with the road opening on to French Hill and another, smaller one far to the south. The closure of the university-access road is a huge nuisance: the old approach road for taxis—a major industry in the village—is cut off; students who come to the university from Isawiyya have a long, roundabout walk unless they can somehow clamber over the barrier; indeed, the general sense is of being encircled, trapped, and, as a result, deliberately degraded. In this respect, nothing has changed.

We take our seats across the wide wooden table from the officer, who calls in a younger subordinate to take notes. We introduce ourselves, and he writes our names, one by one, on a long sheet of checked paper from what must be the Isawiyya file.

Shai turns out to be soft-spoken, intelligent, humane, impassive. Middle-aged, balding, with many bars of rank on his epaulettes, pistol and cell phone in his waistband; also lively, searching eyes. He knows his city. He was in Isawiyya this morning, is there at least once or twice a week. He claims the road was closed because the council has not kept its promise to stop young boys from throwing rocks at cars on the Maaleh Adumin road. In the next breath he says this is not collective punishment; inscrutable "operational considerations" lead them to open and close the road under various conditions.

We argue mildly with him, and slowly he warms to this moment. The setting is colonial, patronizing, but far from hostile; even if peace comes someday, there will be policemen—Jews or Palestinians—like this one, worrying about kids throwing rocks. Darwish protests that they cannot control every single child. We bring the example of Bar Ilan Road, where ultra-orthodox Jews sometimes throw rocks at cars traveling on Shabbat; have they ever closed down a main road in some Jewish neighborhood for months on end? None of this seems to have any impact. Yuri, calling on manners learned during his formative years in a totalitarian state, says in a neutral tone: "We understand that this road is in a gray area, not something absolute. All we ask is that you think of it on the brighter side of the gray, not the dark." This is by far the most effective intervention any of us makes during this long hour. Alon's trenchant legal arguments seem to carry no real weight with the policeman. Shai speaks with the elaborate patience of a weary grown-up, explaining "facts" to innocent, well-meaning children. The Isawiyyans are also, it seems, classed as childish (though not innocent); the tone is unintentionally, unconsciously condescending, and Darwish's pleading, in a jumble of semi-fluent Hebrew syllables, falls flat; eventually he lapses into silence. Stirring uneasily beneath the tall ceilings of this grand nineteenth-century Russian building—where pilgrims once slept—I watch our Palestinian friends almost visibly shrink and grow mute.

Daud, however, suddenly insists on having his say, in his own language. Perhaps he has grown tired of this familiar game, where he must lose again and again. He speaks a simple, dignified Arabic, slow enough that I, too, can understand. "Are we not citizens like everyone else? Do we not have the right to security, to move freely in our own neighborhood and in the city? You are the police—it is your duty to protect us and to ensure those rights, not to impose punishment arbitrarily, not to threaten us. Are we less human than the rest of the people of Jerusalem? Do we not breathe the same air as you? If you hurt us, do we not feel pain?" Perhaps, I think, were this Venice, were we inside Shakespeare's play, policeman Shai might be moved to act. "If you prick us, do we not bleed? . . . If you poison us, do we not die?" I can hear the lines—not so long ago they were ours—whispering inside my head, and for me it is suddenly enough, too much, too bitter an irony, to hear them issuing from the lips of this elderly, sun-parched Palestinian man, speaking his truth. Zion Shai smiles, stands up, extends his hand. We file dutifully out into the dying afternoon, like good colonial bourgeois.

August 5, 2004   *Isawiyya*

Someday, when "it" is all over and all the futilities and absurdities and failures have been reckoned and recorded, the barrier at Isawiyya will remain in my mind as the most absurd of all.

It is impossible to make sense of it. Our attempts to get the police to unblock the road have borne no fruit. The other roads in and out of the village, on French Hill and to the east, are still functional; so why have they put up this ugly barrier, mostly clumsy cement blocks in two uneven rows with a small space between them, right here on the one road that would make life a bit easier for these people? Unless, of course, the whole point is simply to humiliate and embitter them, to show them who is master. The barrier in its present form would stop no terrorist, even one fainthearted or inept. A steady stream of villagers on foot pours over and through it, like mercury from a broken thermometer. They clamber up the steep hillside, slither in between the rows of blocks, climb a small pile of jagged rocks with rusty wires sticking out, and emerge triumphant onto the flat footpath that will take them to the university or the hospital or the city. In the winter, the hillside will be muddy and slick, so it will be harder to reach the cement barrier; but for now, in the sun-baked summer, almost anyone can do it.

Or could until Sunday, when, out of the blue, an army bulldozer appeared and chewed a shallow hole out of the hillside. It isn't much of a hole, but it's enough to stop most of the pedestrians. Athletic teenagers and young men can still easily make the climb. Anyway, it's not clear that the police really intended to seal off the route entirely. It seems to be more important to them simply to turn the screw a little tighter each time.

So there it stands, a sloppy, half-dashed confabulation: the forlorn gray slabs, some of them gaily painted with graffiti; the untidy heap of earth and rock that the bulldozer dumped on top of the hill; the unfinished trench or pit gouged from the slope; the boulders still in place from the first barricade of two years ago. Beneath this unkempt, stony sentinel spread the lovely stone houses of the village, and beyond them are the shocking hills, purple under the sun. It is almost as if they had picked a spot at random to make their point—somewhere in this violent and sorrowful landscape there had to be a site, however small and ineffectual, where the Jews could proclaim their control and the villagers could gather, angry and bewildered, to protest.

We join them this Thursday afternoon at 3:00. The original plan, conveyed to us last evening in Hani's home over tea, was for the younger villagers to appear with a hundred sacks full of earth; together with our activists, they would fill up the recently opened trench, so that pedestrians could again climb the hill. Even this pleasant image has a paradoxical aspect: more sand and rocks on the sandy, rocky hill, at the center of Nowhere. We know, of course, that the police are unlikely to let us carry out this grand design.

Still, a handful of activists straggles in. It is very hot in the sun, especially for Ruth Nevo, who just turned eighty, and upon arrival we learn that the Isawiyyans have moved the time back by half an hour, to 3:30. There isn't much we can do about it. We play at climbing through and over the cement blocks; we stare down at the foolish pit; we look uneasily over our shoulders at the police jeeps and vans that are arriving, right on time. A few journalists are taking pictures. It is my turn to give the briefing, but there is rather little to say; we are not even sure if our friends from the village will turn up with the sacks of earth and the shovels. Hani and Muhammad are suddenly full of doubt: where are all the young men, the real foot soldiers prepared to face the police? I run through the standard scenario: this is a nonviolent action; we will not seek any confrontation; we are to mingle with the Palestinians, for their sake, to protect them; if the police attack us, those who are unwilling to get arrested should move to the rear; the medic's pouch is ready; we have Manal, the Ta'ayush lawyer, with us; we know why we are here. But it all seems a little silly and unreal, like the barrier itself.

We wait, milling around aimlessly. The border policemen are heavily armed, though I am relieved that this time, at least, there are no horses. Still, Hani is reluctant to move ahead. The shovels turn up at last, but it is clear that once we start to use them—the idea is now to shovel the earth from on top back down into the pit it came from—the policemen will charge. No one is eager for that moment. We are too few, hardly more than the police themselves; they are likely to arrest us all, and some will be hurt. I don't like the thought of Ruth or Anita or Nita being exposed to a charge of soldiers wielding clubs. The Ta'ayush representatives consult: perhaps we should send the villagers home and fill in the trench ourselves, as Chen suggests—the police are less likely to use violence against Jews. But the whole point, I say, is to do it together, if we do it at all. In any case, no one imagines that what we do will make a difference—the army will dig the trench again later this evening or tomorrow morning. Maybe the journalists will take a few pictures of the police charge and the arrests.

Supervising the police contingent is Avi Cohen, a high-ranking officer, with three bars on his epaulettes, very well known to the villagers; he seems to have overall authority for Arab East Jerusalem. The villagers know him and seem not to hate him—the one they hate is a lower-ranking Druze officer who enjoys showing off his power, threatening and mocking, swaggering through the village, sending in the border police to explode tear-gas grenades as a sport. This officer is the one who, they say, stands behind the blockade. He is not here today. For the moment, the police are keeping their distance, watching us, weapons drawn.

If we are not going to get into a clash, we have at least to say something to those who have come—some fifty or sixty altogether, by my count. We assemble as many as we can on top of the barrier itself, a photogenic group, legs dangling down over the cement. Hani and some of the elders climb the hill, and Hani speaks: "Thank you for coming. We welcome you in the village. We are troubled by the barrier, which has no intelligible purpose, which is here only to punish and cause pain; but our real fear is the new settlement, with four thousand housing units, recently announced by the government. It has a name already: Mevo

Adumim. We are not sure, but it seems it will be built in part on our lands. The first confiscation orders have already arrived. We need your help, all the help we can get, to fight it." He is right, of course—the barricade is nothing compared to this plan that is clearly part of the overall devilish design to create a stranglehold around each of the Palestinian villages in the area, cutting them off from one another. We will have to organize as best we can and to bring this case to the courts in the immediate future.

As he is talking, Darwish suddenly arrives in his long brown robe. He heads straight for Avi Cohen. Something passes between them—many words, not only words. He pulls the police officer down into our space, with villagers and activists on every side. Cohen starts to speak: "There is not much to say," he says. "We thought we had some arrangement with the village, and that there would be quiet, but things are, it seems, not so orderly around here. . . ." At this point Manal cuts him off: "It's bad enough that you come here with your soldiers and put up this idiotic barricade—why do I have to listen to your lies as well? Can't you see what you're doing to these people? Who gave you the right to torment them?" Cohen falls silent, then turns and walks away, up the hill.

The villagers are, at last, aroused. Debate swills through them. Darwish is angry: why did we have to insult Cohen? Darwish thinks, still, that he can persuade them by sheer persistence and force of personality, the familiar tools of the Old Guard. Others are less sanguine: "For years we have tried to talk to them, and look where we are today. Nothing works but force. We can't take it lying down anymore." Tempers rise; there are heated words. Darwish turns to me and says, "Let them argue. Come with me."

The two of us climb the hill to where Cohen stands among his men. "Why haven't you given us an answer?" Darwish asks him. "You were supposed to initiate the meeting," says Cohen. "So when can we meet?" Darwish presses him. Silence. "Tell me," I say to him, not knowing what else to do, "why did you dig that trench? Can you explain to me what purpose you think it serves? Is there any logic at all to what you do here?" Cohen looks at me, looks away; he has nothing to say. Who am I, anyway, and what am I doing in Isawiyya? Suddenly, he says to Darwish: "Call me on Tuesday. We will meet and settle the whole thing once and for all."

Darwish rushes down to inform the rest. Maybe this time it will work. He seems relieved. We will go as a delegation—he, Hani, some of the professors, our lawyers. The sadistic officer will also be there; maybe his superiors will rebuke him. But I am left with the futility and the rage: Cohen, the lord of the manor—probably not a bad man, probably a reasonable man—treats these people like fractious children. His manner is supercilious, his world apparently rich in certainties. "You have to show them who is boss. Never give away an iota of your power, your control, your assurance. The slightest weakness will be the end of you. Be a man, be tough, listen to them, but give no ground. They understand only force." Some of the same words I heard in Arabic, at the barrier, only a minute or two before.

Still, I am a little sorry they didn't let him speak—though I, too, caught up like all of them in the craziness of this afternoon, am unwilling to give any ground. In Cohen's eyes, I know, I am useless, at best a nuisance, at worst an active traitor—helping *them*. Long ago I have given up the hope of making him and those like him understand even a little of what I see and hear, what I heard last night in the village—the wounds rankling from long insult, the acid in the soul, the bitter taste that never leaves the tongue. Does he really think his soldiers and their guns will save him from that, from the final consequences of that, from what he has done and continues to do day by day, not to Isawiyya but to his own mind?

July 2, 2005   Workday, al-Bustan, Silwan

Ankle-deep in the pungent, turbid water of Silwan, we stand in the old, ruined aqueduct, hoes and pickaxes in our hands. It is 9:30 in the morning and already hot. We have come to clean the aqueduct and make it functional again; so we scrape away at its muddy bed, filling buckets with sandy clay and rocks to be emptied out on the hill below, where a new terrace is being built by our Palestinian friends. The task is Sisyphean; the Palestinian locals keep reassuring us that we will hit bottom after fifteen centimeters or so, but as the day progresses, the channel becomes deeper and deeper—with no bottom in sight. The water flows downhill from an ancient spring somewhere up-mountain—so we are told—a spring older than King David, who lived here in Silwan, older even than the Jebusites from whom he captured the city three thousand years ago. The Silwanis think the spring was here from the beginning of time.

In the old days, the aqueduct carried this clean springwater in a carved stone channel just under the wall of heavy stones that lines the road; in this way, water reached down into the village for drinking, washing, irrigation. At some point in the last years, the Jerusalem municipality blocked it at one end and built a large concrete cesspool just below it. So now the water still emerging from the ancient spring mostly stands stagnant in the aqueduct, evaporating in the hot sun of the Jerusalem summer. The people of al-Bustan have long wanted to unblock the channel, to clean it and let water flow back toward their neighborhood; but they have been afraid to do this on their own, knowing very well that the police or the border police would almost certainly intervene to prevent them. Only our presence here today—some one hundred volunteers from Ta'ayush, Bat Shalom, Machsom Watch, and the Committee Against House Demolitions—has given them the freedom to put their ready plans into operation.

We are here, however, not just for the water and the terrace but mainly because of the municipality's plans to demolish eighty-eight houses in al-Bustan—in fact, to wipe out the neighborhood altogether, ostensibly in order to create an "archaeological park" in the heart of Silwan. In fact, the intention is very different and altogether transparent: these houses will fall victim to the latest attempt to Judaize East Jerusalem, pursuant to the settlers' stated goal and the government's clear policy of making the lives of Palestinian Jerusalemites as difficult as possible. The sheer scale of the current attempt—some one thousand people will be rendered homeless—has sparked considerable protest as well as this collaborative venture between Israeli peace groups and the local committee. We have come in the hope of drawing international attention to what Israel is planning, and thus of forcing the government to back down. We have come in solidarity with innocent victims. And we have come to work.

There is a lot of press, including a South Korean TV journalist making a film about life in Israel-Palestine, a reporter from the *Berliner Zeitung*, and a Chinese crew; if they manage to get a few seconds on the evening news in China, possibly many millions will see this happy moment. Several video crews are filming continuously, and indeed the hillside looks, to my eyes, strikingly photogenic. There are teams of volunteers cleaning up the debris of decades—rusted spikes wrapped in barbwire, blocks of concrete, huge broken branches, and moldy piles of tin and plastic; others are breaking up the caked top layer of soil just down from the aqueduct, readying it for the grassy terrace it will soon become; some are filling buckets with rocks and earth and pouring them out on the hill below to build up the emerging terrace. The whole hillside is alive with color and movement; young men from the village, and some children, work side by side with the Israelis, and the site is changing rapidly, minute by minute, the long neglect over at last. Amnon, only recently recovered from a broken shoulder, is working heroically with his one uninjured arm, hoeing and raking and carrying buckets and branches and heavy stones.

Jim, one of my closest friends, is with us for the first time. Thirty years ago we were in the army together; an irrevocable bond. He is working—hard—on the Sabbath. He rode the bus down to the village with the rest of us; he is an observant Jew, a rabbi. "How does it feel?" I ask him. "Like Shabbat Bereshit," he says: the Torah reading about the creation of the world.

From the start, the police are also with us, seeming, on the surface, rather benign—at first two blue jeeps, reinforced later by a detachment of border police. They have promised that we would not be stopped on our way down into the village, and they do not appear to be unduly troubled by the notion of this workday. It is not, after all, a demonstration. But around 11:00 a settler appears, dressed in his white Shabbat clothes, with conspicuous skullcap and fringes and a well-fed belly. He looks scornfully at the Jews working beside Palestinian Arabs. He lives in a house seized from one of the Silwanis, overlooking this hillside. He stops for a word with the police commander. It is not allowed, he claims—and, as usual, the settler calls the shots—to pour earth to make a terrace, or to plant a tree, or to repair a stone wall, without specific permits. We are intending to do all of the above, but now the officer informs us, bowing to the settler's mysterious authority, that we can go on working so long as we refrain from these clearly criminal acts. They will stay here to make sure we keep within bounds.

The man working beside me says to me in Arabic: "He—the settler—is living in my house. He took my house." He is, of course, enraged. "All the problems," he says, "come from them; only from them. They won't let us live. They won't let us breathe." Another Silwani bursts out in a torrent of curses, and for a moment the rhythm of our hoes and buckets is rent by the pulsations of rage. The moment passes. We will wait awhile before deciding about the tree.

Amiel has brought it, a huge mulberry, *tut* in Arabic and Hebrew; he and Ezra scoured the nurseries of Jerusalem looking for it, because this place was years ago known as Tut Junction, after a famous, ancient mulberry tree. That tree is gone, and we intend to replace it today, also to restore the street signs with the original names. Ezra, meanwhile, has been imprisoned by the army for visiting our friends in the South Hebron caves; tonight he will be brought before a Jerusalem court for an extension of his remand. They seem, this time, intent on punishing him. Nothing, truly nothing, threatens the army more than a man of peace.

There is a magic in Silwan, the most ancient part of Jerusalem, this dense hive of houses spilling down the steep slope south of the Dung Gate and the Old City. People here are proud of their neighborhood. Muhammad, one of the activists in the local committee, asks my name. I tell him: David, Da'ud. His face flowers into a vast, craggy smile: "Da'ud, King David, he was from here—he was a Silwani." For one brief moment, the entire mad overlay of identities and claims, bulldozers, houses, Jews, Palestinians, their flags, the guns, the wickedness of power—all of it falls away before this simple, undeniable fact: whoever he was, if he ever was, King David was a Silwani. Maybe that is all that matters. He would certainly be astounded, also horrified, to see what one party of his children was doing to another, in the name of the all-consuming inanity of the nation-state. This David was, they say, a poet. Muhammad, still smiling, watches me as I think this through. But there is more: Ayyub, the prophet Job, was also here; his well, Bir Ayyub, is just around the corner. So Job—he whose pain was beyond bearing, who questioned God—was also a Silwani, as seems only fitting.

Never before have I been so needed as a medic: there is a host of minor cuts and wounds that require cleaning and bandaging. I almost exhaust the medical supplies I brought with me; it is time to refresh my medic's pouch. By now I am covered in mud and reeking of the stagnant water—will the stench ever leave my shoes, my jeans? I am also very thirsty, as the day wears on, an endless and relentless thirst no liquid can quench.

After lunch I climb with Jim into the Roman antiquities farther uphill—a bathhouse in the shadow of an overhanging cliff. Ta'ayush, Jim says, reminds him of our days in the army; there is the same stark, unfamiliar eros of body and sun and smell, of the group living its life as a collective, of the simplicity of eating and working and using your hands. "Yes," I say—suddenly memory cascades back to Shomron and basic training; "I can smell it again—but there we were slaves, and here we are free."

They ask us to climb up into the cemetery above the road for a few photos, for the Arabic newspaper *Al-Quds*. Only men— women should not go into this space. We somewhat comically, artificially play at cleaning the gravestones, mostly marked as children's graves, for the sake of the picture. Why didn't they photograph us working furiously downhill? Perhaps the sight of Israelis cleaning Muslim tombstones will have some power. Pictures over, we go back to work. A little later someone climbs the tall electricity pole and ties a newly painted signpost on it, in Arabic and English, another fruit of today's labors: *maqbarat al-atfal* above, and below, an unconscious touch of poetry: "Children's Symmetry."

By now it is 3:00; the day begins to wane. Time to wind down: and time for the tree, come what may. Amiel carries it into the newly hoed plot. It is a splendid specimen, and within minutes it stands embedded in the soil, lightly tied to an iron stake; wrapped around the stake, covered in plastic, is a huge enlargement of an aerial photograph of the village, with a bright circle tracing the boundaries of this neighborhood threatened with extinction. We pour buckets of water over the base of the tree, and a cheer goes up: "Silwan! Silwan!" People clap and sing and shout. But now the police wake up, since we have at last broken the law. They march back and forth on the road, barking into their cell phones. (What are they saying to their superiors? "Send reinforcements. They are planting a tree!") The border police look restless, or agitated, as well, and for a few minutes I wonder if at this final moment we will have to face a fracas, a police charge, or the arrest of some of our friends. In a way, I don't much care. There is something about planting a tree that stands outside and beyond all other categories. It is always and ever autotelic: its own intrinsic justification. I am glad we have planted this mulberry tree here, glad to have been part of it, glad also for the defiance. And now, as the policemen look on with anger, apparently hesitant to move, the Silwani spokesmen rise to speak through the loudspeaker to all of us who have worked here today.

"This is the day of Silwan," says Muhammad, in Arabic, "a famous day, a day of peace. I thank you on behalf of the people of Silwan. You have come from all over, even from distant countries, to help us, who have been targeted by the Israeli authorities—one thousand men, women, and children from al-Bustan. I thank you for the sake of peace. Let all people know. In Silwan we are not free. We want our liberty; we want our livelihood; we want an end to our agony. Make sure that the Israeli government knows and the Jerusalem municipality knows: we will never give up our homes. Make sure for the sake of peace, the peace we all want."

Again the cries: "Silwan! Silwan!" Mixed in with them is another shout, almost a rhyme: "Salaam!" Now Khulood speaks for Ta'ayush in a swift, crystalline Arabic, every syllable a promise of human hope. "We are not afraid," she says, "not afraid of the border police or the police or the soldiers, not afraid of anyone. We came here to stand beside you, and we will never abandon this struggle. Your struggle is ours." Someone suddenly thrusts the loudspeaker at me; I try to escape it, try to push it back at Amnon, at anyone, but they insist and I can see there is no choice. They want someone to say something in Hebrew, and it will have to be me. I have no idea what to say, but I press the button and start, without thinking. "We had the honor, and the pleasure, of working here today as your guests. Thank you for inviting us. We loved this day, as we love and honor peace. We want you to know that we are with you and that we will never allow anyone to destroy your houses. We will come whenever you need us, whenever you invite us here, as your friends."

I stop, the loudspeaker mercifully passes on to another, but one of the young Silwanis hurries over to me, takes my arm. "You don't need an invitation," he says to me, speaking of all of us, his eyes full of light. "Silwan is your home."*

July 23, 2005 'Anata: House Building

If you want to see the face of peace—the peace that we could have had already, the peace that someday will be—you have only to look at Arafat Musa Hamdan. He is thirty-seven years old, a housepainter; married, with five children and another on the way. He has the strength of a working man. He is direct, forceful,

---

*The public campaign by the Silwan Committee, Ta'ayush, and the Israeli Committee Against House Demolitions was successful in saving al-Bustan.

clear. He hates no one. He says of himself that he has a good heart, that he wants to live in peace with everyone, whoever they are—Palestinians, Israelis, he doesn't care. He likes people. He has worked in Israel for many years. A certain self-evident integrity, almost naive, radiates from him. He belongs to ʿAnata, to this rocky hill, the way a tree or a terrace belongs. It is his house that Israel has destroyed.

In fact, it's the second time this has happened to him. The first was in 1992, when he was still living at his father's home, farther up the hill. There was another house that belonged to the family, a house intended for Arafat Musa after his marriage. One day the army came with bulldozers and destroyed it. Always the same pretext too: they claim the house was built without a permit. Of course, it is impossible for a Palestinian who lives in ʿAnata to get a building permit; the municipality automatically refuses to issue them. Catch-22. In the end, under constant pressure for space, they build without the permit. So it was with his more recent house, into which he had sunk whatever money he earned, day by day and week by week. The family has no resources, and Arafat Musa has been the main provider for his father and his brothers— ever since his mother died of diabetes when he was a boy. He built the house with his earnings and lived there with his wife and children until June last year, 2004, when the army arrived.

All around us volunteers are busy rebuilding the demolished house, mixing cement, passing the buckets inside to where the walls are being finished. Arafat Musa speaks an excellent Hebrew, far better than my Arabic, and he is an eloquent witness. First the demolition order arrived together with a jeep of border police; the paper was signed by the military commander at Beit-El, the army base next to a nearby settlement. Arafat Musa had no real recourse; to go to court, even to submit a simple appeal, would have cost him some twelve hundred shekels, and he had no such resources. So he waited and hoped for the best. Early one summer morning another set of soldiers arrived and knocked fiercely on the door, as if hitting it with hammers. They gave him a few minutes to get his family and some possessions out of the house. He spoke politely to the soldiers, offered to give them cold water, coffee, but they treated him with disdain. They brought a big dog into the house to sniff around (for explosives?); ever since then his youngest son, who was three when this happened, is terrified of dogs. One of the soldiers opened the refrigerator and found some frozen meat. He called out to his comrade: "Do you want this food or should I throw it away?" That one heartless sentence, says Arafat Musa, still burns in his heart. First they humiliated him, then they knocked down his house. There was also a beautiful fence he had built with his own hands; that, too, the bulldozer destroyed. Since then he has been sleeping, "like a donkey, like a horse," in a small, cramped room at his father's house.

A week after the demolition, police picked him up in a random check in West Jerusalem, in Beit Hakerem, where he was working as a painter. He was detained for some hours, threatened with all kinds of punishments; eventually they drove him somewhere in the hills south of the city and let him go, telling him never to come back. "When bad luck comes," he says, "it doesn't stop with one thing."

"Why don't they think about what they are doing?" he asks me. "People who were alive a hundred years ago are all dead now and we, too, will die; why be so cruel, why ruin everything while we are still alive? Why are they hurting us? They should stop and think. There is a house just over the hill—Beit Arabiya—which they knocked down four times. Each time it was rebuilt, with the help of the Israeli volunteers; and each time the army came and destroyed it again. Today it is standing again, but who is to say that the soldiers won't come back? If it were just one crazy person doing this, that would be one thing—one could somehow survive; one might make sense of it—but here an entire country is doing it, over and over, with its soldiers and bureaucrats and politicians and police, causing stupendous pain to so many simple people. At times," he says, "you feel crazy." He wants to live in peace.

Some fifteen volunteers are working here today, and the work is going well; within hardly more than a week, the stone walls have gone up, the roof is in place, and what remains is mostly the flooring, the finish, the paint. It will be a beautiful house—like the one they demolished—with a view over the gaunt and haunting hills to the south and west. Standing here, I can see, from behind, the tall university buildings on Mount Scopus. I am clearly in Palestine: the roads are full of potholes; there are horses, goats, ragamuffin children, and the wrecks of other demolished houses only a hundred meters away. I ache inside. Aside from a few Israelis, there are volunteers from Japan, Switzerland, England, Sweden, the United States; most are young, and some have done this work before, in previous summers, at the invitation of ICAHD, the Israeli Committee Against House Demolitions. The army regularly destroys these Palestinian homes, and ICAHD doggedly helps the families rebuild. I greet Lucia, from Mexico, directing operations here together with Arafat Musa; I last saw her in the autumn, enfolded in the branches of an olive tree.

Meir Margalit, who is devoting his life to this Sisyphean task of saving houses, arrives with a box of hot *bourekas*. His is another face of peace—the face of a man who never gives up, and who knows what to do. He seems to be everywhere, wherever a house is threatened with demolition. He is modest, effective, wise, and—in my view—truly exceptional. He has good news from Silwan: the public campaign seems to be bearing fruit; the government will perhaps not be able to carry out its proclaimed intention of wiping out the al-Bustan neighborhood. The Americans have apparently put their foot down; they will not allow this act of wanton destruction. But there is still the danger that the municipality will try to demolish a few homes there, for good measure, when no one is watching.

Since food has come, there is a pause in the work, and people take shelter in the shade inside the emerging home. This is my opportunity; they have invited me to come to speak about Ta'ayush, so I briefly tell the story, speaking first in Arabic for the sake of our hosts. I speak of South Hebron, Salfit, Beit Liqiya,

Yanun. There are some questions. "Someday," I say to them, "the suffering will end, and there will certainly be peace."

Afterward I work for some time, under Arafat Musa's guidance, mixing the cement. It is another first for me; I realize that until this moment I have never paused to consider the peculiar alchemy of cement—what it is made of, how it is prepared, how it goes into the making of a house. Arafat Musa explains it all to me with a certain bemused tolerance as I shake the liquid mass through a metal mesh meant to winnow out residues of gravel. As always, the physical work is the best part of the day, the most satisfying, far better than any words. Soon, in a few days, this house will be ready. "The art," Meir explains to me, "is to get the family inside as quickly as possible—at least some furniture, some laundry drying outside, signs of habitation—before the Civil Administration can issue another demolition order. Once people are living there, they can appeal such an order, and the legal process can, with a little luck, take years."

By midafternoon I am home in Katamon. The contrast shocks me: I am back in the first world, in a manicured suburban street with its elegant stone houses and cypress trees. No one seems to be outside—perhaps they are all having their Shabbat sleep—but the cars along the curb speak eloquently enough: many of them have an orange ribbon tied to the antenna, a sign of support for the settlers of Gush Katif, a sign that their owners reject Sharon's plan for disengagement in Gaza. My neighbors—many, perhaps most of them—stand with the settlers and the right. They don't believe in peace and, what is worse, they are completely and utterly indifferent to the fate of, for example, Arafat Musa and his house. Arafat Musa is, after all, a Palestinian Arab, thus somewhere on the edge of being human, a person—if he *is* a person—of little or no consequence. So why bother about his house? Suddenly, as so often, a terrible loneliness courses through me. I briefly consider turning around and driving back to 'Anata, where I have friends.

4

Samaria: Salfit, Yanun, Banu Hassan

Northern Samaria is one of the harshest settings in the territories—a land of fanatical settlers and their Palestinian counterparts; as always, the civilian population of Palestinian farmers pays the price. Taʿayush has been active in this region from the beginning. In the autumn of 2002, when settlers drove the entire population of the village of Kafr Yanun from their homes, Taʿayush managed to entice them back and for weeks kept a small satellite contingent of activists in place in the village to protect them. Here, then, is one small microcosm where a determined group of volunteers made a difference.

In addition, there have been many convoys bringing food, medical supplies, and other necessities to blockaded villages in Samaria and along the western "seam line." We were active in the olive harvest, which, as in the South Hebron Hills, required the presence of Israeli peace activists if it was to take place at all—in the face of settler violence. Relations between Taʿayush and many of the villages are lively, continuous, and close; we have also distributed food to the refugee camp at Jenin and elsewhere, at a time of severe shortage and near-total siege. What follows is a brief sample of efforts concentrated on the northern West Bank.

July 6, 2002   Salfit

Saturday, summer, dry and hot. It is the turn of Salfit. We start off at 9:00 from Binyanei Hauma, the Jerusalem convention center. Two buses have been ordered, and they rapidly fill up, so Amiel and I drive in his car, in air-conditioned freedom, speaking mostly about Latin, to Kafr Qasem, where the Ta'ayush convoy is assembling. Amiel's father died about a week ago, and last night I dreamt that my own father, long dead, was dying again; I lift up my eyes from my desk in Iowa and see him sitting across from me in the room. Amiel has been dreaming of his father all week.

Upon arrival we hear that the bus ride was an ordeal; all have been roasted and cooked. Misha was on the bus, also Iva, Maya, Amnon, Karen, Ronnie, Yuri, and the other Ta'ayush stalwarts.

There is time for coffee and cold drinks before we move on to the briefing. Salfit has a regional medical center that the army has vandalized. We are bringing them an ultrasound machine and some other piece of modern medical wizardry, at a cost of some $10,000 per unit. But will the army let us through? Salfit, like everywhere else, is under curfew. It is unlikely, Gadi tells us, that the army will permit us to go there; more probable is a complicated move through the wadi, by foot, to Palestinian taxis that will take us from another village on to Salfit. Salfit is in Area A, under nominal Palestinian control, so we are breaking the law by going there. He announces in biblical fashion: "If there is anyone who doesn't want to risk legal complications, arrest, and so on, this is the time to turn back; honorably, without blame." Maya, standing beside me, is very unhappy at the prospect of violent clashes with the army, but she gathers up her forces; I can see it clearly, admiring her spirit. I take the medic's pouch from Yigal, as so often before.

Six buses take off in the fiery sunlight toward the villages across the green line. Kafr Qasem has its own share of traumatic memory; everyone knows how the army murdered forty-seven (some say forty-nine) innocent fellahin here on October 29, 1956, because they were supposedly in violation of a curfew they had heard nothing about; and how the military trial of the officers and soldiers responsible, which first produced the Israeli notion of the "black flag"—the clear case of criminal orders that should have been rejected by all the soldiers involved—ended by fining one of the officers one agora, the smallest coin in existence.* The price of forty-seven human lives. Today Kafr Qasem looks like all the small towns and villages of the Arab "Triangle"—nondescript, dusty, cluttered.

We hit the first roadblock. We stop and negotiations ensue. To everyone's surprise, after a half hour or so, we are given good news. The army will let us drive straight to Salfit. First the soldiers come on board to check the buses and the lists of participants. Then we turn off the main Ariel road—open only to settlers—to a smaller paved access route that, we are told, has been closed to Salfit for the last five years. Only tanks have used it. We are the first civilian traffic to travel this way.

We pass Ariel. There are settlements all around, the familiar scene. I think of the old road, not far from here, from Beit Lyd to Shomron, where I did my basic training in 1978. It was hardly the same world as ours—long before the cancer of permanent occupation set in for real. They had only recently allowed settlers to live inside the army camp, while we, new recruits, were supposedly defending them. From time to time, they would hold the settlers' presence as a threat over our heads when we did guard duty: "You have women and children here; you must protect them." All this was irritating or worse but nothing like the sorrow and terror of today. And I—was I akin to the sorrow of today?

Salfit is like Kafr Qasem. Two-story concrete houses, dust, junk, rocky hills, a few trees—the Mediterranean world at its most impoverished. For this people are killing one another? For a few more dusty cypresses? The streets are deserted, though the curfew has been lifted for a few hours, until 3:00. We transfer the medical equipment into the rather sad-looking medical center.

---

*Several of the officers found guilty were sent to jail but served relatively short terms, in no case longer than three years.

There is a delivery room for women, the only one for miles around. I wouldn't want to be dependent on whatever care is available here. But they are proud of this place and grateful for the equipment and the many boxes of medical supplies that we carry in.

By now it is 1:00 and, in effect, we have done what we came for. Three hundred volunteers wander aimlessly under the midday sun. Eventually we gather ourselves into a march, carrying a few signs: "The criminals of the occupation to International Court" is mine. Young men emerge from the street to talk to us. They are apparently glad we are here, but they are, of course, angry. A conversation develops: do I understand what my sign says? I do. "Sharon," one says to me, "is a war criminal." Have I heard of Sabra and Shatilla? I have. Do I agree? I agree.

Maya, meanwhile, has produced the real story of this young man who is haranguing me. He is about to be married. But he isn't happy. He has an Israeli girlfriend in Petach Tikva whom he hasn't seen in two years. Probably only a woman could elicit this information, but suddenly I am skeptical. Maybe he saw an Israeli woman in Petach Tikva. . . . Maybe he has fantasized the whole thing. Anyway, he isn't happy. This I believe.

Or maybe it is all true and deserves a story by some Palestinian Isaac Babel. Yesterday two old people died in the village. The army permitted only four people to come out to bury them. "But are the soldiers bad to you?" "No"—this is surprising—"they are OK. The occupation is the horror and the misery; the soldiers aren't worse than anyone else."

"Why are you here?" they ask us. "You are very welcome, but you should be in Tel Aviv. You should make the Israelis understand what they are doing, how they are producing only terror. You should change their hearts." "We are trying," I say. They are impressed, hundreds of good people from all over Israel came to Salfit today, to be with them, they keep repeating this truth, but we should be in Tel Aviv—that is where the task lies.

We file into the Salfit Civil Center for the speeches, which drag on and on. The mayor, an officer from the Palestinian security forces, Gadi, various others—all have their say. Cold drinks are brought out in an endless series of trays. We sit, restive. The first to speak mentions, in his first sentence, the blood of the *shahids*. A bad start. A huge portrait of Arafat hangs at the entrance. But none of the speakers today has anything good to say about him; what they repeat, over and over, is that they, the Palestinians, will choose their leaders for themselves. No one can make them choose someone they don't want. Abu Dhabi Television and Aljazeera are photographing madly, and this, Gadi tells me later, is the real point of the entire exercise. These Palestinians, who work with Taʿayush, are addressing their own internal audience in the territories. Everyone watches Abu Dhabi. So here they are broadcasting these speeches in which one speaker after another holds out the vision of two peoples living side by side, two independent states, not harming one another, not oppressing one another. "We want to free the Israeli mother and the Israeli sister and the Israeli wife from this fear for the life of their son or brother or husband," says the last speaker, a simpler, straightforward man.

Finally, mercifully, it ends. There is a short period of mingling outside in the streets, the best part of the day. Human beings being human. Kids play, beg cigarettes. But one teenage group has grabbed a loudspeaker and is starting up with the usual chant: "In blood and spirit we will redeem Filastin. . . ." Misha, walking beside me, is immediately tuned in to this and horrified. Others try to hush these young men—or are they boys? They seem to know this is not a good idea. Misha, however, has seen through the veil. We come, we want to do good, we have to do what we can, but so often there is that residue of asymmetry, the readiness to choose violence. I know this from long experience: just at the point where you yearn for some Gandhian voice—for someone to say, "On no account is killing justified, not for any goal on earth; violence is the wrong path"—at that point you get these muffled but unmistakable tones. Blood and spirit. These teenagers are not Gandhians, not now, not ever. We can understand how much they hate, we can imagine our way into their minds, but a recalcitrant discrepancy always survives this empathic move. There is no escaping it. Better to do without the wishful thinking and be clear. We are trying to end the occupation for our own sake as well as for theirs. Of course we want them, too, as friends; we honor their yearning.

Misha takes me into a shop, miraculously open, for girls and women. We buy a small dress for the daughter of his friend in New York—twenty shekels. Later he forgets it in the bus, so those were twenty shekels invested in the stagnant economy of Salfit, a pure donation without even letting the recipient know, the best kind of charity according to the Jews. The buses pull out, and there is a long wait at the roadblock on the way out of the village as the soldiers check and recheck. Then, within minutes, we are back in Israel, at Kafr Qasem. It was easy; it was complex; it was fun; there was hope; there is the ongoing despair. Next year I will take an evening a week to study spoken Arabic, Palestinian dialect.

October 30, 2002   Aqraba and Kafr Yanun

We are the third wave. Two weeks ago Ta'ayush sent volunteers up here to help with the olive harvest. Four or five settlers opened fire, aiming at the feet; Amiel was hit in the stomach by a ricochet. He says it's partly his own fault, since when the shooting began he faced the settlers and yelled, "I'm a Jew and I came here to help pick these olives, and I'm going to pick them." The Palestinians, used to such moments, immediately ran for cover; Amiel felt the sliver of bullet enter him but decided to ignore it. He worked for the rest of the day, reached home, and, when the pain became severe, went to the emergency room. The doctor on duty didn't take it seriously, refusing to believe that settlers really shot at Jews. Probably some leftist hallucination. The next day he had surgery; he'll be OK.

The second wave was the foreign volunteers who came to stare down the settlers at Yanun and were ferociously attacked by them; there were many severe injuries. One elderly woman volunteer says she is convinced they were trying to kill her. The settlers bashed them with rifle butts and other blunt instruments. By this time the villagers of Yanun were so terrorized that they left their houses and fled to Aqraba. That, of course, was what the settlers wanted. Everyone knows that this is about transfer, one more pointillistic piece of the jigsaw. The idea, in short, is to drive them out.

To this end, olives are a potent instrument. One of the settler rabbis has declared that Jews have the right to steal the olives of the Palestinians; after all, the land is ours, so what grows there is ours too. Whole families in the village subsist on the olive groves alone, and this year the settlers in northern Samaria have set about systematically depriving them of this sustenance. They have stolen the sacks of freshly harvested olives on their way to the olive press; they have swooped down on the olive groves and taken over the trees, chasing the owners away with guns.

All of Israel, these days, knows about the olive trees, hence the Peace Now visit today. We are going to help with the harvest and to keep the settlers away—for the few hours we are there. Many TV cameras and journalists are with us, as are the famous men of letters, Amos Oz, Meir Shalev, A. B. Yehoshua, David Grossman. I sit in the bus beside Yael, the daughter of Haim Guri, a presence from the distant past; he, famous poet of the 1948 convoys, is being interviewed today at Sebastia. He was there, the local officer on the spot, in 1978, when the first settlers took over the site, only a few kilometers from our villages of the olives. He was the one who negotiated the fateful compromise that allowed those settlers to stay within the bounds of the army camp. He is going there today, with reporters, to articulate his shame, his grief at his mistake. That was the beginning; Rabin was prime minister, perfectly aware—so they say—of what was at stake and too weak to prevent it. Now there are settlers everywhere in the territories, and violent theft is the norm.

I remember Sebastia, as I remember Shomron, basic training in these same hills: 1978 in my life, the oil-and-canvas smells of the army, the shock and newness, the feel of handling a gun, the poetry of its parts, the birth of profound friendships. All this is in my mind as the bus, bullet-proof (to everyone's relief), sails smoothly across the Trans-Samaria highway toward Aqraba. It is the same season as then, the same light, with a hint of rain to come. The hills are, as always, watching us, a stark and haunting chorus of witnesses. I remember marching with our guns and boots through one of these villages in the early morning; I remember our idiot of an officer stopping us nonchalantly in the middle of the shops and houses and saying—a born colonialist— "Notice the quaint atmosphere of this Arab village as the day begins. . . ."

We are the third wave, a somewhat elderly bunch, nothing like the determined squads of Taʿayush. Already in the parking lot at Gan Hapaamon in Jerusalem, I see how the age quotient is reversed: in Taʿayush I am aging, a good twenty years older than the mean, but today I am one of the younger volunteers, surrounded by grandparents, veterans of decades in the peace movement. They move a little more slowly. The original idea was to bring a group of Israelis from all slices of the spectrum—left, center, and right—to demonstrate the solid national consensus that olives should not, after all, be stolen. This proved impossible, however; no one from the center or right was prepared to come. Harpaz, who came up with the idea, then turned in desperation to Peace Now, who have produced this eager but weary crowd. There is one exception: the well-known, unconventional Rabbi Forman from the settlement of Teqoa has joined this pilgrimage. He has brought with him a heavy pile of Jewish books—Gemara, Shulchan Aruch—this to show that the texts actually forbid stealing olives from non-Jews. I don't know which is more amazing, the physical apparition of a rabbi in phylacteries and long, straggly hair, arms laden with texts, sitting next to the die-hard secularists of the old Israel on the bus, or the fact that this obviously humane man thinks it necessary to bring proof texts from the classical sources to convince people that stealing isn't quite right. God, luckily, has ruled it out. We know this because our sages said it, and he has the books to prove it.

At Kafr Qasem the Jerusalem contingent joins the others from Tel Aviv. It is midmorning, getting hot. This time the army creates no obstacles—unlike the standard Ta'ayush sequence; no doubt they have been prepared long in advance for the arrival of the famous novelists and poets. They will let us pick a few olives. The road weaves through a seemingly endless series of settlements, new and old. The villages are hemmed in on all sides. On the hills around Aqraba, the Itamar settlers have put up electric poles in all directions. Itamar, with some eighty families, has taken over thousands of *dunams* of land and stretches over miles upon stony miles. The Itamar settlers, like those at nearby Tapuach, are hard-core, fanatical, and violent; many are Kahanists. At the moment, two years into the Intifada, they are riding high.

We move out of the bullet-proof bus into a series of Palestinian vehicles that carry us the rest of the way, over dirt roads, to the trees of Kafr Yanun. A large field spills over the hill, easily hundreds of trees. To harvest the whole field is a month's intensive work for the whole village, but this year is different; the harvest will not be complete. The settlers have already seen to that. They are watching us from the hilltop; we can see their tractors. Our hosts say: "While you are here, with the TV cameras, they will stay away; but as soon as you leave, they will be back here with their guns."

We start to work. Heavy plastic sheets are spread under some of the trees; the idea is to clear the branches of olives that cascade onto the sheets, which are then folded up with the fruit inside them and carted off to the olive press in Aqraba. It is thirty-four years since I last harvested olives—at Kibbutz Ein Harod, with an upside-down poncho tied to my waist to catch the olives as they fell. October again; my fingers seem to remember, gliding along the dusty, silver branches as the olives fall gently to the ground before them, a sweet raindrop-like sound murmuring from tree after tree. I climb to reach the higher branches, and I relish this moment, touching fruit and leaf.

Beside me, at first, is an old Palestinian farmer, his hands completely silvered by olive dust, white stubble of beard on his chin. We work steadily together, saying nothing, yet somehow almost dancing, aware of each other's movements. To my left is a young Palestinian woman in a shapeless brown dress that efficiently hides her from any eyes. David Grossman, by now engrossed in the work and happy as I am, says: "I have wasted my life writing; it is this that I was meant to do."

Perhaps an hour goes by. I move from purple-black olives to green ones; the latter are much harder to see as your hands slide through the branches. The physical memory becomes stronger, shapes itself into the young woman I knew and worked with and was too shy to approach. Am I in any way continuous with that remembered, awkward boy of thirty-four years ago? But how did this nightmare overtake us all? Is causality ever coherent? The upper reaches of the trees escape us; Menahem offers to raise me onto his shoulders so I can at least make an effort to harvest the thick, full bunches at the top—"the blind man carrying the lame," he suggests. So far, no one has shot at us. I notice, from some distant place in the mind, that the slight fear I had earlier, nourished by bitter experience, has dissipated completely. It is a simple matter now: olives, sun, a subtle smell, the dusty field, thirst, the eerie hills, the mute, incipient opening of friendship.

When we go, they come to shake our hands and bless us, one by one, their eyes wide open, focused, seeking ours. It was not for nothing.

But there is more. We drive up over the hill to the center of Yanun. It is afternoon by now; the men of the village are waiting for us beside a long stone fence, with a plastic table set up before them, bottles of mineral water standing like forlorn sentinels. I am amazed by these men's faces. Some are wrinkled, at once hard, emotive, and gentle; above all, hurt, or so it seems to me. A line of schoolchildren has placards draped around their necks: "Yes to peace, No to the occupation." "Settlers and Army, go home." We mill around, not knowing what to do or say. These people have been chased from their homes; they have come back, they will keep coming back, but there is no doubt about the trauma, the fear. The worst, they say, are the teenage settlers, hardly more than fifteen or sixteen years old, with their machine guns. They are the ones who have been shooting. They killed a twenty-four-year-old man in the next village, they beat a pregnant woman who is now in the hospital, and they very nearly killed one of the village elders, a dignified man set upon by these trigger-happy adolescent boys. Rabbi Forman suggests we think of the latter with tolerance. "All of this," he tells us, "is only their adolescent revolt. In fact," he says, "they have a certain charm."

As for me, I feel hate and a dark, crumpled despair. Why deny the hate? Do they not deserve it, these Jews who have stolen and desecrated not only olives, not only land, but also the dignity that once belonged to Jewish books, the love I had for the relatively harmless Jewish God of my childhood, the musical Hebrew of my early poems? I know, too, that I am seeing what can only be deadly real, the ground-level, human reality of attack, depredation, expulsion, the prelude to the vast expulsion that these Jews are planning for these people, all three million of them. Let no one say he did not know; let no one talk of vast historical forces, of wrongs piled on wrongs, of generalities and abstractions; let no one speak philosophy. What is real is this overriding anguish. It is in their faces; it is in my body; it is in these rocks and trees. There was a clean well here, at the foot of this hill; the settlers brought a dog and washed it in the water, a deliberate gesture of poisonous insult. There was a small electric generator next to the well. Both well and generator are gone, destroyed.

A few days ago I was in India, absorbed in the goddess Paiditalli. What am I doing on this hill? Am I contiguous to these trees, these people, this random sample of human misery? Why is it for me to defend them? Why do I fail in this yet return, again and again, to these same scenes, these fields and villages, always failing, always ashamed? There is a Ta'ayush man, a young Israeli, stationed, it seems, in the village, and as we leave he suddenly unleashes a torrent of fury at Amos Oz and the rest of these well-intentioned artists or professors who have come for a few hours to work in the olive groves, who have been elegantly interviewed by the international TV crews and are now about to leave. "Don't come here any more," he yells at us. "Your visit was patronizing and insulting; send a letter next time, but don't come back. You didn't listen to them at all. You didn't speak to them." They are hurt. I take his word for it. As we bump over the dirt track back to Aqraba, the usual rationalizations spring to lips and mind.

We were, at least, spared the standard ritual of long-winded, flowery speeches. But perhaps it is this that the villagers wanted more than anything and that we denied them. They need someone to hear them, for they are completely and absolutely helpless in their hour of need: the Palestinian Authority, in whose territory we have been working for these few hours, is incapable of protecting them; the army stands with the settlers, harassing the villagers; the police are nonexistent in this wild area—as soon as we go, or when dark comes, the settlers will be at their throats again. These people need no spokesmen to speak for them; they need no one to give them voice or words. They need listeners. They are astonishingly eloquent if you only listen, as they tell you the simple facts: the settlers came here, they did this, they killed that one, the soldiers stood by and watched, then the families started to flee. . . .

Our driver told us all this on the way up to the village; on the way down, I am in the open back of a trailer, bouncing up and down in full view of the wavelike hills of Transjordan, just beyond the next rocky ridge and across the Rift Valley. Olive trees everywhere, like Crete, like Spain. "Beautiful country, and very empty," says Ian Buruma, the English writer who joined us today; "a good place to settle."

March 22, 2003   Banu Hassan

In Iraq, day three of war. The territories have been sealed off, and food is scarce. For the whole of last week, Ta'ayush has been distributing food by convoy to villages all over the West Bank. Some 130 tons of food supplies have been transferred, volunteers working around the clock. Today, Shabbat, the biggest convoy heads for the Salfit region.

Some 350 of us meet, as usual, in Kafr Qasem. We crowd together to hear the briefing, by now familiar, in Hebrew, Arabic,
and English: "This is a nonviolent action. We seek no confrontation and will not meet violence with violence. We will bring the
food we have stocked to these villages." It is the end of winter,
clearly: heavy clouds cross the sky, but mostly there is sun on
the green hills, still soaked with rain. It is cool, the land fragrant.
Gadi, eyes afire, greets me warmly. Nita has come, still weak from
weeks of chemotherapy after a double mastectomy. Itai, as always, is here, on crutches. Yuri, Yasmin, Karen, Udi, Iva, Yigal,
Amnon, Irit, Neve, and Catherine: by now we have done this
many times; Ta'ayush works effectively, without drama. In the
villages, they know many of us by name.

We drive—several buses, two heavy trucks filled with sacks of
flour—to the roadblock nearest Banu Hassan, well inside Palestinian territory. The roadblock is, in fact, a set of three large
staggered earthworks packed with boulders and soil, completely
cutting off the village from the road. Between each of the heavy
mounds, there is a space of some fifty meters. No vehicles can get
by. We emerge from the buses, peer around. Immediately above,
dominating the hill, is a large settlement, fenced in, demanding
notice with its red-roofed villas. On the next hilltop is our village.
We have to get the flour past the roadblocks, onto tractor-drawn
carts that can wind their way up the hill.

We have several hundred heavy sacks to unload. A line forms,
and the sacks start making their way along it, through sets of
facing volunteers. There are many women, more than eager to
bear these burdens, some stationed high up on the trucks—like
in old-fashioned Soviet propaganda films. We load one tractor,
which slowly chugs toward the village. A second one backs into
the line, and once again the heavy sacks are passed from hand to
hand, over the first, the second, finally the third barricade. How
easy it would be without these barriers; how clumsy and slow it
is this way. Within a few minutes I am completely covered in
white flour, except for my feet, which are coated in the fresh, wet
mud.

For an hour, then another, we work happily like this. A bus turns up at the roadblock, and several dozen Palestinian women and children pour out. They have to get to the village—some three kilometers away—and they will, of course, have to walk. Among them is an old woman on crutches, slowly hobbling through the mud past the roadblocks. I watch her, horrified and sad. One of the Palestinian villagers sees me staring, comes up to me, and says: "When I used to work in Israel and traveled by bus, I would get up and give my seat to any woman who got on— and look what you are doing to our women!" This humiliation of the women is a particularly sore point to them. It happens literally under the noses of the settlers on the hilltop; indeed, it is for them, to secure their road, their houses, their existence on these plundered lands, that the entire black farce of blockade and isolation is being enacted. How can they sit in their villas and look down, day after day, at these scenes? Does it never touch some small part of their soul? Or is this the heart of the mystery, that dependable and devastating human failure to feel?

Like everything else in the territories, the scene is visually surreal. A long line of flour-caked volunteers passes sagging sacks of flour from one side of the first roadblock to the other side of the third. Tractors from the village drag them up the rocky slope. Women, young and old, draped in long robes, are spilling over the barricades and climbing the hill. Sheep graze among the rocks. The sun darts in and out of cloud. Settlers huddle in their houses. A Japanese photographer, Toyoji Uchida, is filming it all, as if he had been parachuted down from some Buddhist heaven into an incomprehensible, absurdly beautiful landscape where a melodrama is being performed by two ferocious, inexplicably hostile tribes. A few soldiers watch from the sidelines. Two or three Palestinians stand on the hill juggling, clownlike—long white pins, bright colored balls. They have no work—what else is there for them to do? Juggling seems perfectly appropriate this afternoon in the slight space between Banu Hassan and the reality of soldiers and settlers who hem them in. Chaim Yavin, Israel's most famous newscaster, is with us, interviewing the villagers for a film he is making about the settlers. One of the Palestinians is explaining to him, as if to a dull student, how deeply foolish it all is: how no one in the village has ever harmed the Jews, even when their lands were taken for the settlements; how ineffectual the roadblocks are if the aim is to stop terrorists—they can easily just walk around them—but what bitterness they cause the village; how pregnant women and the sick cannot reach a hospital except by the laborious trek over roadblock after roadblock; how the government is poisoning the remnants of hope, the hope of peace someday. But then they don't want peace, do they?

By 3:00 we have finished unloading the flour and can now walk up the hill to the village, where they have arranged plastic chairs for us and large cases of orange and grape drinks and chocolate bars. The strong Arab coffee I have promised Nita fails to appear. We listen to the speeches, mercifully short this time—probably because suddenly the sky opens up and we are drenched with rain. The main speaker, clearly the man of authority in the village, speaks of *sumud*—holding steadfast. They will hold fast, he says, until peace comes, the peace of two peoples living side by side, neither harming the other. Yasmin, who knows this village well, tells me the story of Isa, our host's brother. Last year this young, vigorous, athletic man, newly married, was sleeping when a jeep of soldiers pulled up and started shouting. He woke in fright, ran outside to gather in the children. The soldiers shot him for no reason. He is totally paralyzed today, his life wrecked, without hope. Another random, unnecessary casualty. The peace groups put together enough money for him to go to London for treatment, which helped a little—he is no longer entirely incontinent.

From Banu Hassan, the settlement stands out as even more of an eyesore, as if sucking into it all available space and attention, blackening the mind. Beyond it, the hills stagger toward the horizon, each lovelier than the one before. Horses and donkeys are grazing beneath us. One of the villagers says to Guy: "What really matters is that you came here. It is not so much the food, though we need it, as the hope you bring. All the villages in the area will come to know of this. You cannot fully understand how much it means to us."

A young Palestinian takes shelter under my umbrella. Then, with Mediterranean suddenness, the rain stops. "*Khalas*," I say— it is over. "*Khalas*," he smiles. Someday we will say this of the violence and the foolishness and the pain. Someday I will come back here just to visit, as a guest from abroad, from Israel; maybe I will look for this man, and we will talk, remembering this day with its dust of flour, its cloudburst, its simplicities. Bringing food to the hungry is something very simple. Trying to be decent, at least decent, is also simple. Even binding up wounds could be simple. Undoing evil, the evil that comes from within—from yourself and your own people—is not simple.

5

Saying No

What happens in a bloody tribal war when a soldier says: "No more"—when he takes a look at the whole absurd situation and decides that he is no longer prepared to be part of it? What if the *Iliad*, instead of telling the long story of Achilles' lunatic anger and destructive pride, had focused on some anonymous hero in the Greek camp who suddenly realized that he was to be killed for nothing, and that no measure of posthumous glory, the much-vaunted *kleos*, was worth his life? Living in Israel, on a certain level, is like living inside the *Iliad*. Israeli society feeds on notions of the heroic, of self-sacrifice in the name of the tribe. Anyone who has served in the Israeli army knows the rhetoric of selfless missions and glorious deaths; it is the everyday cliché of the commanders, which most soldiers unconsciously assimilate, at least in part, as a possible, if unlikely, rationale for the suffering involved in being where they are.

Of course, it is not only a matter of words and rationalizations. Men sometimes have feelings that are commensurate with such words—among many other ambiguous and constantly shifting feelings. I remember being driven into Lebanon in the half-track that took me to war in 1982. I was certain that the war was a miserable mistake—utterly unnecessary, essentially a crime. There were many arguments among the soldiers in my unit, most of them medics and doctors and ambulance drivers. Some supported the invasion; others, like me—a minority at the time—opposed it. We were also receiving reports of casualties and were already treating wounded in our field hospital, *ta'agad*. We already knew something of the price of this foolish escapade. Despite all that, as the half-track charged forward into the Baq'a Valley, I felt a certain elation, the thrill shared by young men on the verge of the ultimate test, along with the intoxicating sense of merging into the collective mass of comrades-in-arms. The official ideology—Begin's self-righteous, sentimental speech in the Knesset, which we heard over the radio—was of no consequence compared to the "high" we got from one another, from the wild, somewhat unnerving adventure of it all. There is also a certain uncharacteristic tenderness for one another of soldiers serving under fire—probably only under such conditions. Such experiences are the default of Israeli consciousness. They have, in profound ways, constituted the cultural core of this society, and they cut through political affiliations and viewpoints. To opt out of them, by an act of will, is difficult beyond imagining, an act of private courage, insight, and self-assertion that is beyond the capabilities, or the wishes, of most Israelis.

And yet by now thousands of Israeli soldiers have taken this path, often paying a severe price in lost friendships, isolation, ostracism, and a sense of guilt for having abandoned one's comrades in the unit or, even worse, the soldiers one has commanded as an officer. Each decision is deeply private—in this domain, there are no rules. Support groups have organized around the *sarbanim*, or refuseniks; and they have each other. They come in different shades and types: some are out-and-out pacifists who refuse to touch a weapon of any kind; others—the majority, those of greatest interest here—are selective refusers who would be prepared to fight in a defensive war of survival but are no longer willing to take part in the occupation of an entire people and the seizure of their lands. To the best of my knowledge, there is no legal precedent for this kind of selective refusal.

Among these men are the brightest and the best of Israeli

society. Some come from elite units—the air force, the Sayyeret Matkal,* the paratroops. There are high-ranking officers among them. Among them are articulate, committed individuals capable of offering nuanced, reasoned arguments for the step they have taken. They have, however, failed to persuade the Israeli mainstream, and they are, by the nature of their choice, nothing like a mass movement. Most Israeli soldiers—even those with severe doubts, even hard-core leftists and peace activists—continue to serve when called.

Yet protest keeps welling up from within the army, in various forms. Even those who are not prepared to take the drastic step of refusal may be drawn into highly public forms of dissent. In the spring of 2004, soldiers who had served for long periods in Hebron, arguably the most dreadful setting in the occupied territories, went public under the slogan "Shovrim Shtika"—"Breaking the Silence." They published testimonies garnered from their comrades of a wide range of barbaric acts that, so they claimed, are normative in Hebron. Some five hundred fanatical Jews live in Hebron by the grace of the Jewish God and the rifles of the Israeli army; in order to enable them to remain there, the entire city of fifty thousand inhabitants is under almost constant curfew. Tales of humiliations, beatings, vandalism, appropriation of property, and sometimes even killings are legion. Soldiers routinely fire large quantities of ammunition, including indiscriminate weapons such as rocket-propelled grenades, at poorly defined or anonymous targets—select houses in the Arab quarter of Abu Sneina, for example. Such crimes are now being documented and exposed to the Israeli public at large. Will it matter? Will it help bring a change?

In August 2004 I went to an evening in Jerusalem, at the Van Leer Institute, at which these soldiers from Hebron spoke of what they had done and what they had seen. There was, as always, a panel of discussants, including representatives of the army command. The soldiers were eloquent, direct, hard-hitting.

*General Staff Reconnaissance, a prestigious commando unit.

They will not refuse to serve, but they leave no doubt about their sense that Hebron is the site of continuous abuses on the part of the army. Yet to my mind, the most amazing speaker that evening in Jerusalem was Noam, an officer formerly in command of the Nahal—one of the army's core fighting units. He was speaking for himself and has no connection with the soldiers "breaking silence." Noam is humane, intelligent (he has an M.A. from Harvard), and, above all, a career officer high up the chain of command. He comes from a kibbutz; I wouldn't be surprised if his political views are moderate and to the left. Yet what he said that evening reveals the inner workings of the system that has evolved over the last decades, the system that ensures this nightmare will continue.

What the soldiers reported from their experience, Noam said, is very important. He is glad they spoke out. The army has to learn the reality of what happens in such units (the army, in Israel, is almost always a sentient entity, personified, someone who knows and thinks and decides and acts). Mistakes—that is as far as he would go—have to be corrected. He himself is active in fixing things: he goes to the blockades; he visits the front-line soldiers; he makes sure they are not getting out of hand. He tells them to be nice to Palestinians. And it is always possible to improve things by making cosmetic changes—one barrier more or less, some more senior officers added to the detachment that comes in close contact with the civilian population, and so on. Sometimes soldiers are punished: Noam is very proud of the fact that he demoted an NCO and sent him to prison for twenty-one days for breaking the windows in a Palestinian car. The system calibrates and modulates itself, and the high command is very sensitive to infringements of human rights. "All in all," he said, "we're doing pretty well." Then the critical sentence—almost unimaginable from Jewish lips—slips out: "I [the commanding officer] am not meant to decide about the occupation, yes or no. I have my orders. I follow them as best I can."

This after an hour of unmitigated, incriminating testimony from the Hebron soldiers, who have exposed a situation so deeply corrupt, immoral, and self-destructive that it cannot be meliorated or redressed. Noam follows orders, as do most soldiers and officers in most wars. He doesn't think beyond this. He will never rock the boat. In fact, he will provide slick apologetics for the ongoing situation of severe abuse. He is a good man and, no doubt, a fine officer. It is because of the tens of thousands of Noams, who oil the gears, who collude in systemic oppression, that the system endures.

Refusal to serve in the Israeli army is a personal choice—not, in any sense, a categorical imperative of general applicability. I would not presume to urge such a choice on anyone, even a close friend. The factors involved are manifold, conflictual, and individually configured. I know what I would do today, were the army to try to send me to the territories; but this knowledge is no longer relevant—I was released from the reserves in 1998. What I hope to do in the following pages is to convey the flavor of the public debate on this issue as it has slowly emerged and crystallized in Israel, under very special circumstances, over the last few years. There is something extraordinary about this debate and its particular existential intensity (a staple feature of Israeli life). Among other things, it has produced texts of political philosophy that will, I believe, be studied in classrooms all over the world in the coming decades, like the classic statements by Gandhi, Thoreau, and Martin Luther King. Israel remains a living laboratory for existential experiment, and at the heart of the experimentation lies the issue of limits: How far can the state go in coercing its citizens? When does a person have the right, or the duty, to refuse?

February 6, 2002   From Iran to Tel Aviv

Navid Kermani, my Iranian friend from Berlin, arrived yesterday as a guest of the Van Leer Institute. They have sent someone to meet him at the airport and help him through passport control. It is not every day that an Iranian activist visits Israel. In Iran he is, of course, close to the reformers and the radical intellectuals. "When I come to Iran, I am met by the secret services. When I come to the land of the enemy, I am greeted with a red carpet."

He has come at a moment redolent of change. Several hundred soldiers—mostly reservists, including officers—have published a statement saying they will no longer serve in the territories. Their first full public exposure is scheduled for this evening, at Tel Aviv University, under the auspices of "The Campus Will Not Be Silent," HaKampus Lo Shotek. Late in the afternoon, we drive down to hear them. Like everyone else, we are mindful of what the late Yeshayahu Leibowitz, radical philosopher and eternal enfant terrible, said decades ago—that the occupation would end when five hundred soldiers said no.

Gilman 144, one of the larger campus auditoriums, is almost full; there are also many television cameras, including foreign press. But the latter are disappointed: the officers who are refusing to serve are also refusing to speak in public. Gadi explains to me later that, as patriots, they are reluctant to appear as "traitors," especially in the eyes of the outside world. I can't help feeling they have wasted an opportunity.

Instead, there are short presentations by a doctor from the Physicians for Human Rights, a lawyer (who focuses on war crimes), a fiery feminist from New Profile, and Yishai from the veteran organization of refuseniks, Yesh Gvul (There Is a Limit), which came into being during the Lebanon War. The doctor passes around photographs of mauled bodies. She is indignant, eloquent, emotional. One man in the audience tries to oppose the refuseniks and is more or less hooted down.

I scan the rows of faces and wonder, as usual, if this pacific army stands any chance. They are mild-mannered, hip, self-indulgent, a true Tel Aviv crowd; even their language has the somewhat slick register of Dizengoff Street and the bohemian Shenkin Street cafés. Will these people join nonviolent Palestinian resisters—someday soon—to face the tanks and the guns, as in Moscow in 1992? It seems incredible to me. Gadi explains the principle: in order to make that day possible, it is important to avoid doomed heroics and to create a moderate program with potential mass appeal.

In the end, it is the silence of the soldier-*sarbanim* that is most resonant tonight. Although many soldiers have refused before, we are seeing the birth of a far more massive, and more public, protest. In the past, and today as well, many soldiers simply came to an arrangement with their units or their commanding officers; they made it known that they would not serve in the territories, and the army generally preferred not to pursue them. Public confrontation, with its potentially demoralizing effect, was seen by the army command as far more damaging than the loss to active service of a few hundred combat soldiers. This new wave, however, represents a real change; these men are forthright, clear, and prepared to stand behind their public statement.

We have dinner afterward, Navid, Gadi, and I. Navid has already managed a visit to Acco, on the northern coast—largely a city of Palestinian refugees from 1948. He spoke to those he met at shops and cafés, took in their sadness, felt the burden of their memories, the future killed off by the past. In some ways, of course, they are the luckier ones; their cousins are in camps in Lebanon or Jordan. He asks us: "Do the Arabs of Acco have a stake in Israel; is it a part of their identity?" "States," says Gadi, "are not for identity. They are for running the buses and taking care of sewage. If you make them arenas for identity, everything goes awry." So simple, this lucidity. But he is pessimistic; one possibility is that the occupation will return in full force. Israel will crush the Palestinian Authority and take over their territories de facto, though perhaps this time around, in contrast with the past, without assuming any responsibility for the fate of the civilian population. There is a long struggle ahead. I sense in Gadi the slight detachment of the truly charismatic; he has thought it through—it is clear now, one must also act, but there is at best a slight hope that the Israelis will behave like human beings and let others live like human beings.

May 14, 2002   *An Unjust Law Is No Law*

The seminar on refusing to serve in the army finally takes place this evening on the Mount Scopus campus, after being postponed on various, mostly flimsy, pretexts for over a month. The law department gives its auspices, but apparently only by setting various severe conditions, such as excluding from the podium any signatories to the letter of support for the refuseniks that we have been circulating on campus (we have collected several hundred signatures among the faculty). Some deals were apparently struck. It's not clear how all this has evolved, but in the end the speakers, for and against, are uniformly serious and engaging. Merely holding the debate on campus is a victory, since Limor Livnat, the minister of education, and perhaps others did everything they could to prevent it.

Reality is a very strong drug, perhaps the strongest. Arguments sail back and forth like missiles; there is much shouting and heckling. "Where is the boundary?" "When does one say no?" "Who can help decide?" All the speakers agree that the occupation is a deadly poison and must end; but to refuse to serve is to attempt to bring the army to its knees. "Israeli democracy is anyway dying," says Yoram Shachar; "refusing to serve may kill it." As soon as it is truly dead, he will be the first to refuse. Listening to him, I am suddenly afraid: perhaps it is true and I am refusing to see what he can see. The extremists are there, actually already in power, merely waiting for their opportunity.

Yet this volatile, reality-rooted, powerful debate—tearing at the soul, baring the soul—seems to show the opposite: that here, at least, there is still space to think and speak out. What will happen on the other side once we leave? Palestine will perhaps be another ugly Algeria or Iran. Mota Kremnitzer reminisces about a lecture he gave in Beit Sahour, the site of our first dialogue group so many years ago: at first they applauded him for attacking the occupation, but when he tried to suggest that they make an elementary distinction between means and goal—that they might even feel some empathy for victims of terror attacks, for example—he was nearly lynched.

The leitmotif is South Africa. How close have we come to something like the old apartheid regime? Inside the territories, Palestinians are entirely disenfranchised, barred from using the roads, terrorized by settlers, and so on. Why paste over this truth, whatever the differences between Israel and South Africa? Along with this pressing example, there is the eerie presence of "history," sitting as judge. Who is this strange, fictive ghost at our banquet? Time folds and unfolds, and we cannot see it. The winner's history, the story he tells, tends to erase the loser's, as we know; still, everyone seems to think that this blind and ignorant arbiter will make a "realistic" pronouncement, ultimately giving out points and settling the score. In one sense, this is true. It is always foolish to have died for some long-dead cause. Who can imagine, even, the mental universe of a seventeenth-century soldier—killing Protestants, or Catholics, because they were the fashionable barbaric threat? Or for that matter, going off to die in horror in the trenches of the Great War, for what today can be clearly seen to have been nothing, only nothing, a terrible and lonely nothing? Soon, very soon, people will wonder how anyone could have chosen to risk his life for a fantasy, the nightmare of Greater Israel, and the heroes will be those who had the prescience to advise against following orders, doing as told, internalizing the sick nationalist myth.

But the boundary of negation changes hour by hour, maybe minute by minute. Does anyone know where it runs? To refuse to serve is a deeply subjective and private choice colored not so much by argument and reason as by recalcitrant feeling, memory, rage. There is no universal rule of thumb, no signpost in the sand. To be honest, one can only feel one's way along, hoping the decision is more or less right.

Mota thinks it is a legal question, moral within those terms. "Even if you accept the Palestinian reading of what happened at Camp David and assume that the Israeli proposals were inadequate, still it is impossible to accept the violence they have adopted as their weapon while still faced with an Israeli partner who wanted to reach a solution. It is not clear what the Palestinians want—for us not to be *there*, in the territories, or for us *not to be*. They have a right to end the occupation, but not at any cost. Killing us is too high a cost. But the Israeli right uses Palestinian violence to its own advantage. Thus, worst of all, we may well find ourselves in a paradoxical, soul-destroying situation of having to serve in an army that is bent on illegal acts." The South African scenario is all too possible.

Mota knows of what he speaks. He is worried about what will happen to Israeli democracy—under any scenario. So am I. There is no way to know with certainty what to do. Suddenly, very dramatically, a young man in the audience stands up and starts to speak in clipped, compelling tones. A year ago, at a similar symposium in Tel Aviv, he was convinced by such arguments. It is better, they said to him, that the sensitive and moral ones be there, in the territories; that they should do what has to be done and not leave it to the brutes. It is too early, they said, to espouse refusal as a collective strategy. Too dangerous to democracy. And so on. So in November he went to Gaza with his unit. They told him to detain Palestinian cars at the roadblock for three hours, and he detained them. They told him to blow up some house that was blocking the view, and he blew it up. They told him to search for suspected terrorists in some other house, and he searched, turning the house upside down, the children crying in fear and shame—and found nothing. They told him to keep in his gun sights a Palestinian family walking barefoot over the sands, impoverished to the edge of what is human—the same night that the government minister Danny Naveh complained, with odious self-pity, when he had to leave his house in response to a security threat and move for twenty-four hours into a posh hotel. The contrast, says this young soldier, was unbearable. He read Naveh's whining remarks in the newspaper and felt sick at heart. When he got home, he held his head in his hands and thought: "What the fuck are we doing there? It is not a particular act or order that is illegal; it is the very existence of the occupation that is criminal." "It is unreal," he says, "to talk about this in academic terms. What is real must be known and experienced. Once you feel it, there is no longer reason to hesitate."

The auditorium falls silent under the impact of this passionate torrent. What is left to be said? Elyakim Rubenstein, the government's legal adviser, has sent a letter that is read out, in spite of vociferous protest ("Why should the commissar be given a voice here?"). He doesn't much like resisting service. At least not at this time (what time would be better?). The letter is vacuous and rhetorical, convincing no one. It pales before the voice of the resister, who has shown us how and why he has changed.

The occupation will end; the settlements will go; the Palestinians will stew in their violent juices or work their way free of violence; new mythologies will spring up; the problem, it will turn out, was buried elsewhere, somewhere unimaginable today. Meanwhile, the debate is open and merciless, and it is true—the heart does tear. I feel the anguish, and I am glad to be touching what is real. Augustine is quoted: "An unjust law is no law." Surprisingly, everyone seems to know this. Israel has begun the business of freeing itself, none too soon.

June 13, 2002   Tel Aviv (2)

Déjà vu: another evening in Tel Aviv on refusal to serve. At first the hall is rather empty, but it slowly fills up. Sidra arrives with Talya, who has a fresh item to report from Emeq Refaim, down the road from my house in Jerusalem: a settler, armed to the teeth, decided to pick on two Arab teenagers who sell odds and ends on the street. They are always there, but suddenly this sheriff-style bully had them bent over on the pavement, backs to the street, army style, and was calling the police, who discovered they had no permits. . . . No one apparently was able to intervene, and the settler no doubt enjoyed swaggering over the streets of the leftist German Colony, self-appointed defender of the state and the Jews' supremacy. The two boys were carted off to the police station in the city center.

A flyer is making the rounds, "Women Who Refuse"—a peace tent for these women is going up in Tel Aviv next week. This is pure Aristophanes, *Lysistrata*, though I doubt Israeli women will ever renounce sex to get their men to stop making war. But there are now female refuseniks too, some incarcerated for long periods in military jails.

Yaniv Itzkowitz, the soldier who stood up from the audience in Jerusalem last month, is the first to speak, quoting the poet Yehuda Amichai: "Every man is tied to his lament like to a parachute. Slowly he hovers until he touches something hard."* No sooner has he said the words than a row of right-wing toughs erupts, shouting and screaming, near the platform. The ushers eventually drag them from the hall, Yaniv calling out to them from the platform, "I love you, I love you"—not ironically, I think. I cannot hear what they are yelling, probably screeches of hate. A Gandhian moment. "Always," says Yaniv, "it is a small bunch of fanatics who ruin life for everyone else." The audience is with him all the way; they clap and drown out the obscenities still echoing from the doorway. The posters announcing this evening's speakers have been defaced all over the campus and a new motto inscribed: "Death to the Refuseniks."

Yaniv launches into his j'accuse. "I accuse those who prostitute words, prostitute language, and then prostitute life itself." And a further long list. I am moved by him, by his struggle to find language—a tough and lyrical Hebrew, heart-language—minimally commensurate with what he knows and remembers. I wonder for a moment if such sentences can only be stated in Hebrew—if this kind of "no" is utterly unique to the visceral experience of Israel, and resistant to translation. Each word seems to be cleansing itself, cleansing us, of pollution stemming from the government, the media, the army. This is the true miracle of human language: its uncanny gift of *aletheia*, as the Greeks called it, the removal of the veil.

---

*Yehuda Amichai, "Tiyul Yisraeli 15," in *Patuach sagur patuach* (Jerusalem and Tel Aviv: Schocken, 1998), p. 75.

Elia Leibowitz, son of the late Yeshayahu Leibowitz, looks astonishingly like his craggy, rugged father. He is an astronomer and shows transparencies that look like galaxies. Mostly black holes. Perhaps, after all, they are appropriate to politics. Perhaps, as Elia says, they point the way to our future if we continue on the present, self-destructive course. I think back fifteen years: June 1987. The army radio channel was celebrating the appearance of the hundredth volume in its series of the "Broadcast University"—sets of thirteen lectures on all subjects under the sun, broadcast twice each day and subsequently published. I, too, delivered such a series of lectures—on Indian poetry—and had thus been invited to the celebration. Since the Ministry of Defense paid for this huge project, Rabin, the defense minister, was the chief guest. Several of us had been asked to speak; I read a few poems. Finally, Yeshayahu Leibowitz, inveterate iconoclast, rose to the microphone. "I have a German friend," he began, his back bent low toward the mike, his craggy face moving from initial mildness to a vast, almost terrifying fierceness. "I told him about this Broadcast University, which the army initiated, which the army pays for. I told him of the courses and the topics, the wide range of humanistic and scientific fields that have been covered, the large audience that listens to these lectures week after week. He, my German friend, was impressed. He said to me: 'No other army in the world would do such a thing. Only in Israel.' And he is right. I agree." Then, raising his voice to a thunderous pitch, like a biblical prophet, looking straight at Rabin, seated only a few yards away: "And perhaps this one good deed atones, in some infinitesimal way, for the thousands of ugly, intolerable crimes that this same army is committing hour by hour and day by day, even as you sit here before me now." I can still see Rabin squirming in his plastic chair.

Ishay Rosen-Zvi, one of the most articulate among the refuseniks, has a rule of thumb. "The great enemy of refusal," he says, "is not the ideological right, a relatively simple target, but the bourgeois ethos. The bourgeois can't be bothered. To go outside the rules of the game is a bit scary; the bourgeois wants safety

and dull comfort. The situation is obviously complex: there are
the legal and the moral and the strategic niceties—who can understand it? But there is an 'ignorant self-extrication': you cannot
know the whole picture; you cannot even comprehend everything you see—all you can know is that there are things that you
cannot and will not do to another human being. That is all, and
that is enough. That will bring about the change."

He is magnificent: young, lucid, complex, full of feeling. Listening to him, I think: To be able to say no defines the human
being. That, and a talent for empathic imagination—so strangely
rare among us. Perhaps it is because imagination is so active a
mode, the first antidote to passivity. Violence corrupts precisely
because of its subtle mutedness, its way of happening somewhere
else, around the corner, out of sight, in Ramallah, in Jenin.

I think of Ahmad, our aged gardener who turned up today
from near Bethlehem, braving the roadblocks. He hates Arafat;
in general, he is gentle, smiling, honest, modest. For years he has
come to sweep and weed and wash. He tells me in melodious
Arabic that life is impossible now—there is nothing to eat, nothing to do. They sit imprisoned in their houses; the streets are full
of soldiers; nothing is left except the emptiness and the misery.
He is one, the one I know; one of three and a half million.

Michael Sfard, the lawyer who represents the refuseniks, concludes the evening. Two of his clients are demanding a full military trial, something the army has so far avoided, for obvious reasons. All cases of refusal are judged by the commanding officer,
who can hand down sentences of up to thirty-five days in prison.
A military court-martial, which a soldier can demand, allows for
the whole show: witnesses, evidence, reasoned judgments delivered in writing. The military advocate has the authority to refuse
a request for such a trial if the offense is considered "trivial." So
far he has responded with this argument to each demand by the
small number of refuseniks willing to take the risk—for a military
court can give up to three years in prison for the same offense.
Next week the Supreme Court will render judgment on one such
request, from a young soldier of immense courage (or, as Eileen

says later, immense rage). He wants a chance to make his case, to defend himself, to put the army itself on trial. He is staring down the army, unblinking.

I have a moment of sudden hope, irrational but certain: we will win. I can see it. We are not there yet; a certain leap is still required—there is a vast gap to be crossed before this movement of rugged individuals saying individual "no's" reaches inwards to the core of this society, rearranging its imagination of itself. But we will get there: the parachutes are waiting to open, each of us tied to his or her lament.

November 9, 2002 Damun and ʿAtlit

There are no more free weekends; each Shabbat one now has a menu of possible activities, and one has to choose; the need is great everywhere, despair deepens, anger deepens. It is a time for acting. Out of loyalty to Yigal, who has been moved to Military Prison no. 4, I choose the Taʿayush demonstrations in the north—at Damun prison in the Carmel hills, and then at Military Prison no. 6, ʿAtlit—in lieu of more olive picking, for example (the bitter end of the olive harvest).

Yigal is on everyone's mind as the bus drives north along the coastal road. His story is a success of sorts: the army has given in to the intense campaign from within Israel and from abroad and moved him from Ketziot, where he was being held in deliberately humiliating, shameful conditions, to Zerifim, Military Prison no. 4. At Zerifim, at least, he is no longer required to wear an army hat at all hours of the day and night; and he is even allowed to sleep on a pillow. At Ketziot, deep in the desert—I remember it well from my own reserve service in the early '80s—he had been forbidden to speak with any other soldier. Refuseniks are apparently considered dangerous; they might corrupt an innocent mind.

Yesterday there was a full-page ad in *Haaretz*, the first time the refuseniks have been given this kind of outspoken, full-hearted support in an Israeli paper; over five hundred signed, from all over the world. My son Misha and I appear there side by side. As we approach Haifa, a call comes through from Yigal to Neve, who passes the phone to me. He sounds well; it is the story, he says, of the Rebbe and the goat.* After Ketziot, arriving at Prison no. 4, passing through the walls of barbed wire, felt like freedom. Now, at least, he can read. Yuri takes the phone from me to say to Yigal: "Just remember, at this moment you, alone among us, are doing political work at all times, even when you are asleep."

Yigal has published a letter from prison in one of the local newspapers; copies are circulating on the bus.

Dear Friends,

I would like to share some of my thoughts as I pass the long hours peeling bags of onions or washing oily pots. Why does a man of my age—married with two children—need all this? Why is it "worth my while" to refuse to serve?

Such questions have forced me to examine my actions from the perspective of the other prisoners. Here is a man, 36 years old, who is imprisoned with soldiers half his age. He is separated from his family, forbidden to take off his hat (even when sitting in his cell or while eating), forbidden to use a pillow or sheets, to wear a watch, to eat in the dining hall (instead, he eats on a folding table in the hallway near his cell—all the while behind bars), and to speak while working or while eating. He is forced to work fourteen hours a day (in the kitchen or cleaning the bathrooms on the base), to stand at attention and yell "Attention!" every time an officer passes, and to obey a long list of other commands and prohibitions, whose sole purpose is to humiliate him. Why would anybody in his right mind subject himself to this?

To answer this question, one has to recall the alternative—what it was I refused to do.

There are, of course, those who claim that the presence of people like me in the Occupied Territories can make the occupation more humane. It's true that you can politely destroy the orchard of someone you don't know, you can wreck a house quietly and in a civilized manner, you can perhaps even expel an entire population from their village—as has been done in South Hebron—in an organized and less violent way. It is possible, it

---

*A poor man with many children and only a tiny one-room house came to the Rebbe for advice. The Rebbe told him to bring his goat, his chickens, and his tools into the crowded room. After a week the man returned to complain to the Rebbe, who advised him to take the goat and the chickens back out—leaving him with a sense of vast spaciousness and relief.

*seems, to calmly dispossess and oppress an entire people. The question then
arises—are these actions that a person who wishes to retain his or her
humanity can carry out?*

*So when we, the refuseniks, declare that there are certain things that
a just person simply does not do, we do not mean working in a kitchen.
No, such work is dignified. We mean actions that humiliate and deny the
humanity of the other. There is no doubt that it is better to sit in jail,
isolated, wearing a hat, silent, washing dishes, and peeling onions.*

There are jails within jails. By 11:00 we roll up the hill at
Damun and emerge from the buses. I have been away over the
summer, so there are friends I have not seen for some months. We
chat; we embrace; we meet some of the newcomers. As always in
Ta'ayush, there is a wide range of ages: most are young, twenties
and thirties, but there are also the seventy-year-old men and
women who have come to make their protest, who have seen the
state that they helped build twisted almost beyond recognition.
Ta'ayush Haifa has organized the day's activities, and we follow
their lead.

Damun was once like everywhere else: a small, apparently
peaceful village on a ridge overlooking the sea. Sometime in April
or May 1948, during the fighting—no one knows exactly when—
the villagers left. A prison was built in the '50s, they say, on the
ruins of the old houses. In fact, you cannot see any of the old
rocks here; perhaps, indeed, the prison has subsumed them. Two
years ago Ben-Ami, then minister of internal security, closed
Damun prison as "unfit for human habitation." It was reopened
last year to house "nonhumans"—some four hundred Palestinian
workers caught without work permits in Israel. They are held
here for months in terrible conditions, vastly overcrowded cells
(approximately two meters allotted to each prisoner), virtually
nonexistent sanitary facilities, no leave, no telephones, almost no
visits from outside. Most are simple laborers whose crime was to
look for work in Israel, like thousands of others, at a time when
there was no work in the territories because of the war.

We gather up our banners and posters and take our stand on
the hill across from the prison. We can clearly see some of the

prisoners on the roof, deep inside: they wave to us; they dance to the songs we start to sing. We are a mixed group of Jews and Arabs; some are singing "Biladi," the Palestinian anthem. Policemen stand together, a thick contingent, at the entrance of the prison. We have brought food for the prisoners—it is Ramadan—but the police will not allow us to bring it in. There are also jailers who would lose their jobs if our demand—to close Damun down again, as the ministry had decided—were to be accepted. But there seems little chance of this. On the contrary, a violent synecdoche rules. First there was the village, then the prison built over it, now Palestinians have come back to Damun as prisoners, re-encapsulated by the nightmare that displaced them, the nightmare they once fled. Jewish jailers stand at the outer periphery of this dizzying set of deadly circles.

The landscape is entrancing on this incandescent autumn day. The hills circle down to the sea, stretched out before us, almost within reach; row after row of pines and cedars twist up the slopes. The air is fragrant with Mediterranean smells, delicious to breathe in, but the human suffering densely packed into the ugly walls of this prison poisons the taste for me.

Someone is speaking on the loudspeaker, a Palestinian—apparently an Israeli Arab—whose brother had been imprisoned here, at Damun, some years ago; he was eighteen, and his crime was to have waved the Palestinian flag. "Once again," he says bitterly, "Israel wants to eat the Palestinians' olives and to keep the Palestinians in jail." Today this is the prison of those who are not Jewish enough, the foreign workers caught without permits and, of course, Palestinians of this category. Someone hands me a huge poster in Arabic and Hebrew that reads: "They were guilty of trying to feed their families." Others read: "Their freedom is our freedom." "Curfew there, prison here." There is a strong breeze from the sea, it is hard to keep the poster aloft, and the day is hot now; I am thirsty.

Eventually we get back into the buses and drive down the hill to 'Atlit. Another futile scene: we clamber up through shrubs and thorns to a point looking down into the prison, where nine refuseniks are being held. Of the three hundred or so who were with us in Damun, only about half arrive in 'Atlit. Here the demonstration is organized by Yesh Gvul, who have been through it many times before. Our loudspeakers carry over the prison walls, and we invoke the prisoners' names, one by one; we reach one of them on his cell phone. We can see soldiers studying us from a distance, from within the prison complex. The Crusader castle of 'Atlit is just beyond, and across from our hillside perch are the Neolithic caves in the Carmel hills, one of the oldest sites of human habitation in the world. Were those people as tortured as we are, as cruel to one another? Is this what being human means, the constant struggle, straggling up one rocky hill after another to try to melt some stony heart, some stony part of ourselves?

My interest is flagging by now; Leena distracts me with another botanical demonstration—she shows me *tarris*, pronounced with that astonishing roll of the tongue, a sturdy green bush whose leaves sweeten water; she picks several stems of fresh *marwa*, so strong in fragrance that I hesitate to put them in my bag with the books and the bandages. She grew up in Galilee among these trees and bushes, then came to Jerusalem to study law because, she says, she had hopes of attaining justice, *tzedek*. By now she is a lawyer, doing her apprentice year in a big law firm, and she has given up all hope of justice. She wants to go to America to study subjects linked to human rights. I wonder if she will miss anything from here, like the pita, fresh from the flames, filled with *labane*, olive oil, and *za'atar* that we buy from a Druze stall after climbing down.

On the way back, she shows me something else that I have never noticed in thirty-five years of living here. Where once a village stood, before 1948, you now see clusters of thorny sabras, the only plant that thrives around such ruins. Sometimes you can see a few of the old stones, too, covered with these cacti. Nonchalantly she points to just such a concatenation of rock and thorn beside the great highway, Road Number One. We sail past it in seconds; there was once a whole world there. Everywhere you go there are these ruins, or the cities built around or beside them. Luckily, her village in the Galilee was so remote that it was virtually forgotten until the 1980s. Her parents still live there, and she goes from time to time to see them; but, she says, she belongs nowhere, not in the village, not in Jerusalem, nowhere.

And there is more still to lose. All day long I fail to shake the gloom nesting inside me, another embedded synecdoche. Something has changed. For the first two years of this war, we believed that it would crack open again someday; that negotiations would resume, that the self-evident, the only possible solution—two states, side by side—would compel even the blind politicians and those who voted for them. This Intifada was another disaster to be survived, like so many others. But perhaps we were the blind ones. Perhaps the damage is by now too great, the sinister collusion of the violent forces on both sides too compelling.

We are back in Jerusalem before 5:00. Night approaches; the bus driver, fasting for Ramadan, can now drink and eat. He is in a hurry to get home to Abu Tor. We hug each other good-bye. At home I unpack my two books and three gray-green branches of *marwa*, pungent, bitter-sharp, stubborn, like stabs of hope.

December 16, 2003   *The Questions*

The real sensation was caused by the pilots: twenty-seven of them have published a statement declaring they will no longer carry out missions in the territories. Specifically, they will refuse to take part in "pinpoint assassinations"—always a matter of dropping bombs on suspected terrorist targets in densely populated areas of Gaza or the West Bank, where innocent civilians are certain to be killed along with the intended victim. Among these pilots are famous names, including Yiftach Spector, a legend in the air force—one of the pilots who bombed the Iraqi reactor in 1981, among other heroic feats. Debate is intense, and there is much anger. The pilots have been ignominiously dismissed from the reserves, and they report much suffering—lifelong friends no longer speak to them; they have been subjected to threats and abuse. One or two have been pressured to recant. The pilots are the very symbol and self-image of Israel—how can they refuse?

Dan Halutz, the commander of the air force, rushes to give an interview in the press; he is shocked and bitter and self-righteous. He has no doubts about giving orders to attack densely populated civilian areas where terrorists might be hiding, and he is prepared to pay the cost in innocent lives. He has no regrets and feels no pain; he sleeps well at night. When he himself drops a bomb on such a target, all he feels is the slight bump when the ordnance leaves the plane.

To our surprise, Menachem Magidor, president of the Hebrew University, has agreed to participate tonight in our panel about refusal to serve. He will speak against refusal, along with two others; but his presence has generated much excitement and attention. For once, distributing flyers was relatively easy, and when the security people on campus tried, as usual, to stop us, we happily pointed to the president's name among the speakers.

But there is also a price. Hooligans from the right have threatened to break up the evening. Threats have been published on one of the right-wing media websites. Once the threat became explicit, we felt we had to inform campus security; and they at once tripled the security costs borne by the organizers, The Campus Will Not Be Silent, an entirely unsupported, unfunded group of volunteers. The familiar progression: we are a peace-driven organization, and the evening is intended to provide a free and open debate of a critical issue on a university campus, where such debates should take place; the threat of violence comes, as usual, from the right, and we are saddled with the cost.

The auditorium is filled to capacity—not a single empty seat. Outside, lines are forming, and dozens have been turned away; the guards allow one to enter only if a seat becomes vacant inside. Otherwise people would be sitting on the steps and spilling out the windows, like in the old, heady days of Vietnam.

I am chairing this panel; trying to set an even tone, I read two passages, beginning with John Rawls:

"The refusal to take part in all war under any conditions is an unworldly view bound to remain a sectarian doctrine. It no more challenges the state's authority then the celibacy of priests challenges the sanctity of marriage. By exempting pacifists from its prescriptions the state may even seem to display a certain magnanimity. But conscientious refusal based upon the principles of justice between people as they apply to particular conflicts is another matter. For such refusal is an affront to the government's pretensions, and when it becomes widespread, the continuation of an unjust war may prove impossible. Given the often predatory aims of state power, and the tendency of men to defer to their government's decision to wage war, a general willingness to resist the state's claims is all the more necessary."*

And, more simply, Mahatma Gandhi:

"If man will only realize that it is unmanly to obey laws that are unjust, no man's tyranny will enslave him.... So long as the superstition that men should obey unjust laws exists, so long will their slavery exist."†

Somewhat sternly, expecting trouble, I tell the audience: "This is an academic forum; we are addressing a serious issue. We will do so with the decorum and mutual respect that are proper to a university."

Magidor, given his choice of when to speak, has elected to start. "When," he asks, "must one refuse to serve?" His answer: "Only when the state becomes entirely predicated on evil, a state of wickedness. Until such time, in a democracy, one is ruled by the majority. The consequences of refusal, for the democratic system, are potentially devastating. To refuse to serve is to undermine the institutions that safeguard all of us; we have not yet reached the point where the Israeli system as a whole is irreparably corrupt." He is clear and forceful and, as the evening progresses, evidently uncomfortable, unhappy at his decision to speak tonight. I sympathize with his predicament. When does

---

*John Rawls, *A Theory of Justice*, 2nd ed. (Cambridge, MA: Harvard University Press, 1999), p. 335.

†M. K. Gandhi, *Non-Violent Resistance (Satyagraha)* (Mineola, NY: Dover, 2001), p. 18.

a public figure, such as the president of a university, reach the point of speaking out, of taking a stand? Magidor has a university, an entire academic universe, to protect. Everyone has his own private threshold for saying no.

Now one of the pilots, Yoel Piterberg, makes a melodramatic pitch. "Midnight. Gaza. Your orders: a targeted assassination in a heavily populated neighborhood. Will you fire the missile, knowing innocents are certain to be killed?" Yoel has reached his threshold. He is tough, fanatical, every inch a pilot, cut in the heroic macho mold. I don't much like the mold, yet I admire the man's courage. He has a certain retrospective claim to truth. For years, he says, he piloted helicopters over Lebanon, hundreds of missions, shooting at this or at that, following his orders—and now, looking back, he can honestly say that, with one exception, all these missions were a complete and utter waste, a pointless folly. The exception was when he rescued some soldiers stranded in some remote valley, pinned down by an ambush.

Yoel is openly, explicitly scornful of what we are doing here tonight—talking, heaping up words about refusal, thinking it through. He wants only deeds, believes only in deeds. University professors are, it seems, a useless, ineffectual lot. I tend to agree. But why, then, has he bothered to come here to address the campus audience? Eventually the derision becomes too much for me. Using my privilege, I say to him—aiming at the audience—"We are not here for some theoretical exercise. We are here for one purpose—to change a situation that is unbearable, cruel, and unjust."

Avi Ravitzki and Moshe Halberthal—both strongly identified with the left and the peace camp—now speak strongly against refusal to serve; Shula Volkov, from Tel Aviv University, argues equally passionately in favor. The debate goes back and forth, with deep, intensifying emotion; and still the fatal question remains: Precisely where, or when, is a person to draw the line?

Leibowitz, it seems to me, was wrong. By now thousands have refused to serve in the territories, refusals that are "hard" or "soft" or totally silent, and still the occupation continues. Or was he?

It is always the few who make a difference, who precipitate the long business of change. The miracle is that in Israel, driven by the madness of war and terror, the refuseniks can speak freely, can argue and persuade. And, as always in such conditions, the burning vision finds its tongue, as in the days of the prophets. David Enoch, a refusenik himself, philosopher and legal scholar at the Hebrew University, rises to speak.

"There are," he says, "important legal issues involved in the refusal to serve, but the beauty of refusing lies in its being an extralegal act, one that reveals the limits of the law's legitimacy as such. For even if all the judges of the Supreme Court were to tell us that refusal is legal, the basis of our decision to refuse is not legal but moral. We refuse because what we are asked to do—in the occupied territories—is morally reprehensible.

"They tell us that our refusal legitimates refusal by our opponents on the right—who may refuse an order to evacuate settlements, for example. Let us look at this claim. The causal argument will not hold. Our opponents are not waiting for us. In fact, they don't care in the least what we say or do. For many years they have been engaged in systematic violation of the law—violation that is brutal in effect, driven by greed, that generates strife and contention, and that has changed the entire national agenda and transformed the nature of the Israeli-Palestinian conflict. What is more, there is no moral symmetry between the two types of refusal. No one can claim that there is no difference between justified and unjustified refusal. It is one thing to refuse an order in order to defend certain basic human rights, and another to do so with the aim of sanctioning theft and oppression, in the name of a messianic racism and the alleged supra-rational sanctity of the Land of Israel.

"What about playing by the rules? Are we not committed to the rules of the democratic game? Yes, in general we are. But a majority vote is not enough to legitimate a crime. The other side, to repeat, does not play by the rules. There are flaws in the democratic process: at present we find a tiny, extreme, and violent minority coercing the moderate majority. The extremists have effectively hijacked the system. Moreover, as Rawls has said, principled refusal to go along with destructive or unjust policies may constitute a kind of check or balance on the system—so we may actually be playing by the rules after all. Most important: how can we speak seriously about democracy in the context of the occupation, which denies fundamental rights to millions of people?" Enoch invokes, again, the ghost of Leibowitz: "There is, as Leibowitz was fond of saying, no kosher way to slaughter a pig.

"They tell us we are undermining the rule of law and weakening the state, the sense of shared destiny, and so on. This kind of claim needs to be supported by evidence. Is there any evidence, any historical precedent, to show that nonviolent refusal to obey has caused catastrophe? There is not. So stop trying to terrify us with nightmare scenarios. What is more, such arguments have to be pitted against the alternative. Even if massive nonviolent resistance were dangerous, would it be any more dangerous than going along with our present self-destructive course?

"It would be easy to go on, analyzing argument after argument, but what we must bear in mind is something else. Think about the occupation and what it means—the continuous repression, the large-scale seizure of land, the humiliation, killings, disposessions, the impoverishment of millions. Think about arrogance and domination, about arbitrary injustice, about the planned route of the Separation Wall. Think about the abysmal disregard for human rights, the cynical contempt for other human beings. Think about the lies we have been told and continue to tell ourselves—as if all this were really related to the war on terror (terror, in itself, is of course an abomination). Were the war on terror truly the goal, the means would certainly be very different. Think about how Sharon and his people have lied in saying they genuinely want to reach an agreement, and about how the army likes to claim it is a moral, honorable army, with only a few, negligible exceptions that are supposedly self-investigated and punished.

"And since to obey always implies a certain faith and trust, we must also talk about our leaders—about the commander of the air force, for example, who sleeps so soundly every night. Let us talk about the officers who toe the line, who do what they are told without question. About the horrific record of the decision makers in this war, and in earlier ones. And once we have thought about all this, we can ask ourselves: Is it right for us to put aside our grave doubts, and our knowledge of the inhuman price paid by the civilian population in the territories, because we trust the wisdom and integrity of those who are making the decisions? When you receive some order there, in the field, can you proceed to carry it out without wondering if those who gave the order have taken into account how many innocents will be hurt, or without wondering if our leaders understand the depths of the humiliation they are causing, or if they are sincerely trying to bring this terrible situation to an end?

"When it becomes clear," says Enoch, "that these are the questions, then I, for one, am also clear in my mind about the answers."

He sits down. The audience, contrary to my fears and expectations, sits in near-total silence. It is a serious moment, perhaps the most serious I can remember in many years of struggle and debate. A choice—real, urgent, and agonizing—faces us. Each will have to answer. With the agony comes the gift—of looking deeply, of deciding, of becoming more fully human; also, for me, the gift of sharing a podium with David Enoch. After a few moments, there are questions, debate resumes, but there is little rancor or bitterness tonight; we are all, I think, sensible of the burden and the sorrow. And of doubt—another young reservist in the audience cries out, toward the end: "Be careful. You are playing with fire. I have just come from Nablus. I know what it means. Be careful. If I am called, I will serve again, but I want to know that when I leave, I will never have to go back into that hell again."

6

The Wall: Maskha, Abu Dis, Ar-Ram, Bil'in

Confusion dominates discussion of the Separation Wall. Most Israelis want the barrier and believe it is the only effective means of stopping suicide bombers. There are those who argue against this—claiming that once the wall is built, the bombers, nurtured by despair, will come from within the vast Arab population trapped on the Israeli side of the wall. And there are some who oppose the very idea of "fencing off" or "fencing in" as a violent and self-defeating mechanism that effectively perpetuates the conflict. But, in general, the campaign led by Israeli peace groups against the wall is not aimed at the idea of a wall as such. It is a protest at the route that the government planners have mapped out, a route that penetrates deep into Palestinian territory and protects, before all else, every possible settlement and outpost. This trajectory virtually rules out a peaceful solution based on partition and the idea of two states for two peoples in Israel-Palestine. It also perpetuates a regime of terror inside the territories, leaving most Palestinian villages encircled, isolated, essentially ghettoized, and at the mercy of bands of marauding settlers. It also appropriates large tracts of Palestinian land, practically annexing them to Israel.

This basic distinction—between the wall as an anti-terrorist barrier, acceptable to nearly everyone, and the trajectory of the wall as planned by the Israeli right—has to be kept in mind in any discussion of the legal or moral situation. Those of us active in the struggle have been involved, primarily, in an attempt to redress the gross injustices inherent in the planned route—above all, the seizure of Palestinian land, the consequent ruin of the villages and their economies, and the creation of a nightmarish world of fences within fences, walls within walls. This struggle was rewarded with very partial success in the decision of the Israeli Supreme Court of June 30, 2004, described below.

May 16, 2003   Maskha

Could Jews really build ghettos for Palestinians? It seems unlikely, given Jewish history. If anyone knows what life in a ghetto means, we do. But, as Isaac Babel says, reality has no need to be probable and is only too happy to follow a well-devised story. In this case, there is perhaps a certain tragic logic to the story.

Our bus drives past Qalqiliya, where we get our first glimpse of the wall from various sides and angles. Tall gray slabs circle the city. There is only a single opening, both exit and entrance, controlled, of course, by the army. Qalqiliya has, in effect, become a large prison; similarly, Tulkaram, the other major city along the "seam" between Israel and the territories. The market that once flourished in Qalqiliya—the main outlet for this part of the West Bank—is now dying. The roads that connected the villages to this small town, and to one another, are completely blocked. We drive along one only to see it come to an end; after a hundred meters, there is the standard ominous, immovable boulder. The end of the road. At the turn, a tank sits phlegmatically, a soldier standing beside it, guarding the new wall that snakes and slides over the hillside above. It is not yet finished, but that won't take long.

The bus parks at the bus stop for the large settlement of Elkana, still growing, metastasizing through the hills. We proceed on foot past another blockade, another set of boulders, to

Maskha, where a fleet of ancient, banged-up cars and Transits will drive us over the rough tracks toward the protest tent. We have crossed into another world: I remember crossing the Sheikh Hussein Bridge into Jordan and finding these same rickety old taxis waiting to take us to Amman. But here they are manned by unemployed drivers with literally nowhere to go, nowhere to drive to anymore. The wall hems them in on every side.

We get out at the bottom of a hill, climb up to where the wall-to-be is suddenly before us: a huge gap in the surface of the earth, two deep trenches in the middle of which the electrified fence itself will soon pass. Slightly to the north, the fence is already in place, mostly wire and steel and visually somewhat less menacing than the Qalqiliya segment. But appearance is deceptive, for what becomes clear as the eye adjusts to the terrain is the true meaning of this new border. It meanders, wanders, loops through the hills, extending to include every possible Jewish settlement, circling the towns, cutting villages off from their fields and hinterland and from each other. We are several kilometers east of the Green Line, the border of pre-1967 Israel; and what we are seeing is the basic path of this fence, which chews deep into Palestinian territory, swallowing huge, savage bites of land. No one knows exactly how much land is being appropriated in this way. The government and army refuse to publish exact maps while the land-grab is in process.

Still, I am somewhat less horrified than I had expected to be. It is, after all, no more than a wall (plus trenches, patrol paths, prison-style watchtowers, secondary fences, tertiary fences, and so on). What human beings can erect they can also take down. Look at Berlin. One of the villagers tells me as we walk along the trench: "I don't care so much about the wall itself. It can be removed some day. What I care about is that the Israelis will not talk to us, don't treat us as human beings, don't want to live together with us. We could solve the whole problem if they wanted peace. The terrorists are a tiny minority. The rest of us just want to live."

We clamber down into the trench, slipping a bit on the rocks, climb up the other side, straddle the concrete base for the wall-to-be, another trench—and find ourselves at the foot of a hill dark with olive trees. (Tens of thousands of olive trees have been destroyed in clearing a path for the wall.) We climb up to the tents where Palestinians, Israeli peace activists, and a few foreign volunteers have been coordinating the doomed struggle against this fence. Nazih—articulate, lively, focused—sets out the basic facts as we huddle in the shade of the olives. There are now several distinct territorial zones in this small area. There is the large space between the Green Line and the fence: many thousands of *dunams* have been expropriated in this zone to create the fence, and the owners of the fields have, of course, not been compensated. Some eleven thousand villagers here, where we sit, are directly caught up in this limbo, effectively imprisoned within it. They belong neither to Israel nor to Palestine; their homes are now a no-man's-land, though they are hemmed in on all sides by settlements and by the Israeli army. Then there are those villages that, like Maskha, are just on the other side of the fence, in Palestine, thus cut off from their fields, which are in Israel—the third zone. In theory, the army intends to open gates for these farmers to enter the no-man's-land so they can work their fields—at ten shekels per entry, five shekels for a donkey. But it seems the gate will be open only for half an hour in the early morning, and half an hour again in the late afternoon. Farmers need the possibility of constant access to their fields, and the sense is that these Palestinian peasants will very rapidly be alienated from their lands. In any case, the settlers are constantly encroaching, stealing more and more. Tens of thousands of villagers will be stripped of their holdings in this way; they will be able to view, impotently, their former fields from the other side of the fence. The process is already far advanced. The army is preventing access; the future looks grim.*

Actually, says Nazih, he is left with only three options: (1) He can sit at home doing nothing, that is, starve; (2) he can emigrate

*For a detailed discussion of the situation in this region, see Shlomi Swisa, "Not All It Seems: Preventing Palestinians Access to Their Lands West of the Separation Barrier in the Tulkarm-Qalqiliya Area," *B'Tselem*, June 2004 (also available at www.btselem.org).

to Lebanon or Jordan as a refugee; (3) he can put on an explosive belt and blow himself up in Tel Aviv. The Israeli right obviously wants him to select option 2. This is the devilish cleverness of the fence: it so radically impoverishes the Palestinians caught up by it that they may well "transfer" themselves voluntarily. There is no longer any need to put a single Palestinian on a truck or bus and dump him or her at the bridge or the Lebanese border. Transfer will happen of itself, perhaps relatively quickly.

It is thus not accurate to call the fence an "apartheid wall," as some of the Israeli left has been doing. True, conditions on the wrong side of the fence are horrific: roads that are open only to Jews, total confinement in prison-like enclaves for the Palestinians, and so on. In reality, however, this is a wall for transfer—or, as Nazih says without pathos, for taking the land.

Nazih's in-laws live in Bidiya, a village hardly three kilometers away from Maskha—but Bidiya and Maskha are divided by the fence. For him to visit his wife's parents means, now, a long nightmarish trip over the tracks and back roads and past the army roadblocks. When the fence is finished, even this may become impossible.

Various Palestinian ecological groups have tried to map the new reality. Since the fence is also meant to include the Jordan Valley within Israel, what is left for Palestine is a ludicrously reduced bubble in the north, including Jenin and Nablus and Ramallah, and a discontinuous bubble south of Jerusalem. And even these enclaves have settlers ensconced at points within them, breaking them up into still smaller units. It is worse than any Bantustan, and no Palestinian leader could ever accept this. But then no Palestinian leader is expected to. They no longer matter. What is more, a large portion of the most fertile fields in the West Bank lie exactly in this area near the Green Line in the north, from Jenin south to Qalqiliya, in the limbo zone of the fence. Some say a major percentage of the good land, the breadbasket of Palestine, is being annexed to Israel. The same applies to the available water, for the fence controls perhaps 80 percent of the mountain aquifer.

As we begin to take in this reality, with the fence coiling through the hills beneath us, past the red roofs of settlement after settlement, the police and army turn up in force. They have already ordered the Maskha people to take down the protest tent and evacuate the foreign volunteers. Today they are, it seems, only checking, and we are happy to be here at this moment when they happen to appear. Perhaps our presence deters them, but they will surely be back soon. Monday is the deadline, and there is no hope. Naama, my former student and the leader of today's expedition, says that what is needed here is a Gandhian *satyagraha*, a campaign of nonviolent resistance, but where are the thousands of Israelis who would join it, where is the Gandhi to lead it? Nearly all Israelis like the promise of this fence. They have, and seek, no idea of its human cost and no understanding of its deeper purpose. They also probably have no particular compunctions about taking a little more land.

As we leave the village—clambering over the trenches and concrete a second time—one of the young Palestinians starts to harangue me. "There was an opportunity," he says, "but already it is wasted. Is it not true that the Israelis don't want to make peace?" "No," I say, "it is not true; most Israelis want peace very much and would agree to any reasonable compromise." "But they elected Sharon," he says. "The Labor Party, Meretz, all the left have lost everything. Israelis want Sharon. They don't care what happens to us." There is no way I can explain to him, no time—it is very hot, and we have to leave; my Arabic begins to fail me. Still he follows me to the edge of the roadblock, the boulders that cut him off from the world, crying to me: "Why won't they let us live beside them?" I cross the roadblock, picking my way over the rocks to the edge of Elkana, brutal, immovable Elkana.

Maybe all will change nonetheless. Maybe the fence, someday, will be another pathetic, scorned reminder of these times. Maybe the Bantustan model is not, after all, our fate. Who can say? But I am more disheartened today than at any time in the last two years, more sick in soul than I was that day the settlers beat me in Twaneh. I can't reconcile myself to the human suffering that we are knowingly inflicting. Some part of me is still incredulous at the fact that Jews are the ones who are doing this. I am the witness who cannot believe his eyes.

By 4:00, dusty, burned, I am back in my fenceless, well-appointed house in Jerusalem. Edan is home for Shabbat from basic training. Despite everything, I am proud of him as I see him coping, even thriving, as if I were reliving an anachronistic memory from the time when it was all right to be proud of a soldier-son. At dinner he says with his usual casual sweetness: "It's quite a challenge doing the army with parents like you."

September 7, 2003   Al-Quds University (1)

It has been over three months since I was last in Palestine. I have breathed other air. In Oxford it rained, and I reveled in cloud. I have read poetry, written books. Others, too, had a brief respite. There was the transient hope of the Hudna, the precarious cease-fire declared by the two sides. Now we are back again to the vicious cycle. Yesterday Israel tried to assassinate Sheikh Yassin and the whole Hamas leadership. Abu Mazen has resigned. The fence, meanwhile, is expanding. Sari Nusseibeh, president of Al-Quds University, sends a message to his colleagues at the Hebrew University, members of HaKampus Lo Shotek: they are cutting into the Al-Quds campus for the wall; can we help?

We met last week with Dmitri, Sari's secretary, a volatile, articulate Italian-Palestinian with a charmingly incongruous New York accent. We saw the maps. It is not, after all, much of a case. In a sense, given the magnitude of human suffering caused by this fence, the loss of a few dozen *dunams* belonging to a university is trivial. Their soccer field and botanical garden are to be swallowed up. They will lose maybe a fourth, maybe a third of their land. Is it worth investing energy in this?

Yes, it is worth it. Every small victory counts. They are our colleagues and friends. We cannot just stand by.

Today Menahem surprises me with an invitation to join Janet, Avishai, and Tzali for a visit to Abu Dis, to meet Sari. Last week we were told not to come: the students are enraged—they don't want to see even a single Israeli there; our safety could not be guaranteed. This has not really changed, but Sari wants us to come, so we drive through the winding, tortuous roads to Al-Quds—only a few kilometers as the crow flies from Mount Scopus, but far indeed if you have to negotiate the barriers and roadblocks and back roads. At one point we find ourselves driving on the old Jericho road through Al-ʿAyzarīyah, which I remember well from many years ago. There was the day I walked there with a friend to see Lazarus's tomb: token of the dream that what dies can live again. At Abu Dis, the first part of the cycle—killing something living—is still in force.

So close, yet a different world. You know you are in Palestine because, under the same blazing dry sun, you see children clambering barefoot over the rocks behind the goats. You hear their sharp, thin calls. The walls are rich with violent graffiti. Old cars, shuttered shops, an impression of long neglect, incurable poverty. At the same time, the breathtaking swirl of stony hills. Driving through the town, we run straight into a piece of the new wall. We are lost: Sari has to guide us in by cell phone, past the gray, ugly slabs that will mark the end of the line, the boundary of Palestine, the end of hope. It is moving closer day by day. From Al-Quds University, you can look back, westward, toward Mount Scopus and the Mount of Olives, a few minutes' drive and worlds apart. But the first world has its claws in the third: the army bulldozers are parked on the hill over the campus, waiting for the sign to chew their way through it.

Sari's security man is waiting for us. He says to us in Hebrew: "Don't speak Hebrew here." He is worried, even tries to scrape away the Peace Now sticker on Tzali's back windshield. There are violent factions on campus, Islamic Jihad, the Muslim Brethren. Students stare at us as we walk into the huge tent spread in the heart of the confiscated area. Sari is there, seated at a plastic white table.

They bring us water, very welcome in the choking heat. We walk with Sari along the ridge to see the line of the wall. The mind doesn't fully take it in, this coil of wire and concrete slabs that is about to cut the landscape into two separate entities—Israel to the west, and the rump of Palestine, a warren of discontinuous ghettos, to the east. That is one level. Then there is the micro-level of this one piece we have come to see. Why must the fence cut through the university's soccer field? There seems to be enough room along the outer perimeter. There is, of course, the matter of the perimeter road, to which the university agreed months ago—thinking this new thoroughfare would serve them too, would allow access for students, for spectators at the sports stadium, for visitors. That was their mistake. Once they agreed to the road, the fence was bound to follow. Now the road will be in Israel, and they will be fenced off from Jerusalem, their natural hinterland.

We sit and talk about what to do. Does he want us, I ask, to organize an international campaign of signatures? He does. What about a demonstration in Abu Dis by our students and faculty? He seems unsure. Is it safe? "We work," he says, "only by consensus. It is slow work; we have to persuade all of them, even the radical Islamicists. Last week," he says with a smile—this urbane, contemplative, skeptical man sitting on a plastic chair in the dusty field—"I had to pray two times."

We agree we will bring a small group of professors on Thursday, when work is scheduled to begin again. For two days they had a little hope; in the standard Middle Eastern mode, the army told them: "Don't worry, we'll work it out." Today, however, it became clear that this means only: "You have lost." Their contacts with the Ministry of Defense and the government have produced nothing. The legal battle is still going on, but will the bulldozers wait? And can Sari, who seems bemused at the active role that has been thrust upon him, Sari with his cultivated Arabic, his Oxford English—can he move the fence a hundred meters west?

Everywhere it is the same story: the fence is reinventing the map of Palestine, leaving hundreds of thousands in limbo, at the mercy of the settlers. No one in Israel seems to care. Indifference has seeped into the Jews like an intravenous anesthetic. *Fence them in.* It is an apotheosis of the old, familiar Zionist response to attack, coupled with an insatiable hunger for land. No one seems to have noticed that this "solution" has never really worked.

The drive back reminds me of Amman, a mirror image of the ascent through the cypresses and olives. It could also be Greece or Turkey or Cyprus. Greece—where the violence ended fifty years ago. No, in between came the colonels. There is always this potential for barbarism when humans are involved. Still, Greece, I could sit and read Homer. . . . My mind wanders away from the relatively minor distress of our colleagues and friends in Al-Quds, away from the intense political discussions going on in the car. There is talk of a new initiative, a document signed by leading public figures on both sides that sets out the basis for an agreed settlement to the conflict—the Geneva initiative. Maybe it will change, in some measure, the rules of engagement. Perhaps there will be a new hope. I listen, halfhearted, my attention wandering. It is hot and I am tired—tired of fighting and losing, inch by inch, in this endless battle. I will organize the petition and the visit, I will do what I can, but it will not be enough. The anesthetic is dripping into me as well.

September 19, 2003   Al-Quds University (2)

Second time around, everything is more familiar. As a result, the reality is more malignant. I already feel at home on the Al-Quds campus: the tent outside the football field, the rocky ridge, the hill with its cypress trees, the makeshift gate, the glistening new stone buildings. It is Friday morning, the day of prayer, and most of the students are at home. I cannot bear the thought that this piece of Jerusalem, which I have now taken in and recognize, will soon be devastated by the bulldozers.

They are a little closer, and already the army has been marking the line of advance. Yesterday morning Dmitri called, then we reached Sari, and both were unequivocal: they want us to come. There is a good chance that everything will come to a climax within hours. So hurriedly we put together the lineaments of this visit and prepare the activists; they may, we think, have to face down the bulldozers.

But by late afternoon yesterday, the news is a little different; another apparent delay. Another small victory? By now we are committed to coming; the message has gone out. So we meet this morning at Gan Hapaamon. Janet is there ahead of me, with the signs she has made herself. The bus is waiting.

We head through the Maaleh Adumim tunnel—for many, the first time on this road—then weave through Al-'Ayzariyah and into Abu Dis. Like last time, we get lost and have to be piloted in over the telephone by Sari. They are expecting us; they greet us warmly. Stephanie from *Le Monde* has already arrived. There are other cameras clicking, but none of the big Israeli papers seems to be represented. Dmitri gathers us around him and briefs us. Al-Quds has given up on the legal struggle; past experience with the Israeli Supreme Court is not encouraging. The international campaign is gathering speed—some six hundred glittering names will sign on tomorrow in Paris—but so far nothing seems to have changed on the ground. The Defense Ministry calls, talks politely for half an hour, and again says no. They are planning to go ahead, to slice away a third of the campus.

Sari appears, as always, gracious, self-ironic; distressed, yet in control. He shows us the maps, answers our questions. I tell him I have written a few words; he can take them and use them as he wants. No, he wants them spoken aloud. I would be happy not to have to speak them, but he takes hold of my shoulders and pulls me into an open space at the other end of the tent—prayers will soon commence where we were standing—and asks that I read out my morning's text:

> *We are students and faculty of the Hebrew University and other Israeli institutions of higher learning, activists within the Israeli peace movement, Peace Now, Ta'ayush, and other groups. We are here to protest against the attack on Al-Quds University, the seizure of a large part of the university's lands in the interests of building the so-called Separation Fence or Wall.*
>
> *For a thousand years, since the first universities were founded in Paris and Pisa and Naples, and from even earlier times when great academies*

and madrassas were active in Baghdad, Cairo, Nishapur, and in India, the institution of the university has embodied certain basic values— human dignity, a respect for the other and his or her dignity, tolerance, freedom of thought and expression, unfettered curiosity, and the rejection of all forms of violence and coercion. These values are the foundation of all our activities on campus; we seek to educate ourselves and our students to fostering and nourishing such values day by day. Let there be no mistake: An attack on a university is an attack upon these key concepts. It is our simple human duty to stand here and protest when such an attack is imminent.

There will always be people who think that academic freedom, mutual respect, and tolerance are dispensable; who think they can be set aside in the name of some instrumental goal and who use the coercive means at their disposal for this purpose. Such people are wrong and must be resisted. A university is a sacred place—at least as sacred, in our eyes, as most of the so-called "holy places" in this city that people on both sides are fighting to possess and to control exclusively. A university must have immunity from walls and fences and barbed wire; it is the space of human freedom, the space where our future and our hope can grow.

Al-Quds University and the Hebrew University are sisters; they share various cooperative scientific projects and collegial relations, but more than that, they share a vision and a set of values. What can be done to Al-Quds University today, in the name of the brutal and narrow-minded vision of the Israeli government, can easily be done to us tomorrow, at the neighboring campus on Mount Scopus, hardly three or four kilometers away. We have made our protest heard throughout the world, and we are here to say to you today: We stand beside you; we will not be silent; we will face these dangers together; we will not give up on the hope of peace.

They say Sari is visibly moved, but I cannot see it. Anyway, I am glad I have spoken, the words a little bitter on my tongue, released into the hot noon air like bubbles blown by an angry child. Sari shakes my hand and thanks us for coming. Now he has to go join the prayers.

We clamber up the slopes of the hill, past the massive bull-dozers—I am speaking to the Arabic radio from Dmitri's cell phone, ashamed not to be able to do it in Arabic—and a breath-taking panorama presents itself. Al-Haram al-Sharif from an angle I have never seen, much smaller, perhaps more beautiful than from close. The sweep of these hills soaked in the light. From above, the path chosen by the army engineers seems even more arbitrary and unnecessary. As we climb down, some of the children start throwing rocks at the bulldozers, perhaps to impress us. Our hosts are getting nervous: prayers will soon be over; the streets will be full of people; we may not be safe. They usher us quickly into the bus, hurrying the last stragglers, and guide us out.

On the way back, Samira, born in Beit Safafa,* speaks of being a Palestinian-Israeli. What is this strange creature? She herself finds the amalgam amusing. When there is a bombing, however, she gets confused—which side is hers? "Every single death is an unacceptable tragedy," I say, and she agrees at once. She is on the side of peace. She doesn't want to leave her home. She has a sister in Abu Dis—on which side of the fence? Will she be able to visit her when the fence is finished? With Dr. Zvi Mazeh, a deeply humane, religious man from Netivot Shalom, we discuss the unnerving fact that the Jews, the heirs to the prophets, are perpetrating such crimes. I speak of my father, of my mother and her still indomitable hope. But he cites the *Kuzari*, Yehuda Halevi's classic philosophical text: the Kuzari king says to the *chaver* that if the Jews were one day to have power, they would use it like everyone else—to kill. And since, says Dr. Mazeh, he believes in Providence, believes that we are judged by our deeds and will be punished for evil we inflict, he sadly concludes that we will not be living in this land much longer.

October 2, 2003   Al-Quds University (3)

It is one small, almost invisible point in the maze. Still, we are not prepared to give up. We prepare a letter of protest against the appropriation of lands from the Al-Quds campus, and the rectors of five Israeli universities, led by Haim Rabinovitch at

*A Palestinian village incorporated within the municipal borders of Jerusalem.

the Hebrew University, sign it and hand it over personally to the minister of defense. We use whatever contacts we have within the defense establishment. We visit the campus and make it clear to our hosts that we are prepared to come at an hour's notice to stand, arm in arm, with our Palestinian colleagues in the path of the bulldozers. The army knows this too. We garner some sixteen hundred signatures, including those of famous scholars and activists from around the world, and fax the list to Sari Nusseibeh in time for him to present it to Condoleezza Rice when he meets her in Washington. Maybe the list is the least of it; some say that when he explained to her that his university was about to lose its football field, she—an ex-provost of Stanford—at once understood that this, at least, was unacceptable, even in Palestine. Some verities are eternal.

Meanwhile, on this same football field in Abu Dis, a new form of nonviolent protest has emerged. At one point when the bulldozers were about to advance, the students raced to take out a ball and began to play; the soldiers retreated. Since then, a steady program of Palestinian folk dancers and soccer matches has kept the field engaged, filled with people, throughout most hours of the day and evening. All this has bought precious time for the international campaign to gather force.

Will any of it help? At 3:00, as I sit at my desk in the institute, the phone rings. Dmitri, Sari's secretary, is on the line. His voice is excited, intense. "They have given in," he tells me. "The campus is saved." He reads me the text the president's office is releasing to the press: "As a result of combined pressure from the world community on the outside and from Israeli academics and activists on the inside, the Israeli army has informed us that the Separation Wall will run to the west of the campus. Our land is now safe." There is a moment of silence on the line, then Dmitri continues: "That is what we are saying to the media, but between you and me"—his tone suddenly changes to a wild crescendo—"a freaking great thing happened here today!" Another pause. "Tell all your people that we thank you for what you did."

It worked.

November 8, 2003   Sawahreh

Is it too late? Or is something changing in Israel, tentatively and slowly and mostly invisibly?

On the one hand, there is the reality of the wall, remorselessly moving forward, uprooting whatever is in its path. On the other hand, nearly a thousand people, from both sides of this fence, came together today—the anniversary of the day the Berlin Wall came down—in Sawahreh to protest, in the name of some imagined future peace. The number far exceeded any prediction; at the last minute, several extra buses had to be ordered. Perhaps something is stirring, after all, percolating from the bottom up.

It is a short ride from the German Colony to Sawahreh, over the terrible back roads of Palestine. We pass first through Abu Tor—past the very house where I stood with my father in 1962, staring with a child's curiosity and fear at the Jordanian soldiers stationed on a roof a few meters below us; past the building where Eileen and I were married in 1972, the whole city of Jerusalem glimmering at our feet in the frozen night.

Those days and their axioms have been lost. Historians will someday tell us, with their habitual confidence, how it became possible, this black, murderous travesty of the old values that guided the Jews in Palestine; but we will not believe them.

We have been prepared for confrontation with the police. Thinking back over the last three years, we realized that our very worst moments have been here in Jerusalem—at Isawiyya, in Abu Dis, and elsewhere. So the briefing in the bus focuses on what to do if the police attack us with tear gas (everyone is given an onion, which dilutes the effect of the gas) or with clubs. We are also issued cans of spray paint for use on the wall. There is a choice of green and red; two volunteers cheerfully move through the bus, plying their wares. The idea is to cover the concrete slabs at Sawahreh with graffiti, to join up with the Palestinian group coming from there and the surrounding villages, to gain the attention of the media (represented by a large array of Israeli and foreign journalists and TV crews), and to climb the hill to see the planned trajectory of the wall in that part of the city with our own eyes.

The police are there, of course, when we arrive, but for once they make no attempt to interfere. They watch us from on top of the hill, sitting in their jeeps. As we emerge from the buses, a Palestinian column of feigned mourners comes down the narrow path along the concrete slabs of the wall. They are carrying a stretcher wrapped in cloth, as if to cover a body, and they hold aloft signs and flags. They greet us warmly. Ta'ayush has had people here almost every day for the last week or two, preparing for this moment. The "coffin" is to highlight one facet of the new reality; Sawahreh will be divided in two by the wall, and those to the east of it will no longer have access to the centuries-old cemetery at Jabal Mukabbar. They will, of course, similarly be cut off from hospitals, schools, family, places of work, and all the rest. When they asked the army officer where they were to bury their dead, he answered, "Try not to die."

We mingle with the Palestinians, and soon there is a thick mass of people filling the path next to the wall. It is midday, hot in the sun, dusty as Palestine is dusty; the usual caravans of donkeys and scantily clad children stop to gawk at this bizarre intrusion into their world. It is also Ramadan, so we are careful not to eat or drink in the presence of our fasting colleagues. Very rapidly the slabs of the wall turn red and green with slogans in Hebrew and Arabic (and a few, thanks to Yuri, in Chinese): "No to the apartheid wall. Yes to peace." "Make love not war." "Bridges are better than fences." "Yesterday Berlin, today Sawahreh." "Fuck racism." Farther up the hill, toward the village, there are Arabic graffiti that are signed: "Yes to peace, no to the wall—The Democratic Front for the Liberation of Palestine." Once such a slogan, with this signature, would have seemed unthinkable. The Democratic Front dominates this village and has been our partner in this demonstration. As a friend remarks to me, "Who said there is no one to talk to?"

The usual speeches must be spoken, in several languages, the soldiers watching from a distance. It is a gentle moment, and at the same time somehow deflating: we know we cannot block this wall. But then, as the Zen people say, you do not act in this mode, political action, with your eyes focused on results. You act because you must act, for the sake of what is right. The world takes care of the rest—or not. Very soon the speeches are over, and we begin to move back toward the buses. Gadi tells me of his recent work on Hieronymus Wolf, the sixteenth-century German Latinist who fled Erfurt because he felt he was being threatened by black magic. Amnon outlines next week's visit to the school at Umm Tuba. I try to kindle some enthusiasm for Tuesday's teach-in—on the wall. Ta'ayush talk, the elixir of immortality. Life goes on, the wall moves on, the barbarism worsens, the future presses in on us, and it is hard to breathe; gasping, grasping at straws, we do what we can with little thought to the result. On the rear window of a Palestinian car I read, from the bus, in large letters: "NO FEAR."

December 13, 2003   Ar-Ram

The campaign against the wall seems to be gathering momentum. Hardly a day passes without some article of protest in the press—it seems that parts of the Israeli public are slowly waking to the impossible reality the government is creating; meanwhile, the problem has reached the international court in The Hague. Optimists say we will stop it before the eastern segment is completed. If we don't, there will be nothing left of Palestine and no one to make peace with; the settlers will have won.

But in today's winter sunshine, Ar-Ram looks lively and intact. Shops are open, the billboards display a rich range of advertisements, including election propaganda—will there be a free election here anytime soon?—and the stone houses of the Palestinian middle class sprawl over the hill. This is a growing town, prosperous until the Intifada closed them off from Israel. Now the wall is to cut the town in two. As is typically the case in all the Palestinian Jerusalem neighborhoods, the wall is to replace a major street. Families slated to be on the Palestinian side are now frantically trying to buy or rent homes on the Israeli side, where land prices have shot up tremendously; for many this means impoverishment, as they sell their old flats at rock-bottom prices and pay vast sums for a new one.

There are some two thousand of us here to protest and, like the Sawahreh demonstration last month, Palestinians and Israelis mingle together in the demonstration. This is the new Ta'ayush style, a winning combination. I can easily imagine how it will look twenty years from now: our children, from both sides, will be marching together to demand an end to apartheid, a single state for all who live here, equal rights for all, one man/woman, one vote—under conditions of a Palestinian demographic majority. Such a binational state, with all its inherent tensions and potential for violence, is not the solution I am seeking; I assume that most of the Ta'ayush activists here today do not want it. It is the continuing reality of occupation, however it may be camouflaged, with or without a wall, which takes us closer each day to the South African nightmare. And we may not have twenty years.

Signs are in Hebrew, English, Arabic. International press and the local stations, Palestinian and Israeli, are all filming furiously as we walk the length of the street that will soon be a wall. "We want peace, not walls," says one sign. "Freedom of religion, freedom of movement, freedom to work," reads another immense banner, one end of which I am holding aloft. An older Israeli woman is displaying one of her own: "The wall: a ghetto for Palestinians and a prison for the Jews." "Shouldn't it be the other way around?" Iva asks her. "I was in a ghetto," she says. "I was a young woman in Poland when they fenced us in. Then I was sent to Majdanek. I survived and came here. I know what a ghetto means. That is why I am holding this sign."

How, I think, does one contain that kind of story? Or is this the secret of human history, the principle of being hurt and hurting back, the principle of the traumatized soul that can no longer dare to feel? It appears to operate automatically, collectively. Usually it can't be stopped. And yet here is one woman who lived through the trauma and has gone beyond.

Drums are beating; traffic is stopped; the heart of today's action has been reached: a symbolic wall of Styrofoam is being put up along this route, and schoolchildren, those who will soon be cut off from their schools, are to knock it down. The atmosphere is almost festive. I think of India, of the goddess rituals, the crowds milling in the streets, the drummers, the ragged children, the sun. There is a noticeable rise in intensity as the moment approaches. Then, when the Styrofoam is demolished, there are shouts, clapping, cries. I hope the press has filmed it and that someone will notice.

The speeches begin with passion, but we can hear nothing; the loudspeakers are not working well—anyway, who wants to listen to the same old words? There is work to be done, various last-minute arrangements for our teach-in on refusal to serve, just three days away. We are afraid the hooligans of the right will disrupt it, and I go looking for "ushers" sufficiently brawny and intimidating to stand guard. Many are here from the campus. I speak a bit with Nazmi Al-Juʿbeh, one of the architects of the Geneva agreements. A humane and eloquent man, he will come and speak to us when we are ready to run a teach-in on this matter. We stand together, smiling, almost hopeful. Leena runs past, a little worried—an army jeep has turned up; the last time Taʿayush was in Ar-Ram, two years ago, the demonstration turned into a violent clash, with much tear gas. But the soldiers disappear; we mill around aimlessly, walking on the chunks of broken Styrofoam. Some take pieces home with them, souvenirs of the pseudo-wall. I think that soon a day will come when we will have to attack the real monster.

Young boys with cans of red spray paint are inscribing graffiti on the street, and we stop to read them. A few red swastikas appear. Iva is shocked, unable to speak, but Rachel turns to them and asks: "Do you know what this means?" They don't answer. "It means you want the Jews dead," she says calmly, suddenly a teacher in all her soul. "And maybe you do; I can understand that. But we came here because we want to help you. It is not right to insult someone who came as your guest, wanting to help, no matter what your real wishes are." They are only thirteen or fourteen, these young boys, but they listen, a little sheepish. Then they ask to be forgiven. Iva and Galit scrape the swastikas off the road with their feet.

January 27, 2003   Abu Dis (1)

It is like no other wall.

It is nine meters high—the concrete slabs have the measurement stamped on them. It dwarfs anyone who stands near it. There is an insufferable hubris about the way it arrogates the land to itself, splitting Abu Dis down the middle. But it is the pernicious aspect that strikes you most forcefully once your eyes adjust to the new reality. It twists and turns and loops. There is a rather pleasant hilltop covered with cypresses—slotted for a new Jewish settlement, in the heart of this Palestinian town—and the wall slithers around it to ensure that this extra little piece of land, which no doubt belongs, or belonged, to someone, will now become Israel. Palestinian houses nearby are, as a result, squeezed right against the wall, which shuts out their light, renders windows and doors irrelevant.

We walk along it, first on the Jewish side, then, where there is still a gap, unfinished, along the Palestinian side. There are graffiti growing up everywhere. "Sharon knows only war." "Welcome to the ghetto of Abu D"—in big red letters; the painter, Angela, a friend of ours, was arrested by the police before she could finish the sentence that is, after all, "anti-Semitic," or anti-Zionist—anyway, a crime, unlike the wall itself. Perhaps even more poignant is the verse from Malachi (2:10–11), which they say was the first text to be painted on the newly finished barrier: "Have we not all a single father? Did not one God create us all? Why does one man betray his brother, to desecrate our fathers' covenant? Judah has betrayed, and an abomination has been committed in Israel and Jerusalem." In black letters covering four or five whole slabs; the anonymous writer managed to finish the verse. Who, I wonder, is this hidden hero, who knows the Bible, knows what words are for?

A few days later Amalia solves the mystery. She happened by, on her way to a shift of duty for Machsom Watch at the barricade, when the painter turned up with his can of paint. Religious? Secular? No one knows. Anyway, he knows his Bible. When he started spraying the verse onto the concrete slabs, the border police arrested him and took him to be interrogated. He said to them that the law allows you to inscribe verses from the Bible anywhere in Israel. This was a novel argument so, baffled, they consulted with their superiors—one can imagine the conversations going up through the chain of command. Eventually the word came down from somewhere, perhaps the general staff: he's right. So he went back to painting the verse, with the border police officer, a Druze, and Amalia still watching. When they reached the word *to'eva*, "abomination," he suddenly couldn't remember how to spell it: with an aleph or an 'ayin? He consulted with present company; the Druze officer was also unsure, but Amalia apparently carried the day. The 'ayin won.

Only in Israel.

It has been raining heavily; it is cold and a wind whips us as we pick our way among the vast puddles, through the mud. There are not many people around the wall; a street that I remember as full of life only four months ago, when I was last here, is now utterly deserted, the wall slicing through it like a scalpel. Men wrap their keffiyehs around their faces. On the main street, to the right of the wall, I look around: there is another gap here, soon to be filled; in the meanwhile, huge piles of vegetables in sacks are waiting to be heaved over the wall to the other side. The new economic plan for Palestine. I want to bring our students and colleagues here on Thursday to see it with their own eyes.

We sit in the offices of Nihad and Abu Jihad, in a dull cold building over the Akbar Hair Saloon. A man in some distress is filling out a form while our host speaks over the phone in a flood of Arabic. There is a small electric heater, and we hover around it, waiting. How many rooms like this have I known; how many hours have I spent in dusty third-world offices; how much cruelty does it take to effect the alchemy of pure despair? We talk of Thursday. What will happen if the army stops us? There is, it turns out, another route in. Muhammad Abu Hummus, from Isawiyya, knows it well; he will show us. Will there be microphones that work? Where shall we stand? Where will the speakers be most clearly heard? What if, what, when, how, why?

Shie is with us this morning—he is young, calm, soft-spoken, self-possessed, a musician; another one of those miraculous unassuming Israelis who will do anything, risk anything, in this quixotic quest for peace. Or perhaps we have given up on the quest and are doing it now, all of us, merely out of a sense that it must be done, even if we fail, as seems to be the case. Out of loyalty to the others, to our friends, to a notion of categorical values. Because it is right and the least we can do. Where do people like Shie come from? What is it in this tortured country that still regularly produces them and impels them to act? He will spend the morning here on Thursday, getting things ready for our arrival with the large group of students, professors, and doctors.

We poke around the main street; we make our plans. The weather is supposed to improve. "I'll worry about the weather," Yigal says to our hosts. "You take care of the microphones." As we talk, I feel ever more keenly, in my body, what it means for these people to be living here, futureless, encaged. A vast sadness envelops me, fierce beyond thinking. It deepens as we begin the short ride back to Israel—a kilometer or two away. We pass the chink in the wall that still allows people from Abu Dis to reach the hospital, Makassed, on the Mount of Olives. Old women, heavy in their thick black dresses, are painfully clambering across, over the rocks. Soon this crack will be stopped up, and the only way to Makassed will be through Ar-Ram and the army checkpoints—a journey of several hours to reach a point less than a hundred meters away, but separated by the wall. Those who are really sick will die. We hear later that as many as two-thirds of the hospital staff will also be prevented by the wall from coming to work: the hospital, too, may die.

As we drive up to Mount Scopus, Muhammad points laconically to the hillside, now inside the university fence. This, he says, was his family's land; and there was more, on the other side of the road, which has also been seized. He is unemotional about it; it is just a fact, like the rain, the Jews, the demonstration we are planning together, the wintry rocks. He speaks good Hebrew, but still we find ourselves struggling to explain to him in our halting Arabic what the Hebrew word *siyut,* "nightmare," means. "I don't understand," he says. "You know," I say, "there are dreams—some are good and sweet; others are bad." "What is a bad dream?" he asks, still unsure. Shie answers: "Like Sharon."

January 29, 2004   Abu Dis (2)

8:30 A.M.: I check, one last time, that everything is ready: medic's kit, emergency numbers, walkie-talkie, forms to distribute on the bus, camera (fresh batteries), Eileen's cell phone, and something to read, small enough to fit into my shoulder bag, in case we get arrested.

9:10 A.M.: I don't hear the blast, but Edani, in the next room, does. Then come the sirens. Bus 19, Rehov Aza, corner of Arlozorov. We turn on the TV. The usual ritual of horror: maps, police spokesmen, the hospitals, the mangled bodies, the maimed, the orphaned and bereaved, the count. The aching heart.

9:30 A.M.: Yigal calls: Should we cancel? I am against turning back at this point. And will the wall itself not produce the next bombing, and the next, and the next? I vote to go ahead with the program. It is clear, however, that many who would have come won't.

9:45 A.M.: to the university with Yigal. We speak of emptiness. I cannot concentrate; I am thinking of those who died. Calls are starting to come in; many want us to cancel. I explain: "The political reality has not changed in the least since yesterday; we are going there to see it, to learn, and to teach."

On campus I wander around; check in with Catherine, who is preparing signs; force myself to eat something. Wonder if anyone will show up. It is a bright sunny day, a burst of spring. I sit in the sun for a few minutes, waiting.

11:50 A.M.: I go to the assembly point; first to arrive. But within a few seconds, students begin to filter in. I speak to Yigal, on the bus at Givat Ram: the bus is already full. So people are coming after all. Soon the crowd exceeds all our estimates by far, and many, perhaps most, are new faces, young students whom I've never seen before in the demonstrations. We must have made an impact this time—is there a reservoir of untapped frustration and anger among the thousands on campus? Are we reaching them? We order two more buses just for the Scopus crowd. Some are arriving from Hadassah and the Ein Kerem campus; others have come from far away, from Haifa and the north. Amazed, I board the bus, now totally packed, and we start for Abu Dis.

We expect the police to be nervous today, after the bombing. We think there's a high probability that the army will blockade the road, to stop us; but in the end, it's a short, uneventful, winding drive over the Mount of Olives, then down and up to the wall. We get off the buses—some 180 of us, I figure—beside the famous graffito from Malachi. We retrace our steps from Wednesday—uphill along the wall on the Israeli side, then through the still-unfinished gap and down along the Palestinian side to Ras Kubze, the main street that now ends in the wall. In the sunshine, everything looks stark, crisp, the hills drying out, turning green, the cypresses still more beautiful on the hilltop that's been taken over for the new settlement. The wall itself looks, if anything, still more devilish, ophidian, a foreign implant in this passionate landscape. Some two hundred Palestinians are waiting to join us in Ras Kubze.

12:50 P.M.: The speakers begin. For once the microphones are working well—a cable has been drawn out from one of the shops—and the result is that the loudspeakers boom in the direction of the wall itself, which responds with an astonishing echo: "Kibbush [occupation]-bush-bush-bush-bush. . . . " "Sharon-ron-

ron-ron-ron. . . . " The Palestinians speak first and set the tone—
overtly rhetorical and political, and highly emotional, as is almost
always the case; our hopes of actually teaching something, of pro-
viding hard facts and dry description, dissolve. The lecturer we
invited from B'Tselem, the human rights organization, opts not
to lecture under these conditions. But the wall itself, towering
like a gray bird of prey at the speakers' backs, overshadows the
words. Yaron speaks with great passion: "This is a wall of cyni-
cism, meant to foster despair." He suggests the government issue
a postage stamp with a picture of the wall, to form a set with the
menorah-candelabra on the earliest Israeli stamps—to show the
distance we have come. Yohanan—gentle, pained, speaking at
a political event for the first time—says: "What word would we
use for what we see here?" He asks like a teacher in a class, but
before anyone can respond, the microphones go silent. Power
failure? Language fails. There is no word. After some time a
megaphone is somehow produced, and he begins again, names
the word—*zadon*. One of those ancient biblical words that defy
translation, but this one echoes with the resonances of "malice,"
"arrogance," "crime." Language returns. *Zadon-don-don*.

Border police have by now noticed us. Some of them are
standing just the other side of the wall, peering in through one of
the unfinished cracks. A Palestinian man approaches this crack
and starts to climb up toward the top, hoping to cross to the other
side. He is sick, on his way to dialysis at Makassed Hospital; he
has the medical forms in his hands. The soldiers turn him back.
One jeep, then another, comes down the street toward us, closing
it off, blocking us, but they in the end seem reluctant to interfere
in our harmless speechmaking. Irit goes over to confront them,
tells them to go away. Surprisingly—or perhaps not; she is a
formidable, self-assured woman—they withdraw.

Against the backdrop of the loudspeakers, I study the wall
itself. Many of our people are busy with cans of spray paint, and
new graffiti are emerging minute by minute, in many colors, several languages. "Damn to the wall." "Build a wall around Sharon,
for the sake of peace." "Jerusalem is stronger than the wall."

"Peace" (over and over). "The Dumb Wall Is Screaming." Biggest of all, a huge flourish of red: "Scheduled for demolition—Immoral Building." Perhaps most moving, two lines near the ground:

"We are still here.
Forever."

Abu Jihad and Nihad, our hosts from the local committee, are speaking. Soon the Physicians for Human Rights arrive. It is getting late, the light turning to liquid gold; the words are simpler now, more direct. "This wall, this prison, is intended not merely to prevent peace. Even more, it is intended actively to continue the war. This government needs the war, as they need corruption, bombings, terror—they need them to survive, and they need them so they can take more land. They fear peace more than anything." Dr. Abdallah, from Makassed: "This is the first time we have ever seen a wall to divide doctors from the sick." Abu Jihad: "This wall turns every Palestinian into an enemy—so you can kill him." Yigal, trying to bring the event to an end: "Today there are still a few cracks left in this wall. Tomorrow they will be gone. Dialysis patients will not reach the hospital. Someone who has a heart attack will die here, unable to be helped. Women will give birth to their babies right here, where we are standing, at the base of this wall."

As we are about to leave, someone, an unfamiliar face, grabs the microphone; he truly has to speak to the crowd. Such urgency cannot be denied. He is just a simple man, he says, who happens to live here in Abu Dis; he has a shop on this street. He thanks us for coming. He didn't think so many Israelis would come. He wants us to know what it means. His family is now divided—some of his brothers on this side, some on the other side of the wall. "If you want to see what it means to divide brother from brother," he says, "look at me." We are already beginning to move away, back toward the buses; the light is fading, but, overcome with feeling, he calls out behind us, the loudspeaker echoing against the stones: "Thank you—thank you—*shukran-ran-ran-ran....*"

May 1, 2004   Abu Dis (3)

May Day. A dry, hot Saturday. Does anyone still celebrate the workers' march to freedom? Yes. The Palestine General Federation of Trade Unions has asked us to march with them through Abu Dis. Perhaps they haven't heard that the revolution has failed. Or perhaps in the violent patchwork of Palestinian politics, this organization—one of the oldest (founded in the 1920s, rooted in Salfit) and with a long history of cooperation with Jewish groups—has somehow preserved its own peculiar power. Today they have promised to bring thousands into the streets to protest the Separation Wall, which, among other iniquities, keeps workers from their place of work. They have been strenuously pushing Ta'ayush to join them.

The promise fails. Four busloads, they say, didn't make it through the roadblocks at Khizmeh. But it seems they knew well in advance that none would arrive from Jenin, Nablus, or Ramallah. Some internal struggle, obscure to us, has been going on between the Abu Dis grassroots committee and the others from farther north. Still they need our presence and support, so some two hundred of us have made the trip behind Mount Scopus through Al-'Ayzarīyah, through the back of the fence, to Abu Dis. Instead of the two thousand Palestinians we expected to find waiting for us, there are, perhaps, two hundred.

They look like a faded, discordant memory: anachronistic, innocent, and noisy. Children dressed in red are holding flags and marching to the beat of the village drummers. We unfold our Ta'ayush banners, including a heavy, unwieldy new one, with enormous letters, that I am stuck holding at one end. At first our direction is unclear: we are positioned facing south, down the dusty street toward the desert, but the marchers—an inchoate mass, swirling in arcs and waves—finally turn around and head north. With my partner, trapped, like me, at the other pole, I spin

the banner around toward the south, then north, then south and
north again, before we are at last swept into the dizzy current of
drums and flags. As metaphors go, this inelegant spin beside the
wall, toward our equally confused and uncertain friends, tells all.

Red—for the People's Party, largely an intellectual affair of
poets and intellectuals. Green and black: the Democratic Front
for the Liberation of Palestine, with many from Sawahreh (just
down the hill from Abu Dis). Yellow: the Palestinian Boy Scouts.
Leena, in ravishing red, is just ahead of us; Charles M., white-
haired and bemused, walks beside me, as last week he harvested
wheat beside me in Jinba. The first of May means something
to him; he was married to the wonderful, lamented Catherine,
granddaughter of Léon Blum, and his memory spans the whole
history of European socialism and many stormy demonstrations
in France. Perhaps that is why he insisted on coming today, though
he is soon to leave for Paris. Now he is spilling over with intense,
tactile memories: standing at the hill of Al-Quds University, on
the edge of the sports field that we helped to save—the impassive
gray wall now runs along its western edge—he tells me of his army
service in Algeria in 1954–55, of the vast beauty of Kabylia where
he was stationed, of the Arabic he learned there. "What was it
like?" I ask him, and he answers: "It was only the beginning, so
it wasn't so terrible; and I didn't kill anyone."

Sari Nusseibeh is marching with us, and I leave my post with
the banner for a moment in order to greet him; he smiles at me
warmly, perhaps remembering that moment in September when
we came to his aid. This was one of our few real successes, but
nothing is innocent in Israel-Palestine. Leena tells me, her words
laced with rage, that when the army moved the wall westward
to the edge of the campus, they destroyed three private homes
on the ridge of the hill. The people of Abu Dis are angry at Al-
Quds. No gain comes without a price.

The border police drive up in their jeeps; heavily armed soldiers watch us as we clamber up the path, but there is no contact—
to my relief. I have been nervous all morning, expecting a clash,
tear gas, rocks, maybe worse. Previous experiences in Abu Dis

make this likely enough, and this time I am the only medic in the field and the closest hospitals are miles, perhaps hours, away, on the other side of the wall. The fact that fewer Palestinians are present than we expected is, on one level, a relief; it is a small demonstration, no real threat to the soldiers, for all the noise.

At Ras Kubze the wall seems to have rooted itself in the ground. I am already getting used to it. From time to time I come here. I shake the hands of Abu Jihad and Muhammad Abu Hummus and our other friends; I study the old-new graffiti; I wander helplessly down the truncated main street; I note that the gaps that were there last time have now been filled in; I listen to the inevitable, predictable, but impassioned speeches coming over the loudspeakers. A few Palestinian women, wrapped head to toe, have joined the demonstration. Soon even the words fall silent— the drummers have long since marched off home—and we begin to leave.

On the bus back, Charles speaks of the obscene crudeness of the wall—just a line of thick cement blocks rising high into the sky, blocking off the horizon, the view, a future, from those caught on this side, as if they did not matter, had no need of schools or hospitals or a normal life. I tell him of Qalqiliya and Tulkaram, almost entirely encircled by the cement. How can we, the children or grandchildren of utopian idealists and dreamers, have done this to another people? My own grandfather, a Jewish humanist of the old school, would never have believed it possible. I don't think the trauma of terrorism, real and devastating as it has been, is enough to explain what has happened here—the demonic amalgam of greed, myopic hyper-nationalism, and an infatuation with brute coercion that develops only among those who feel vulnerable to the point of impotence. All of these are endemic to ethnic conflict, which inevitably narrows the collective vision and deadens the human heart. The first thing to go is the ability to imagine the world through the eyes of the other, the enemy, the victim-to-be. But the Jews have, perhaps, added something very much their own in this towering gray wall, standing on stolen ground, something that embodies very specific and altogether recent memories. You build—for others—the wall you have known.

May 15, 2004, Nakba Day   Beit Liqiya

We are standing on the hill above Beit Liqiya—another landscape that lashes out with its beauty. These are the last hills before the coastal plain, its green and yellow fields unrolling just beyond the ridge. Here, in the village lands, there are olive groves and vineyards and some cultivated fields and many gray-white stones; sheep and goats graze on the slopes. The hills sweep down in a swirling rush to meet in the wadi, where the olive trees, some of them hundreds of years old, stolidly bear witness.

A deep white gash cuts through this Mediterranean vignette where the wall will stand. It sways and curves over the hills, an open, ominous wound. Some of the old olive trees that were in its path have been torn up by the roots and hastily set down in the earth of the wadi; but they are dried out now and dying, because the soldiers couldn't be bothered to transplant them. Hundreds of years of growth extirpated. "Can't you see?" our hosts ask us over and over, trying to convey to us, with our impoverished city vision, what any farmer can see at a glance: these trees are no longer living, growing beings. "We have lost them too."

And on the other side of the wall-to-be, neatly climbing the hillside, is 'Abed's vineyard. It isn't very big, but it seems to matter enormously to the villagers; maybe in Beit Liqiya a year's crop of grapes is enough partly to sustain a family. Or maybe it's that 'Abed's thirteen-year-old son was killed right there three years ago, when he opened the door of an army vehicle that had been left standing beside the vineyard; it's not clear what it was that exploded in the car, or if it had been left deliberately booby-trapped or not, and perhaps it hardly matters—the subtle distinction between death through malice and death through indifference or negligence is no comfort in Beit Liqiya. The place the boy died is marked with a Palestinian flag. Like the vineyard, it, too, will very soon be lost to the village, cut off by the wall.

"You see those olive trees?" says Ali, our guide today, pointing to the other side of the slope. "I am losing them, and my fields over there, and more olive trees, and a vineyard. I am totally ruined." He is, like the rest of these villagers, remarkably innocent in this land of continuous, implicit or complicit violation. Beit Liqiya has been completely quiet for all the three and a half years of the present Intifada. No incidents, no suspects, no arrests, no violence, nothing. Now it is being systematically stripped of easily half its lands. But this is not the first time: in 1973 many thousands of *dunams* were appropriated by the state; the Keren Kayemet has planted some of them with trees. More significant still, the settlement of Mevo Horon was planted on top of an existing village, Beit Nuba, where Ali was born. What happened to the villagers? Who in Israel cares? They were driven away; most went as refugees to Jordan. You can still see some of the old houses from where we are standing, with the settlers' villas astride them.

Ali's family was a big one, some six thousand souls. Most went to Jordan, but his father had large flocks of sheep and goats and couldn't leave them; so they moved here to Beit Liqiya, on the next hill. Recently Ali went back in search of his grandfather's grave on the hill above Mevo Horon; he was chased away by the security officer, who threatened to shoot him if he ever tried to visit the grave again. Even worse, the settlers' sewage now flows through the old cemetery of Beit Nuba, an offense so outrageous that Ali can hardly bring himself to speak of it.

He should, one might think, be bitter, but he is not—though he clearly aches with endless insults. He shows us where the wall will run and what it will mean. "If you ask yourselves what is good and what is bad about the wall, you will conclude that there is nothing good about it; and the list of what is bad is so long I don't know where to start. It is destroying our village and robbing us of our lands. Shepherds who will graze their herds too close to it will be shot. The olive groves and vineyards will be lost. We have done nothing to deserve this. But I still think this is the best time for making peace. Right now. There is room enough for both peoples in this land, and today is the right day for peace. Let us start here." Shai, the remarkable photographer who has brought us here, echoes this tone. "Governments will never make peace. It has to come from the roots." He is here each week with small groups like ours. Today his father has come with him; he should, I think, be very proud of such a son.

"What are they thinking?" says the young villager who drove us up the crazy, rocky footpath, at breakneck speed, to this outlook. "Everything has always been quiet here. Now they are taking whatever we have—and they don't realize that there will be trouble?" So far, Beit Liqiya, like Budrus, Biddu, Beit Surik, Qatana, and other villages—some seventeen in this area—has kept to the path of nonviolent resistance. The army has used its usual methods to disperse demonstrations—tear gas, stun grenades, rubber bullets. An empty tear-gas canister lies at our feet; they are everywhere on the hill. Lately, however, the demonstrations have died down; perhaps the army has successfully crushed them, for now. There are many wounded.

On the way down we chat with another man, who spent twelve years in Israeli jails. He has, he says, always believed in peace. He was a member of the Popular Front; he knows the politicians of the Israeli left, has hosted them overnight in his house. Yesterday his son was shot with three rubber bullets in the head; he had been throwing rocks at the soldiers. The boy is in the hospital and will, it seems, recover.

Back in the village, we take our leave of the elders. Last to speak with us is 'Abed, of the vineyard, 'Abed of the murdered child. "It isn't enough for you to come here and see it," he says— gently, but with an inner urgency. "You must do something to stop it. Demonstrate, write to the prime minister, write to the Knesset, find a way." I wonder if we have time, if we can be effective, this assortment of tormented activists who have spent the morning in Beit Liqiya, who have watched the video and drunk the tea and wandered among the stones. I think of another vineyard, Naboth's, and of the prophet's voice that came too late to save it, and its owner, from the greed of another malevolent king. Maybe there is always a vineyard on a hillside waiting to be stolen; and we know from experience that there is always some rapacious and self-destructive Ahab or Sharon. But here, in village after village, *dunam* by *dunam*, the rape of land and tree and vine and hope and dignity and simple decency is on a scale not even the prophet could have imagined.

Lawrence Cohen, the Berkeley anthropologist, has joined us today—a soft-spoken, gentle man. Tours like this have, it seems, become standard parts of the visiting anthropologist's itinerary; a year ago we took Val Daniel from Columbia University to South Hebron. Maybe somehow the news will get around. Lawrence grew up, like Eileen, in Jewish Montreal, learned Hebrew, knows Israel. He tells me, just before we part, that there was a decisive moment when he was a young student, teaching Hebrew school to pay for his education. He was telling his pupils the Midrashic story of how Abraham smashed the pagan idols, when suddenly he realized that he couldn't accept it. He stopped the story in the middle (and went on to become a South Asianist). Monotheists have no monopoly on greed, on ruthlessness, on indifference; and there were also, after all, the Micahs and the Jeremiahs (they are said to have been Jewish). Still, like Lawrence, I'm on the side of the idols and against destructive fanatics. Abraham misunderstood. No Jewish God, if he knew his texts, would want to harm Beit Liqiya.

June 30, 2004   Supreme Court Decision

Occasionally there is a good day, a ray of hope. The Supreme Court has rejected the planned route of the wall in the area west of Jerusalem, between Pisgat Zeev in the north and Modiin to the west, including Highway 443 that serves the Modiin suburbs but also a series of Israeli settlements in Palestinian territory on both sides of this road. A unanimous decision of three judges—Barak,

Heshin, Matza—forces the government to come up with a route less injurious to the Palestinian villagers. Although the judges did not accept the villagers' argument that the wall, as such, is not a security barrier but rather an instrument for seizing land, they did articulate a principle of proportionality: the damage to the villages has to be weighed against any "pure" security considerations. The army and the government will not have carte blanche to determine the route. Beit Liqiya, Biddu, Beit Surik—and so many others where we have demonstrated and petitioned and appealed—may be saved.

On TV the government's counsel, Danny Tirza, the man entrusted with planning the route, speaks in the mean-hearted tones of the nationalist settlers. "It is a black day," he says, "for the state of Israel." Channel 2 has dug up some footage of this man, an M16 slung over his back, marching over the rocky hills somewhere in the territories: a conqueror, occupier, settler, utterly secure in his narrow world. Disgust at the court's decision echoes in his words.

Next the reporters interview a Palestinian man from Beit Surik, who speaks haltingly, not adept at Hebrew words, about the Israelis from neighboring Mevasseret Zion who co-signed the petition to the court, who fought to save the lands of their Arab neighbors: "They are"—he searches for the right word, stops, waits, hesitates, then he has found it—"they are human beings."

November 6, 2004 Olive Harvest, Umm al-Rihan

She sits on the dry earth, folded into her long robe, a thousand wrinkles on her face, her silver hair gleaming in the hot sun like a natural extension of the silver-green leaves of the olive tree above her, and as we pour out of the bus, she cries out in confusion, or perhaps it is glee, "Al-Yahud! Al-Yahud!"*

We are in limbo: between the Green Line and the wall. The people of this village belong nowhere—they are not Israelis and

---

*"The Jews! The Jews!"

cannot move freely beyond the confines of the village, and they have been cut off from Palestine, from their relatives in Tura, two kilometers away, from the nearby cities of Yaabad and Jenin with their hospitals and stores, and from any kind of livable future. In a way, however, they are lucky. Anin, their closest sister-village, is on the other side of the wall, but its fields and olive groves are in limbo. This year the army has prevented the people of Anin from completing the olive harvest, which is now all they have left to live from. The villagers were given three half-workdays in which to pass through the fence—a slow business, each permit has to be examined by the soldiers—and harvest as many of their olives as they could before crossing back, before dark. Nothing like enough time: much of the harvest will rot on the trees. What is worse, since Anin, like nearly all the villages along the line of the wall, is prevented by the army from tending the olives and working the fields on a regular basis, it stands to lose most of its land, which will revert to the state. The next step will no doubt be to start building a settlement on the new, ill-gotten property.

We are here to prevent the nightmare from coming true. All along the wall, on both sides, the villages are in distress, fearing the worst. A little deeper in Palestinian territory, settlers have been forcing the villagers out of their own olive groves at gunpoint, as in the previous two years.

Today there are some two hundred of us, four busloads of volunteers, committed to harvesting the olives of Anin, Umm al-Rihan, and another three villages together with the Palestinian owners. We will not let the government take these lands, not without a fight. We will ensure that the olive harvest—*qatf al-zaitun*, one of the high points of the year in these villages, a time of festive sharing—is carried to completion, wall or no wall. We are here to defend the defenseless. The bus drops us off in small groups scattered among the groves and fields of these five villages, according to the instructions of our hosts.

We have brought with us large stocks of used plastic banners, the debris of many demonstrations. They read: "Two States for Two Peoples"; "Make Peace and Not War"; or, more simply,

"Ta'ayush, Arab-Jewish Partnership" and "Peace Now." It turns out they are useful after all. We spread them, anchored by rocks, directly under the olive trees. Then to work: once again, the remembered eroticism of light and tree. From this moment on, and for the next few hours, there will be a constant pitter-patter of falling olives, the sweet percussion of an autumn day just before the rains. The olives sputter and spin; the sun beats down upon us through the silvery leaves; there is the good smell of earth and ripening fruit, of dry thorns and bleached rocks, of happiness.

There was a good chance we wouldn't make it today. Arafat lies dying, in effect already dead, in Paris. The villagers called us yesterday to say: "If he dies, do not come; the territories will be closed—it will be dangerous, and for us a time of mourning." Working now, perched high up on one of the trees, I am glad the merciless old man has lingered for another day. Why is it that so few of our moments have this sense of rightness and of balance? Is it the loneliness of the everyday that drives us mad? Here I am far from alone; a friend among friends. I listen, I speak, sometimes in Arabic, sometimes in Hebrew—a liquid counterpoint to the gentle, continuous percussion of the olives.

It is Ramadan, they are fasting, but the atmosphere is light and inviting. A woman nurses her baby at the edge of the grove, her back turned to us. Other children crawl, crying for their mothers, over the plastic sheets. The young Palestinian women want to know where we have come from—can we really be Israelis? It seems unlikely. Lucia, harvesting beside me, tells them she is from Mexico, only recently arrived in Israel. "She's come from very far away to pick these olives," I say to these village girls. They giggle, suddenly shy. Lucia tells me her story: she became interested in Rosenzweig and Fackenheim, wrote a Ph.D. dissertation (in Essex) on their theologies; then she decided that if being Jewish mattered that much, she could not afford not to be here. What she found shocked her. How could Jews do this to other people? She fled back to England. There she reread her dissertation, noticing that the word "Palestinian" appeared nowhere in it. Rosenzweig, were he with us, might have wondered. Now she has come back to live here, made *aliyah*; she is the spokesperson for the Israeli Committee Against House Demolitions, an Israeli activist. She is young, a striking Latin beauty, tough-minded, aware—she will see it through; she will see peace come.

And she is not alone. I think, in the part of my mind that is not entirely engaged in olives, of the cycle that has turned round. It is like A. D. Gordon, the theoretician of the early kibbutzim, all over again: young idealistic Jews who have come to work on the land, to rebuild their own souls; but this time around they are working to save Palestinian land, to save these other, innocent people from ourselves. Other than that, they are burnt by the same Mediterranean sun, driven by the same intoxicating sense of bodily awakening and moral urgency that animated those earlier pioneers, a century ago. Aviad, to my left, has climbed all the way to the top of the tree: "It's no fun unless there's a risk." He is the grandson of one of the leaders of Poalei Zion, the Zionist Socialists who came here to save the Jews and build a country. I know his grandfather would have approved. This is the rhythm of time: always, as Rilke says, there is the first generation, which finds God; the second generation, which binds him in chains and builds stone walls around him; and the third, which breaks down stone after stone and smashes the chains, which sets him free.

I have made a friend, Nabil. At first he doesn't believe I am Israeli; I have been speaking to him in Arabic; he feels comfortable and curious. I assure him, without apology, I am an Israeli Jew. He smiles. "We are cousins," he says. There is a peculiar, wholly uncharacteristic sanity about this day. I am tempted—foolishly—to trust it. Last night the TV news on Channel 2 had an interview, from Prison no. 4, with senior prisoners from Hamas and Islamic Jihad, including one who sent a terrorist to murder a family in Kibbutz Metzer, two years ago. Astonishing sentences come from their mouths. They want peace; they want an agreement; they know what it will mean; they believe it is possible. It is wrong, says the arch-terrorist, to kill children—under any circumstances. He asks forgiveness of the father, who survived the shooting. In war, he says, children also get killed; it is wrong—nothing can justify it. He wants to be photographed eating the Iftar meal, after the day's fast, with Bin-Nun, the Israeli reporter. These men are sending a message to the Israelis. Will anyone believe them? My son Edan, always skeptical, says: "You can't take what they say at face value."

Nabil's uncle shows me his permit, which allows him to cross the wall to his fields twice a day, at 7:00 and at 4:00. Each crossing can take several hours. "What is life like for you now?" I ask. "Where is the nearest hospital, for example?" It is in Jenin, seventeen kilometers away in the old days, before the wall. Now it is a sixty-seven-kilometer journey through the army barriers and roadblocks. Before, it was a 20-shekel taxi ride; now it takes 130 shekels and many hours. What is worse, Tura, where half his family lives, is on the other side of the wall. The army wouldn't let them come to Umm al-Rihan for his daughter's wedding. How could he celebrate the wedding without them? Speaking of weddings, there was one recently in Moshav Shaked, very close to here, a settlement built close to the Green Line—built, in fact, by this very man, who worked there in house after house, who knew everyone living there and was close to all of them. One of the Shaked boys got married in just such a home, one that this man built with his own hands—but they wouldn't let him attend the wedding. He is sad, insulted, hurt. "What do you do with your days?" I ask him. "Do you have work?" No, there is no work; he sits at home. He inhabits the limbo, with nowhere to go anymore; his permit is valid only for this village.

Everything comes around. Amiel has come today to harvest olives. Two years ago a settler shot him during the olive harvest near Yanun. He identified the man who fired the shot, which ricocheted into his abdomen, but, as always, the trial came to nothing; the settler was found not guilty by the Israeli court. This is the standard outcome, no cause for surprise. The sequel, however, is another matter. Sylvia, a veteran Peace Now activist from Jerusalem, working beside us today, has a daughter who traveled recently to India, where she was lightly hurt in a car collision. As it happens, a young Israeli was living not far from the site of the accident; and hearing that an Israeli girl was involved, he rushed to the scene to help her, showering her with care and solving the various bureaucratic difficulties. It turns out, of course, that he is that same settler who shot Amiel. Now Sylvia has a problem: can she write him a thank-you note, knowing what she knows—that he represents all that she loathes in Israeli politics, that he nearly murdered our friend?

There is something in this story that speaks the language of reality, of love twisted and torn to deadly effect, the dependable human talent. For a moment today, the olives have untwisted it, and all of us seem to be feeling the relief. We gather up the olives from the plastic sheets, pour them into the sacks and pails that are waiting; we climb back up to the village. In the distance, in the late-afternoon sun, the hills of Jenin are turning purple; to the west, on the far horizon, sunlight rebounds from the sea. Time to go. Nabil comes to say good-bye. He holds my hand. *"Lehitraot ba-medina shelanu,"* he says in Hebrew: "Until we meet in *our* country"—Palestine. "Yes, may it be soon," I answer him in Arabic, with the familiar blessing: *"Min tumak li-bab al-samaa"*; "From your mouth—to the gate of heaven."

December 31, 2004   Jayyus: The Massacre of the Trees

It is the last day of the year, a glowing, shimmering, midwinter world of sun and rock, the light so intense it cuts your eyes. What light reveals hurts the heart. Even great beauty—especially beauty—hurts.

I have never been to Jayyus, just north of Qalqiliya, now on the eastern side of the wall. Groggy, sleep-deprived—for the last days have been full of pressure, and for some time I was unwell—I peer through the windows of the bus at the hills green with winter rains. "Are you going to a New Year's party?" I ask Amiel, beside me. He smiles and waves his hand at the bus, the volunteers, the rocks and trees outside. "This is my New Year's party," he says.

We cannot visit the village itself; today's action is aimed at the village lands west of the wall, beyond the farmers' reach. Jayyus has lost 72 percent of its lands (8,600 *dunams*) to the wall. These lands are being taken over by the state to build a new settlement, Zufin Zafon, a continuation of the older settlement of Zufin that faces Jayyus on the next ridge. Straw companies owned by settlers are preparing the ground for 2,100 new building units. The bulldozers have been active throughout December; two weeks ago they uprooted 300 olive trees, some of them very old, on land belonging to Tawfiq Hassan Salim from Jayyus, who watched helplessly from his house on the other side of the wall. Moreover, all six wells that served Jayyus are west of the fence, in the area to be annexed; the village now has to buy water from outside. Take this as emblematic: Israel is drying out Jayyus, like so many other villages in this area, the breadbasket of Palestine, with the obvious aim of impoverishing the Palestinians and driving them from their homes.

On December 19 the villagers managed to face the bulldozers in nonviolent protest, which stopped them for the moment. The pattern of grassroots, spontaneous Gandhian-style activism that cropped up in Budrus last spring is recurring here. The courts have yet to pronounce on the legality of what is happening in Jayyus, but what is beyond any doubt is that Jayyus is part of a much wider scheme of accelerated settlement and annexation aimed at obliterating the Green Line forever.

We have come to show our solidarity with the villagers and, specifically, to replant the plundered field with young olive saplings. Perhaps this will stop the bulldozers for another few days. Perhaps not. On one level, our gesture, seen against the grand machinations of the government and the army, is pitiful, ineffectual almost by definition. On another level, if we persist, and if the people of Jayyus persist, there is at least a chance that eventually we will save these fields. It is, perhaps, not so terrible to be ineffectual if you have hope. I am certain—almost certain—that in the end we, the bumbling, well-intentioned soldiers of peace, will win.

The army and the police, as always, are waiting for us, this time in force. There are many jeeps full of soldiers and policemen, most of them heavily armed. They block the road leading

to the Jayyus fields at the very point it turns off from the main
highway. We have been prepared for this moment. Quickly we
disembark from the three buses—some 120 volunteers—and prepare to wash over the soldiers' barricade. Each of us picks up an
olive sapling wrapped in black plastic. There are many posters
and signs as well: "Stop the theft of the land!" "The Wall will
fall." "Occupation and settlements are the opposite of peace."
"They disengage in Gaza in order to settle the West Bank." I am
carrying the medic's pouch and, uselessly, my winter jacket, in
case I get arrested and have to spend the night in some frozen
cell. But at this point, 11:00 A.M., it is hot and getting hotter.
We scatter over the hill, clutching the tiny olive trees and the
signs.

The jeeps follow us as best they can, some of the officers
walking on foot alongside us. Clearly, they are not eager to get
into a clash, at least not at this point. It is a long walk through the
heat, easily an hour, and soon I am thirsty, covered with sweat.
We pass groves of mango and guava, the orchards of Jayyus,
which so far the villagers have managed to care for by crossing
through the wall with army permits. Soon this, too, will become
impossible; once the new settlement is in place, the villagers
will automatically be seen as security risks, and the roads and
footpaths closed to them.

It is always good to have Amiel beside me; we speak, as so
often, of Virgil, a benign and lyrical presence in this tortured
Mediterranean domain. Amiel seems to be at his most serene
in circumstances such as these, which are, in addition, perfectly
suited to discussions of Latin poetry. Yasmin, once a student
of mine, has recently returned from Ladakh. She is a superb
linguist; she tells me how she learned Turkish last year in about
a month. I listen, envious, as she speaks a fluent Arabic with our
Palestinian volunteers. She has been out of sorts for weeks, she
says; perhaps it is the situation—but today, seeing 120 people
carrying their olive saplings, she is happy again, for this moment.
I meet Marty, a Californian, tough and idealistic, specializing
in conflict resolution. There are many foreign volunteers, some

from Germany, others from Scandinavia, also a contingent of wild-haired anarchists in black T-shirts. Meanwhile, I am rapidly bonding with my sapling, though it is a rather scrawny specimen: will it survive the first winter storm, let alone a determined attack by the bulldozers? I feel a strong urge to protect it, though it is becoming heavy in my hands.

We climb the hill to the ravaged field. The ancient olives are gone—apparently to some contractor in Tel Aviv, who will make a killing. We have seen the devastating pictures of three hundred olive trees, roots up, from just two weeks ago. "Is a tree in the field a human being who can take refuge during a siege?"* Now we pause amidst the rocks for the necessary speeches. Abu Azzam, from Jayyus, takes the megaphone. "Friends, comrades. Your coming here today has great meaning for us. It is a very deep act. In a time when the Israeli government and the Israeli army are making our lives into a daily hell, you have come as friends to help us." He tells the story of the fields. First, in December 2000, the Civil Administration renumbered all the plots of land, but they refused to hand the new maps over to the villagers. When the latter received notices that plots 786 and 788 were being appropriated for the new settlement, they had no idea what these numbers meant. Only on December 15, two weeks ago, under pressure from the courts, did the authorities hand over the maps. Now the people of Jayyus knew: they were to lose everything. Then there is the devilish legal rule that a field that is 50 percent stones reverts to the state. Is there any field or olive grove on these hills that is not covered with stones?

Abu Azzam wants one state for everyone, Palestinians and Jews, a state where there is room for all and all will live in peace. Some of the volunteers applaud his vision. Others, like me, are skeptical. But no sooner has he finished than the police officer in charge delivers his expected threat. "You are on private land. You are breaking the law. If any one of you tries to plant a tree here, he will be filmed and brought to justice. We will use all the

*Deuteronomy 20:19.

means at our disposal to stop you." He has been waiting for this moment for the last couple of hours.

This is our signal. We burst up the path to the open, more level stretch of mountainside and start to work. There are not enough shovels, but we begin, somehow, to excavate shallow pits for the saplings. There are a hundred young olive trees in our hands, and we are determined to plant them right here, amidst the rocks and the soldiers. The police photographers are filming furiously, pit by pit, recording our heinous crime. We take no notice. Surprisingly, to my intense relief, there are no arrests, no blows from the truncheons or the rifle butts. In fact, a sweet and unnatural silence suddenly envelops this dry hillside, as if the sheer magic of planting trees had taken over all the other, conflicted, confused thoughts and feelings, as if even the soldiers had become entranced by the vision of these people—young and old, Arabs and Jews—digging with their hands into the hard ground so that something new can grow. I look around: the hillside is covered with small groups of planters, and dozens of tiny saplings are now bravely standing more or less erect in the upturned brown soil. It is another Taʿayush moment, that eerie, unstructured limbo that we enter from time to time, always with the soldiers or the police or, worst of all, the settlers to share it with us, always with a strangely delicious uncertainty about what will happen next. Often such moments are noisy; people scream, some may be hurt, the soldiers snarl, sometimes they shoot their canisters of tear gas or stun grenades, but today, under the blazing winter sun, there is a sleepwalker's quiet. Abu Azzam was right: I feel the depth of this visionary space. In the distance, we can see one or two houses at the edge of the village, across the wall. Perhaps they are watching us from afar as we tend their field.

Gadi appears beside me—I have finished watering one of the saplings, giving it a head start in the unequal battle ahead of it— and he is happy, I think, and, like me, oddly at peace. "If one has to get arrested," he says, "it should happen now, over this—let them try to convince the court that planting an olive tree is an act of treason." As always, Gadi embodies a certain calm lucidity and courage; as always, he is looking beyond this moment, into the menacing future. Dana, beside me, with long black curls, poses mischievously for the police camera that lingers over her face. We finish patting down the fresh soil and prepare to leave.

But it is not quite over yet. Our plan is to reach the wall and make our protest there while the villagers of Jayyus reach the same spot from the other side. We will not be able to mingle with them, but let us at least see one another. So we start off over the hills again in the direction of the vast swath of metal and stone that has cut the land in two. Ahead of me is a Palestinian woman in a black robe, carrying a huge sign in English: "You can't uproot Palestine." We are moving along a path that winds through olive groves; the village emerges fully into view. Suddenly the police officer barks at us through his megaphone: "No farther. You are breaking the law. If you take another step, you will be arrested. We are prepared to stop you."

Gadi rushes forward to negotiate; I catch his eye, and he signals to me to circle through the olives, to get beyond the soldiers. We head off over the terraces, through the trees, stumbling over the rocks. An older woman who has come, it seems, for the first time to a Ta'ayush action is suddenly afraid. "What will happen now?" she asks me. "I don't know what to do." "Don't worry," I tell her, "it is nothing—stay with the others; we are safer together." I help her descend a rocky terrace. Volunteers are pouring over the path; the police have lost control. Their jeeps grind their way, honking wildly, over the bumpy dirt road, forcing the volunteers to the side. Finally they halt us about a hundred meters from the wall. On the other side, barely visible, stand the villagers, waiting. Between us there are suddenly rather a lot of soldiers; I count ten new army vehicles, watch the soldiers unload the teargas guns. Mostly we are worried that they will turn the gas on the Palestinians, as is their wont.

Instead, everyone stops on the brink. Negotiations ensue. Meanwhile, absurdity takes over, as is only fitting for this mad scene of massacred olive trees and yellow bulldozers and settlers and soldiers and the vast monster that is the wall and the motley crowd of volunteers that have come here to cry out against it. A Palestinian man goes off into the green field on my right and prostrates himself in prayer: it is time. A cart and mule, with two villagers, wait behind us, hoping to cross over into Jayyus if the soldiers open the gate. The crazy anarchists begin a vaudeville-like dance routine, right here on the muddy path, brandishing their legs at the soldiers as they sing, in an English drawl: "We're gonna shake off, shake off, that military rule.... We'll never be safe, never safe, with that Apartheid wall." I can hear the policeman arguing with Gadi: "I am just doing my job." "We don't want any kind of violence," Gadi says, not for the first time today, "but we won't be deterred." In the midst of the hubbub, a letter arrives from the other side of the fence—from Tawfiq Hassan Salim, he of the plundered olive grove. The letter is read aloud. "I am sorry I could not come to meet you at the wall. I am mourning my murdered olive trees. For decades I nurtured them and loved them like children. I sit and weep in my house. You have come as if to comfort a mourner, and you have touched my heart. You give me hope. I wish I could welcome you as my guests, but between us stands the wall." Hisham, one of the Taʿayush lawyers, now cries out in impassioned Arabic, his voice hoarse, the syllables tripping from his tongue: "We want peace; we believe in peace, peace without occupation. They must stop stealing the land. You cannot steal the land and make peace. We *will* make peace in spite of Sharon."

We have brought with us a gift for Jayyus: one large olive tree, left behind in the field on the day they uprooted the other 299. The soldiers make way as a group of four volunteers approaches the gate; as it is opened, they hand the tree over to our friends on the other side. That is as much as we could do. It is not enough. It is never enough. It is time to go home. And my sapling? Probably tomorrow it will be gone.

September 9, 2005   Bilʿin (1)

"There will be no more demonstrations in Bilʿin," announced the Israeli colonel in the village—just one week ago today.

He was wrong.

Bil'in has become the symbol of nonviolent Palestinian re-sistance; since January there have been weekly demonstrations, which the army has desperately tried to suppress. Let it be said clearly: Here the route of the wall has absolutely nothing to do with Israeli security and the fight against terror. The wall at Bil'in has only one purpose—to appropriate land for the extension of the Israeli settlements of Modiin Ilit, Matityahu, and Kiryat Sefer. Modiin Ilit is an ultra-Orthodox urban settlement with some 20,000 inhabitants today; blueprints for its development envisage its eventual growth to some 300,000. One can see why they need more land, and what better source is there than this helpless village situated at the top of one of the most beautiful hills in Palestine, with a spectacular view over the western slopes of Judaea to the east and the coastal plain to the west? Bil'in, a village of 1,600 people, stands to lose two-thirds of its land, 1,980 *dunams* out of a total of some 3,000. So far the Israeli Supreme Court has failed to redress the obvious injustice, although the case is scheduled for yet another hearing in the coming week.

The Israeli peace camp has been supporting the villagers' struggle, but the Bil'in demonstrations are not for everyone; the risk of being hurt by army violence is great. Until today, the An-archists Against the Wall and various international groups have borne the brunt of the campaign together with the local com-mittee. But after last week's pronouncement by the colonel—the attempt to put an end to the resistance once and for all—the peace groups decided they had to act immediately. An appeal went out to the activists of Ta'ayush, Machsom Watch, Gush Shalom, and other organizations; thus some two hundred have come to join the protest today.

At first it seems our chances of reaching the village are slim. Before leaving home, I find an urgent e-mail announcing that the army entered the village at 5:00 A.M. and imposed a complete curfew; anyone leaving his or her home would be arrested, or worse. The ten o'clock news on the radio reports clashes in Bil'in between soldiers and villagers throwing stones. (This has been the standard progression, week after week: the villagers march peacefully to the site of the wall's construction; the army attacks them with tear gas, stun grenades, clubs, rifle butts, and, eventually, rubber bullets or even live ammunition; at this point enraged Palestinian teenagers start throwing rocks at the soldiers.) At the briefing on the bus, we learn that the army has closed off all access roads to Bil'in, completely cutting off the village. Our only hope of getting there is by winding our way, on foot, through the hills and wadis.

Four buses full of tense activists rendezvous in Modiin and continue on through the settlement of Modiin Ilit, an ugly warren of huge stone and concrete apartment blocs. The woman sitting beside me, a volunteer from Machsom Watch, points out the utter absence of anything green or growing; unlike other Israelis, ultra-Orthodox Jews do not decorate their windowsills with potted plants and flowers. She also points out that if we have to drive back this way after Shabbat comes in, in the evening, we're likely to be stoned—a danger possibly worse, she says, than anything that awaits us in Bil'in. Another, even more severe problem is the heat; it is midday, still summer in the Mediterranean and, as Adam—a veteran of many Bil'in Fridays—says knowingly, our worst enemy is the sun. We soon discover how right he is. A few kilometers past the settlement, the buses pull up at a spot above the wide, dusty gash in the earth that will soon turn into the wall. We gather our belongings and quickly exit into the burning sunlight. We set off down the hill, walking quickly, before the soldiers turn up.

Soon we see them—several jeeploads—on the road above us. Most of us by now are near the bed of the wadi, picking our way over the rocks. The heat is overwhelming, choking, drenching us in sweat. We scramble up a steep hill and then down its other slope. Where are we, and where is the village? We cannot see it, though our guides assure us it isn't so far, another few kilometers ahead. Where we stand there is no sign of human habitation; this is a wild, still pristine space, full of rocks and thorns, clearly the back route into the village. I begin to worry that some of the marchers may dehydrate; I have only three liters of Hartman fluid with me, for transfusion, and I want to save them in case someone gets wounded in Bil'in. It is a hardly credible scene—two hundred peace activists of all ages, disoriented and already exhausted, melting down under the relentless sun, still far from their goal and not entirely certain how to reach it.

We push on through the wadi. Still no sign of the village, but apparently we are getting nearer. There is a final briefing. We are to do our best to stick together and thus to wash over the barricades and the soldiers. "Don't worry if they stop you," says Einat from Ta'ayush, another very experienced activist; "if one hundred activists are arrested at Bil'in, that will be a great victory for us." This is the moment to take out the onions we have brought as antidote to the tear gas; they are effective only when sliced open, so I borrow a knife from someone and cut mine lengthwise, distributing pieces to those around me. I am in the middle of an absorbing discussion with Ishay Rosen-Zvi, a brilliant scholar of rabbinic literature, about the book he is writing—on the concept of *yetzer ha-ra'*, the "evil impulse" that became the centerpiece of rabbinic anthropology, as he explains to me, and was then, in Talmudic times, linked with sexuality. "Evil" is now internal to the human being and cannot be fobbed off onto external forces—this is a true achievement of the rabbis. The discussion is at once surreal and somehow utterly appropriate to these circumstances, a minute or two before chaos erupts.

We pass the crest of another hill and emerge directly onto the path of the wall. To no one's surprise, there are many dozens of soldiers and policemen waiting for us. Someone calls out to us to move left, keeping some distance from the security forces, so we start picking our way along the lower slope of the hill abutting the dusty path. The first houses of Bil'in are now visible high above us, to the right. Loud explosions shatter the silence: stun grenades. They are not dangerous so long as they don't hit you directly. After a while I hardly hear them. I am busy navigating over the rocks, keeping an eye out for the soldiers who have started grabbing people from our ranks, arresting them, and pushing them into their jeeps and vans. Oddly, a certain calm descends upon me; I have been through this many times, and over the years an irrational belief has taken root in me; somehow they have never managed to stop me, although others beside me were arrested. I am agile and nimble; I always elude them; perhaps I even imagine myself, half-consciously, to be more or less invisible.

But I have made a mistake. Some of our people are pouring over the dirt track; others stumble over the hill, still beyond the soldiers' reach. At some point, however, we have to cross over to the right side of the track and head up toward the village. I pick my crossing point, jump onto the track—and find myself faced with a line of blue policemen. Several are busy picking activists out of the steady stream, but one of them plants himself directly in front of me and says, "Stop. Don't pass this line." "I'm going up this hill," I say to him. "If you take another step, I'll arrest you," he says, impassive, arms folded on his chest. I inch forward, still hoping to get beyond him. "You're under arrest," he says. There is a moment where I can still, perhaps, escape, make a dash for it, but suddenly I see, a few meters away, that they have pushed Hillel—one of the older activists, white-haired and tough—to the ground. They are poking and pulling at him violently. I rush to his aid, yelling to the policemen not to hurt him, but they carry him off, kicking and struggling; and by now I am completely surrounded and forced into the waiting van myself.

Three others are already there, in the forward compartment where they put me, and another seven or eight are soon packed into the back, behind a thin partition. It is very hot. I try to get my bearings. To my left, a young activist is cracking jokes; he is used to this scenario. "Why do they drive these beat-up old vans?" he asks. "I voted for increasing the police budgets." We try to find out who is behind the partition, but there is too much noise and hubbub; through the open door I watch, with envy, activists still making their way up the hill toward the village, through the jagged line of soldiers and police. But my main feeling is the absurd sense that "It's about time this happened"—also, a certain curiosity about what happens next.

A comic moment ensues. They have loaded the van with ar-
restees, but the sliding door on the right has come off its track
and can't be closed; apparently their regulations won't allow them
to drive with an open door. So in the midst of the stun grenades
and the cries of those struggling outside, the officers shouting
at their soldiers, the activists sweeping past them through the
thorns, and, still more absurdly, the sudden appearance on the
scene of a car carrying the famous Peruvian author Mario Vargas
Llosa, who has come to watch this fracas—in the midst of all
of this, three inept, sweat-drenched policemen pit themselves
heroically against the broken door. They give advice to one another; they swear and fuss and pound their hands against the
metal; they try the standard Israeli method—first use force, and
if force doesn't work, use more force—but the door won't budge.
A quarter of an hour passes. Roi, the detainee to my right, seems
to know how to fix it, but naturally he keeps this information to
himself.

Eventually the door gives up its Gandhian nonviolent resistance and slams shut, and the van takes off along the dusty road,
uphill. At the top they tell us to get out and to sit under a large
olive tree directly across from the village, which we can now see
on the next ridge in all its stark beauty, the purple hills of Judaea
gently hovering over it in the distance. We take stock: there are
other activists waiting for us under the olives, including one of
the anarchists who spent the morning hiding from the soldiers
on a rooftop in the village. One of the villagers, Abdallah Abu
Rahmeh, sits calmly, guarded by an armed soldier, under another
tree not far away. We are about twenty, and I recognize Lucia—
the Mexican expert on Franz Rosenzweig whom I first met a year
ago while picking olives in Umm al-Rihan, and then more recently in ʿAnata, rebuilding a demolished Palestinian home; also
Inbal, a Ph.D. student in linguistics from Stanford, the daughter
of my colleague at the university. Her mother and brother have
also come today; perhaps by now they have reached the village.
A middle-aged Israeli woman has been handcuffed and is sitting
uncomfortably beside us; a fiery girl from a kibbutz takes her

seat under the tree while delivering a powerful, fluid stream of invective against the soldiers—many times in the coming hours she will urge them to refuse their orders, to say no, to stop their collusion with the occupation. There is also a lawyer from Tel Aviv and an older activist from the town of Carmiel in Galilee; Adam, who warned us about the sun; and a determined, freckled redhead who immediately rushes over to sit beside Abdallah, despite the soldier's attempt to separate this dangerous Palestinian from the Jews.

There is, unfortunately, not much more I can report. Hours roll by. We hear explosions and shots coming from the village; we see thick black smoke—apparently from burning tires—and many military vehicles rushing to and from Bil'in. By cell phone we hear that several groups of activists, cut off from one another in the mêlée, have eventually succeeded in regrouping in the courtyard of the mosque, where the demonstration continues. Later we will hear of many waves of tear gas, rubber bullets, more stun grenades, arrests, live fire. The reports are confused; everyone sees only one small piece of this violent jigsaw. Dozens more are arrested. We learn that four soldiers were wounded when a stun grenade accidentally landed in their jeep. On our hilltop, the police go through the usual motions, recording our names and identity numbers, filming us for their records. They offer us no water or food, and their greatest fear seems to be that we will succeed in joining up with Abdallah, but apart from that they are actually rather courteous and relaxed. A senior police investigator turns up—he is, we discover, a kibbutznik from Masada in the Jordan Valley, probably inclining to the left, though who knows?—and with a certain incongruous jolliness goes through our names and addresses.

Late in the afternoon they call out five names: they have chosen this number to be taken to the Jerusalem police station at Givat Zeev and charged. Why these five, who include Inbal, L. the anarchist, and an Israeli Arab, Ali? Perhaps the choice is mostly random. An hour later they tell the rest of us that we are free to go. But now we have a dilemma: we are not prepared to abandon Abdallah to his fate. We cluster around him—later we discover that he is a well-known Bil'in activist, a man they call the "Palestinian Gandhi"—and we demand from the soldiers that they summon a senior officer who can make a decision. Surprisingly, they agree. A lieutenant colonel drives up in his jeep. He orders Abdallah into an army van—we are powerless to prevent this; we shout that this is racism: the Jews are set free; the Palestinian is sent to prison. Suddenly the soldier who has been guarding Abdallah all afternoon protests: "It isn't racism," he says. "Didn't you see how I let you talk with him?" He is no more than the smallest screw in this vast machine, but I am glad to see that he doesn't like being classified as a racist; something inside him is offended by our words. Israel is still a kind of big, almost intimate village. Now the officer—perhaps the senior commander in this area, a man who clearly sees himself as enlightened and benign—wants to address our complaint. He explains that he himself had proclaimed the curfew and then, "in order to allow freedom of worship," agreed that the villagers could go from their homes to the mosque for Friday prayers; this on condition that there would be no demonstration, nothing that was not purely "religious." Abdallah, says the officer, came out of his house to stand in his own front yard, where he was being interviewed by Egyptian TV; the officer warned him, once, twice, thrice, that if he refused to go back inside, he would be arrested. That, of course, is what happened. It is all perfectly reasonable, is it not? Never mind the fact that Abdallah is a leader of the nonviolent resistance, that his lands are being annexed to Israel for the sake of the settlements, that he is an utterly innocent human being protesting a crime. In the eyes of our rational lieutenant colonel, a likable, intelligent man like so many who keep the system running smoothly, the protest is the crime.

At 5:30, as the shadows lengthen, we set off again toward the village. A long line of police and army trucks and jeeps passes us in the opposite direction. They are no longer concerned about us; the confrontation is over for today. They wish us a Shabbat Shalom. A deep peace descends on the now silent hills, and the light turns soft and golden in the late-afternoon Mediterranean mode. It is astonishing: only a few hours before, at this same spot, they were prepared to stop us with all the instruments of power; now we walk freely, casually, into Bil'in. It is as if both sides had decided, in some highly ritualized way, that they would clash at the appointed time and space, with all the usual panoply of bullets, gas, and screams; and once the ritual has been performed in its remorseless, proper order, the place reverts to being just another tormented hilltop, like all the others. Human beings cannot tolerate too much disorder. Life should make sense. Next Friday the ritual will no doubt be enacted again.

I am walking with Asaf, whom I remember from Silwan and other actions. We greet each of the villagers we meet, and they answer graciously with the melodious blessings of the host. As we reach the main street, a group of men sitting on a balcony high above us calls down to us: "We thank you. We honor you for coming here." It is the happiest, deepest moment of the day, this simple, obviously genuine statement of welcome, bonding, thanks. It was all worth it—there is no doubt. For them and for us. We faced it together. And suddenly I am aware of a feeling that has been slowly building up in me throughout the day but that only now becomes fully explicit—a breathtaking experience of freedom, perhaps more complete and more satisfying than at any other point in my life. Later I will wonder what such freedom consists of and why I felt it in this way. Clearly, it has very little to do with armies, policemen, jails. It is not, however, disconnected from external things, despite what people (especially those of a romantic temper) sometimes say. Above all, this sense of being free must be linked to a mode of being *with*—*ta'ayush*—of acting, or caring, or caring enough, of overcoming fear, not looking away. It is not so easy not to look away. Perhaps it is obscurely connected to the curiosity that seemed to rush through me earlier. Perhaps it is a function of the play of shadows and light as evening falls in the hills. Probably there is no point in analyzing it. I remember, from out of the intoxication of this moment, with its sadness, too, that today is my father's Yahrzeit, ten years since the day he died.

I look around me. Activists, weary, smiling, mill around in the street beside the mosque, chatting with the villagers of Bil'in. I see ordinary people who have, all day long, been doing something extraordinary. My eyes take in the graffiti that cover every inch of wall space on this street, most in Arabic, some in quaintly idiosyncratic English. *Al-jidar yaqtul al-jami*ʿ: "The Wall is killing us all." "The occupation destroys us, in rejecting it we are free." "Isrel [*sic*] creates hatred." Most touching, most simple, at the edge of the village, sprayed with red paint several times on the gray stone walls: "No Fair."

January 1, 2006   8th Light of Chanukah: Bilʿin (2)

We scramble down the wide dust path into the wadi, then up the gentle slope. Heavy trucks loaded with rocks and soil pass us in both directions, stirring clouds of white dust. Bulldozers sit phlegmatically on the hill to our right; every once in a while, they rouse themselves with a dissonant roar of metal tracks and metal jaws, and for a few minutes we watch them gnawing at the hillside until, satisfied, they desist. Trucks carry off the debris. It is like a gigantic building site, replete with wire fences, prefab huts, security guards, and the inevitable detachment of bored soldiers in their jeeps. Between two deep gashes in the surface of the wadi, a small green patch of grass and ancient olive trees survives, last witnesses to the world of terraces and rocky fields, of goats and shepherds, that has been torn apart to build the huge settlement of Modiin Ilit, on the one hand, and the Separation Wall, on the other.

We cannot see the wall itself, which follows the course of the next wadi, to the east; but we can clearly see the houses of Bilʿin and the white stone mosque scattered over the gray-green hill. And where we are walking is also Bilʿin, though these fields are on the "wrong"—that is, the Israeli—side of the wall. To be precise, they are in the territory that is being annexed to Israel to make room for the future expansion of Modiin Ilit. Yet another session of the Supreme Court is scheduled to address Bilʿin's appeal on February 1.

In the meantime, the people of Bilʿin have proven themselves remarkably creative. As one of the old villagers says to me, with pride, in his colorful Arabic: "Bilʿin is the Number One Village of

Palestine." Week after week, each Friday morning, the ritual of nonviolent protest by the villagers and violent suppression by the army is enacted anew. To date, over three hundred villagers have been wounded. Twenty villagers are still in jail. It is, by now, a stable, familiar, ultimately tragic drama. But two weeks ago something new happened: the people of Bil'in managed to drive a caravan-trailer up the hill where we are standing, beyond the wall, and to declare it an "illegal outpost"—the infamous term used by Israeli settlers when they take over yet another piece of Palestine. Hundreds of such outposts dot the hills of the West Bank; the army and the government, despite their promises to the Americans to evacuate them, in practice never touch them. Most have now been there for years. Bil'in's "outpost," standing on land stolen from the village—and with a permit issued, for what it's worth, by the Bil'in municipality—was of course overrun by soldiers and demolished within thirty-six hours.

With astonishing persistence, the villagers returned with another trailer, just over a week ago. Muhammad tells us the story in a tone of bemused heroics, as if he were reciting a slightly ironic, self-parodic epic. When the soldiers of the Civil Administration arrived, on schedule, to remove the second trailer, the villagers asked them why Jewish settlers can build illegally, without any permits, with total impunity (on Bil'in's land), whereas the Bil'in "outpost" is immediately destroyed. "But those are real *buildings*," replied the bureaucrats of the Civil Administration, referring to the apartment blocks of Modiin Ilit, which everyone knows are illegal. What, asked the Bil'iners, defines a "building"? The bureaucrats answered with disdain: "You know, four walls, a roof, an interior with at least ten square meters, and a window." "What would happen if you were to find such a building right here tomorrow morning?" they asked. "In that case, the law would require that we wait ten days before tearing it down, so that the owners can appeal."

That was enough. It was a frozen, rainy night, and all the paths and terraces had turned to mud, but the people of Bil'in were determined to build the house—knowing it had to be ready, entirely complete, by 8:00 in the morning. It was no simple matter to get the cement blocks and other building materials from the village across the wadi, past the security guards, and up this hill on the other side. One car loaded with material got bogged down in the mud, and the guards immediately turned up, very suspicious. The villagers talked their way out of it and then somehow managed, in driving rain, to extricate the vehicle and move everything uphill. Perhaps the storm helped them in the end, as they made three or four more trips back and forth, unseen in the dark, while a small group worked frantically on the site through the night. By 3:00 A.M. the walls were standing, but there was still no roof, and the cement wouldn't dry in the intense rain. After some hours, despite everything, a roof was in place. Suddenly they realized they had no window—a necessary part of the definition—so they raced back to the village, knocked on a door, and, apologizing profusely to the owners, detached a window to be installed in the new edifice. "We're sorry we're ruining your home, but we really need a window!"

So here it stands, the none-too-imposing Center for Joint Struggle, with its corrugated roof and its gray block walls and, God be praised, its very own window (so to speak). A Palestinian woman reclines on a mat inside. Goats graze among the olive trees. A young man in a wheelchair is chatting with an Israeli girl, perhaps one of the "anarchists for peace" who have been involved in the Bil'in struggle from the beginning. Not far away, soldiers watch the odd group of Israeli peace activists who have come to light Chanukah candles in Bil'in. I study the graffiti carved on the cement blocks, and slowly it dawns on me that they are, in part, an Arabic translation of a well-known song by Uzi Hitman: "Welcome to the Bil'in School. Welcome, Grade 1: 'Here I was born. Here my children were born. Here I have built my house with my own two hands.'" What could be more Zionist than these words? Indeed, the whole enterprise is a savagely ironic replay of the classic Zionist mode of *Choma u-migdal*, "Wall and Tower"—the method used to put up settlement after settlement, overnight, in the heady days of the 1930s, in the face of violent opposition by the British Mandatory police. Let it not be said that the two peoples have learned nothing from one another. I meet Fadi, the engraver, who is proud of his graffiti; someone, he says, dictated to him Hitman's song, which seemed appropriate. He takes me to the other side of the door to show me the sequel: "Here is where I will be."

Can the hope come true? In less than a week, the grace period of ten days will be over. It is all too likely that the army will return to wreck this small sign of human tenacity and human faith. Maybe, who knows, we can stop them with legal maneuvers. One thing is clear: the people of Bil'in remain uncowed in the face of overwhelming state terror. Here is Wajih, a vigorous, bearded man who tells me his story. He has lost sixty-two *dunams* of his own to the wall. He has five sons. The oldest, Ran, is the one in the wheelchair. He was paralyzed from the waist down by a bullet at a nonviolent demonstration in Ramallah, at the start of the Intifada. Another son got a bullet wound in the head at one of the Bil'in demonstrations. Two other sons were also wounded by the soldiers. Wajih himself took a splinter from a tank shell in his neck; he shows me the scar, beneath the beard. The fifth son is in jail, awaiting trial. In addition, he has five daughters. Yonata asks him how he manages to survive, and he says: "It's not so bad. I have a little land left, and some goats." He is full of energy, not overtly bitter; also eager to teach some Arabic to the Israelis who have come today. He offers free Arabic lessons on Friday, an hour or two before the tear gas and the rubber bullets begin.

It is almost time to light the candle flares. A large-scale, somewhat rudimentary Chanukiya candelabra has been constructed, and we gather round to hear the words. Uri Avnery begins. "Tonight is Chanukah, the festival of light, the festival of freedom. The lands we are standing on are the lands of the Maccabees. Here, at Modiin, on these very slopes, the Maccabees raised the flag of freedom. Here the great revolt began. The whole world knows of it, knows of that ancient struggle to be free. And if we ask ourselves today, who is Antiochus, the oppressor, and who are the Maccabees, then the answer is very simple: Israel is Antiochus, and those who struggle against the occupation, both Palestinians and Israelis, are the Maccabees. Bil'in is the Palestinian Modiin. We are here to support this struggle. We will not abandon you until you are truly free." Muhammad takes the microphone. He thanks us for coming today. "We believe this is the only way to expand the fight against the occupation. That is why we have set up this Center for Joint Struggle. We do not see the Israelis as our enemy. Our enemy is the occupation. We want to shorten the life of the occupation. We will never harm anyone physically, not settlers, not soldiers, but we will not give in. We hope that from this place where we stand the great revolution will begin, the revolution of the forces of peace, Israelis and Palestinians together." He tells us that among their supporters is an anonymous ultra-Orthodox man from Modiin Ilit—a settler—who, moved by the Bil'in struggle, came to help the villagers during the long, stormy night when they were building. He tells us the story of that night.

I have lit many Chanukah candles in my life—nearly 2,500, at a rough count (allowing for a cumulative forty-four each Chanukah). I used to think they had something to do with what really mattered, with what the Jews, at heart, were about. I guess I was wrong. But somehow tonight, for a brief moment, on this stony hill amidst the olives and the goats and the crippled son and the unassuming men and women of Bil'in and the ever-so-precarious, ramshackle Center for Joint Struggle, the doomed childish dream flares up in me again. People step forward, a little awkwardly, to speak a few words as they take their turn with the lights. "I light this candle tonight for all those who believe in peace, who will not be silent." "I light this candle for those who overcome their fear." Some, perhaps the most powerful, are texts of defiance: "I light this candle tonight in protest against all those who have defiled the true Jewish values, who have desecrated the holiest of all, the truth of human freedom." "I light this candle in protest at the settlers who steal Palestinian lands without shame." The last is a man of Bil'in, who reads a text in Arabic: "I light this candle in the name of our friendship and our hope." Soon, as the sky darkens, the entire candelabra is alight.

January 20, 2006   Bil'in (3)

The time is ripe. This Friday marks a year since the villagers of Bil'in began their campaign of nonviolent protest. In ten days the Supreme Court is to pronounce on their appeal. So today some four hundred Israeli activists converge on the village to join the weekly demonstration. Everyone knows that Bil'in is unusual—a symbol of grassroots resistance. Palestinians from villages nearby also come to take part along with international volunteers— and a significant contingent of the Israeli media. It is partly for their sake that we are here; we want the judges who are soon to determine Bil'in's fate to read about the villagers' struggle in the papers or see it on TV. Let them know that Bil'in is fighting for its freedom.

This, then, is weekly demonstration-cum-confrontation no. 52. It is a sun-drenched winter day, springlike in its fragrance; the almond trees in the wadi are in bloom, and I see the first blood-red anemone of the season proudly rising out of the grass and mud. The air is cool, the land heavy with the last two weeks of rain. A perfect day—were it not for the ugliness human beings inflict. At first it feels like a nature hike—we slide down the rocky, muddy slope; we laugh and joke, almost forgetting what lies ahead. The bus has let us off here, halfway between Jerusalem and Modiin, because the roads to Bil'in are blocked by the army; our two busloads of volunteers will never be allowed through. We will have to cover these last few kilometers on foot, or until one of the Palestinian minibuses picks us up.

At the bottom of the wadi, we hit a paved access road leading to the village of Beit 'Ur. Five minutes later we discover (no surprise) that the army is waiting for us: one large truck, a jeep or two, and a handful of soldiers who have taken their stand in the middle of the road. They tell us to stop and threaten to arrest us. But it is clear at a glance that they cannot handle a hundred

volunteers—nor is the army legally permitted to make arrests—
so we blithely walk through their blockade. The soldiers quickly
reassemble a little farther up the road, and again we wash over
them, unafraid. Soon we have reached Beit ʿUr; young boys
welcome the straggling line of Israelis of all ages, including even a
few children who are here with their parents—an unusual sight at
a Taʿayush demonstration. There are also several older volunteers,
in their seventies, who take the long climb up to the village a little
more slowly.

We are poised on the verge of the Palestinian election, and
the village is covered with posters. The whole range of parties is
represented, from Fatah and its splinter factions to Hamas. How
far are we from Bilʿin? One of the boys says: "An hour's walk."
It is already 11:30, and the demonstration will begin around 12:15.
We will have to rush. Suddenly we see the army ahead of us
again, straddling the main road in the village center. This time
they are more serious; they shout, lash out, try to pull some of
us out of the line. Amiel pushes his way through the blockade.
Several Taʿayush volunteers link arms and advance, forcing the
soldiers aside. It is one of those moments of mini chaos, all too
familiar. With others, I circle round to the right, down one of the
village lanes, beyond the soldiers' grasp. Last time I came to a
Friday demonstration in Bilʿin, I was arrested at a fairly early
stage; today I am determined to make it into the village and intent
on avoiding arrest. An elderly Palestinian woman, standing in her
doorway, lights up our path with a craggy smile. Daniela, who
has also successfully eluded the barricade, says to me, surveying
the ragged line of marchers, "With our youths and our elders we
have come."*

The first minibuses appear, and some of the volunteers clamber in; I keep walking, occasionally glancing back at the ongoing
tussle with the soldiers on the main road. Our ranks are thinning. Amiel miraculously materializes beside me; I congratulate
him on his "semi-Gandhian" act of resistance. On either side

*Exodus 10:9.

of us there are green fields, incipient spring. Here is Natasha, the veteran Ta'ayush photographer, from Prague; I say to her, with a nod at the soldiers, "It's the springtime of nations all over again!" She smiles too. And so it goes—the soldiers fruitlessly scrambling to stop us, tearing down the road in their jeeps to take up position in front of us only to find themselves, moments later, left behind as we march forward. I lose track of time. How many barricades have we walked through? The sun beats down; I am thirsty, also happy, even elated, and slightly bemused. These minor clashes feel unreal, an empty gesture by the army, which wants to control the number of dangerous peace activists streaming toward the demonstration. Eventually a minibus sweeps me up and races over the winding road into Bil'in. We pass another minibus traveling in the opposite direction, toward Beit 'Ur and the marchers; the two drivers wave the V sign of victory to one another. Bil'in is special, and Friday is their day.

We get out beside the mosque. The main street is filling up with villagers and volunteers—perhaps a thousand or so, at my estimate. Inside the mosque, the preacher is reaching his conclusion; his voice, carried by the microphones, rings through the square. I greet my friends from Haifa and Tel Aviv. Huge red posters of Mustafa Barghouti dominate this space; his party, Filastin Mustaqilla—Free Palestine—seems to have the upper hand in Bil'in. But the other parties are also there in a rich palette of color and slogans. A group of young women, dressed in black, full of energy, stride down the street crying out, "*Min Bil'in li-Bayrut / sha'ab hayyi la yamut*": "From Bil'in to Beirut, a living people that will not die." Are we in a demonstration against the wall or an election rally? It isn't clear. In any case, we are carried along by the torrent, down the street, toward the wall. The whole village is marching, as it does every Friday at midday. It is like being in an Indian film: a truck with huge loudspeakers mounted in the rear, young men in keffiyehs astride them, is blaring out popular Arabic songs. The real danger today, so it seems, is that we will all go deaf from the noise. I fight my way past the truck, away from the speakers. The atmosphere is light, volatile, festive.

A vast flag of Palestine—green, white, black, red—is held high as a canopy over our heads. Soon we have exited the village and are climbing up the hill just beyond.

On one side, on its crest, is the temporary wire fence. Beside it and scattered along the whole length of the ridge stand some forty soldiers, armed, waiting. Not far away, in clear view as we walk, a gigantic orange bulldozer is working, carving out the swath of the wall. You can hear its ghastly staccato echoing over the hills. Farther north and east, a panoply of machines, heavy vehicles, and enormous piles of displaced rock and soil stands guard over the deep gash in the surface of the earth, where the wall will pass. Somewhere nearby, amidst the olive trees, is the Center for Joint Struggle—the small outpost the villagers built a month ago, under the soldiers' noses, on their own stolen lands, on the "wrong" side of the wall.

What now? At first, the festivities continue apace. The soldiers make no move. Maybe today, in the face of so many demonstrators, they'll avoid the weekly ritual of tear gas, stun grenades, rubber bullets, injuries. I have more or less convinced myself that this is the case; surely they don't want a confrontation, especially with all the press photographers there. Anyway, this demonstration is firmly nonviolent. But I am wrong. The first line of demonstrators breaks against the wire and the stolid soldiers. Scuffles break out. Halfway up the hill, Gadi signals to me to lead a group over to the right, to break through the line of soldiers on the crest. I'm not sure why this is a good idea—this is another one of those moments when my lack of true political instincts suddenly becomes clear—but I trust *his* instincts. I head up the hill with the others. Some manage to dash past the soldiers; some are pushed back downhill, rather brutally. The officer in charge is yelling, "Get down from my line!" I reach the top, and a soldier rushes at me; I try to get beyond him, and he blocks me, pushes at me. Soon another one or two run up to stand beside him, and I reluctantly retreat.

The ritual remorselessly unfolds. First the stun grenades, which no longer bother me, though the noise is bad enough; then the tear gas, which is much worse. The acrid taste burns my tongue, my eyes, my face. The Palestinians are rushing wildly downhill, back toward the village, and I follow in their wake—trying to get past the range of the gas. Hamutal has thoughtfully provided me with a sliver of onion, the only effective antidote; I breathe it in, wipe my face with it. My breathing is mostly unaffected, but another few volleys of gas pushes us farther down the hill. We regroup, study the situation. On the crest, the line of soldiers wavers; the demonstrators move up, seem almost to overwhelm them, then are turned away like a wave that has crashed against the shore. There is quite a lot of shouting. I learn later that Gadi, with his remarkable presence of mind, has used the occasion for a little political education. Under his guidance, some of the volunteers engage the soldiers: "What are you doing here? This land belongs to Bil'in." A Druze soldier shouts back: "So what? I have my own land; others have theirs." "But this land is theirs, and you are stealing it by force." A Russian soldier releases a string of curses and is answered patiently by a Russian-speaking volunteer; the soldier hears him and blushes crimson, apparently ashamed.

I move up the hill again, then back, following the rhythm of this strangely disarticulated, mostly leaderless, human mass. In the midst of the hubbub, there is even time for snippets of conversation, time to tell my friends that I am leaving for India in ten days. "Be sure to solve all the problems," I say to them, "before I get back in late August." Tear-gas canisters arc over us, leaving a thick white tail in the sky. We cover our mouths and nostrils as best we can. Still, the quantities are not that impressive, hardly more than a pointed reminder of who has the guns and the real power. At one point it seems that the soldiers have had enough, that they will withdraw—a powerful surge from our side seems to flood the top of the hill, but again we are driven back. This is the moment when the village teenagers, true to their weekly routine, steal up through the olive trees and start slinging stones at the soldiers. They are, no doubt, angry, and they are very young; perhaps they have waited all week for this moment, the test of courage, the sweetness of risk, the hope for revenge. I don't know, and it is not for me to stop them. The soldiers crouch or lie down and carefully take aim. Sharp cracks from the rifles—so different from the blunt indifference of the grenades—punctuate the wild symphony of cries and shouts, the bulldozer grinding away as the background drone.

Surprisingly, today there are no serious injuries; the rubber bullets apparently miss their mark. But even as the demonstrators begin to wind their way back to the village, a new melody is added to the cacophony. The Palestinians pressed up against the wire fence begin to hit at it with pipes and hammers. An uncanny metallic clatter swells and ebbs as the fence itself begins to vibrate and sing. Louder, now, and louder: it is the sound of the prisoners shaking their cage, and soon it has drowned out all the rest, even the thin, high splatter of the rubber bullets and the occasional detonation of the gas grenades. It is perhaps the most unsettling music I have ever heard, this fierce clanging and banging of metal on wire, at times rising to a frantic pitch, at others falling almost to a grinding groan. It has its own unpredictable rhythm, and it refuses to stop. There is no conductor to regulate it, no score, no climax, no apparent structure, only the relentless, endless beating and pounding by hundreds of ordinary, innocent human beings who have been hounded and hurt and shot at and humiliated and fenced in and robbed, and who have, for this one hour, again found their voice.

7

Epilogue

There are really only two ways. The one currently pursued by the Israeli government, in all its agencies, is the path of stubborn, violent coercion. The extreme nationalists of the Israeli right have a vision that is easy enough to comprehend; it is embodied daily in a thousand acts and signs. They want to crush Palestinian nationalism as a historical force, and the Palestinian people as a collective; to hem the Palestinians within isolated enclaves and to cut off any hope of their sustaining a national existence with a basis on the ground; and, in the course of achieving this, to annex as much land (with as few living Palestinians attached to it) as possible. In short, this is an uncompromising vision of domination and control. The right, clinging to all the violent memories of the past, fears the Palestinians and inhabits a mental universe in which the only safe option is to attack, punish, destroy, incarcerate, and contain. Such people perceive any alternative approach or action, based on compromise and negotiation and on acknowledging one's own responsibility for what has happened, as an existential threat. Thus they are prepared to live indefinitely with ongoing occupation, in one form or another; they are also willing to make occasional, relatively minor sacrifices, like the withdrawal from Gaza, in order to ensure the continuation of the main colonial enterprise. A regime of total control, constant application of brute force, the rape of the land—all these are acceptable, indeed necessary, if the Jews are to survive.

This bleak, self-perpetuating vision encompasses all levels and the system as a whole, embracing its most strident and primitive voices. All of us are caught up in this system, from the police officer who terrorizes the village of Isawiyya to the young recruit learning how to handle weapons to the mother who, however fearfully or reluctantly, sees her son off to the army and accepts his (or her) fate. All of us are bound to the wheel of death; at most we can hope that it will, as Rilke promised, "coolly disdain to destroy us"—for the moment. Yet each one of us is also free, truly and authentically free, free to make a choice, though we may find this freedom burdensome, irksome, even frightening.

A somewhat similar, no less violent system exists on the "other," Palestinian side, but it cannot concern me here. This conflict is not a war of the sons of light with the sons of darkness; both sides are dark, both are given to organized violence and terror, and both resort constantly to self-righteous justification and a litany of victimization, the bread-and-butter of ethnic conflict. My concern in these pages is with the darkness on my side. In this respect, looking inward at Israeli society and listening to its public discourse, I tend to agree with the Greek poet Seferis, who, at the end of his life, experienced the terror of the colonels' regime: "There are always," he said, "but two parties—Socrates, and his accusers." One must choose.

There is no doubt in my mind that the nationalist fanatics are wrong; not only cruel and unfeeling, not simply limited, narrow, and mean, but deeply and disastrously wrong. Domination, humiliation, threats, assassinations, raids, missiles, bombs, arrests, demolitions, expulsions, more and more coercion—none of it will work. The strategy of the right is shortsighted and certain to fail. There is another way. It is no secret. The only questions are whether and how we are going to find our way to it, together, and how long it will take. Also, of course, how many will die on the way.

*July 22, 2004   Jerusalem: To Save One Person**

A week of good-bye parties. Leena, Tom, and Itai were sent off on Sunday. Leena is going to New York for five years with a scholarship from NYU. Tom will teach in Richmond. Tonight, at Yigal's, we part from Catherine and Neve, who are leaving for Berkeley for a year.

Everyone recognizes that Neve has been instrumental in building the Jerusalem Ta'ayush group—patiently, with astonishing perseverance and foresight. I look around at the faces I know from the convoys, the demonstrations, the barricades. Salomke. Amnon. Irit. Natasha. Yuri. Anat and Anat. Kinneret. Hillel. Yair. Shie. Muhammad. Tom. Nili. Yigal. Galila. Ezra. Manal. Aviad. Khulood. Amiel. And many more. All of them gentle, determined, good-hearted human beings, who are willing to take risks. It is this willingness to face risk that is, for me, most crucial. As always, I ask myself, uneasily: Have I done enough? Have I earned the company of these friends?

Yigal has spent the afternoon in Sawahreh. He gave a speech in Arabic: "Now is the time," he said, "for nonviolent resistance; now, as the wall is being built between Sawahreh Sharqiya and Sawahreh Gharbiya." Apparently, he fired them up; our next demonstration will probably be there. He is sad tonight; Neve is his closest friend. They met nearly twenty years ago, in a dingy hotel in Delhi. Since then there have been years of political work together, and the inimitable closeness that such shared work brings.

Amnon speaks, poking fun, also invoking honored ghosts. "Catherine is a reincarnation," he says, "of Rosa Luxemburg"— and I heartily concur. Ever since I first saw her marching through the barricades in South Hebron, I have thought of her as an instinctive revolutionary. She was born to the manner, unlike me; I hate tear gas and police charges. I also seem to lack a talent for the unequivocal. I think politics is always equivocal, confusing, and incapable of resolution; that is the necessary ground for acting.

*Jerusalem Talmud, Sanhedrin 22A.

For some reason—perhaps it is the serenity of this summer night or the sadness of saying good-bye—the always latent skeptical undertones break through the surface tonight and, as so many times in the past, we start to ask ourselves if what we have done and continue to do makes sense. We are, for the most part, modern, post-Enlightenment secularists; doubt and irony are perhaps the deepest sources of our strength. Let us, then, look back, look ahead; let us consider the path. We speak of justice, of fairness, of human evil, of the crimes, large or small, that might be mitigated by our actions. But does any of it really matter? The world remains unchanged. In Israel, the situation is worse today than when we began four years ago. The Israeli right continues to rule, to pursue its vicious, autistic program, to determine, by and large, the rules of play. Let us say, moreover, that the Palestinians do someday get their state and their postage stamps and their blood-stained flag; let us say the occupation ends—will not all this, too, seem grotesque in a few years? It is only because we are so caught up in it that we cannot see this. So why act?

Yuri gives, what else, the Confucian answer. "You follow your conscience not in order to change the world but in order to be a noble person. You are prepared to go against all norms, conventions, dictates, and decrees, even to risk your life, in order to remain true to yourself. This," Yuri promises, with uncharacteristic optimism, "leads to immortality. At the very least, you can look at yourself in the mirror without disgust."

Neve answers him. He has a different name for the immortal: history, or History, a transcendent witness. History will know and will judge. He cites Hannah Arendt. "There is a need for stories, more and more of them, stories of resistance to collective evil. If there are enough such stories, the evil will be blocked. If only there had been more at other, critical times. There will be a record, and the record is like God. It is always worth acting for the record."

Yigal, from the edge of the courtyard, disagrees. "We will never have the privilege of knowing what history will think of us. We cannot know. That, in fact, is the hope. We act, as we must, without ever knowing which of our actions and which of our words will make a difference. We cannot know at what point or points, in what hidden or subtle domain, change begins."

But for me, history is fantasy; even time itself is possibly, probably, less than real. I don't believe "history" will ever be able to think about us or anything else. What is real is this moment, these people, the sliver of moon in the summer sky, the Passiflora tree in the courtyard, the crimson wine, the inevitable sweetness of confusion, the musical murmur of the words, and the profound, ironic happiness of doing what is right in circumstances of rooted, inherent, unresolvable ambiguity. Because of the ambiguity. Without thought of consequence. Without calculating this way or that. Without a future, though there is, still, a past rushing away from us minute by minute—partly a Jewish past with its dead voices whispering in my memory. "Bind the wounds. Heal the sick. Don't forget you were slaves. To save one person is to save a world. Don't be afraid. All that lives is holy. Forgive. Wake up. Shake off the dust and stand up. Feed the hungry. Bring the poor into your home. Cover the naked. Break their chains." Did I invent these voices? They seem to speak from some buried, dreamlike domain, as distant and insistent as childhood. It is nothing to be right, and a true disaster to be righteous, but it is everything to do what you can.

Our true enemy is elsewhere, much closer to home, the one who sits, complacent, in government offices or in the army's high command or in the passivity of the home. (Let our Palestinian friends deal with their own violent counterparts to such people; that is not our business.) We will meet our foe at every point—every house he demolishes, every olive tree he uproots, every rocky field he is intent on stealing. We will engage him over and over, without violence. We will watch and record and bear witness, and, from time to time, we will stop him. He has guns; we have each other, determination, and some dogged convictions about what it means to be human. That, and a certain dark hope.

Postscript

September 28, 2006   Beit 'Anun: Refusing to Be Enemies

Distance and the passage of time may impart a certain clarity. I spent the last seven months in India, blissfully removed from the ongoing tribal wars in Israel-Palestine. I lived and thought in another language—Telugu—and I can assure you that Telugu sees the world quite differently from how it looks, say, in Hebrew. Distance exposes the imbecility of tribal war.

Reentry has been uneasy. Israel is gripped by collective depression. During the time I was away, she went to war in Lebanon and lost. No one likes to lose a war, but for the Jews the descent into hysteria is immediate. The war revealed for all to see the limits of coercive force. But in the absence of an option to coerce, Israelis panic. Either one forces one's will on a recalcitrant world, or one is utterly impotent. There is no space in between. For the first time in decades, Israelis feel faced with an all too familiar, and perhaps for this reason somewhat gratifying, existential threat.

One predictable result is the meteoric rise, in the polls, of the Fascist right. Were elections held today, it seems the extreme right—parties openly advocating the physical expulsion of the entire Palestinian population living west of the Jordan River—would garner at least 20 percent of the vote. The dangers to

Israeli democracy, from within, are more severe than before the war. For the moment, people are caught up in what the media keeps calling a "crisis in leadership"—as if the public at large bore no responsibility for the catastrophic slippage over the last years. Almost everyone—with the possible exception of the prime minister, the minister of defense, and the chief of staff—agrees that the war was criminally mismanaged (yes, this is the word they use; war is something to be managed). Decision after decision was dead wrong. Turning the provocation by the Hezbollah into a casus belli was a mistake, and pursuing the war after the first week, indeed expanding it, was an even greater mistake. All this is easy to acknowledge. But when it comes to the continuing occupation, the ever-expanding settlements, the refusal to enter into negotiations, the fateful transformation of the Israel Defense Forces into a kind of upgraded anti-terrorist organization specializing in targeted assassinations—very few, it seems, are prepared to recognize what all this has done to the very viability of a Jewish state. As for the immense devastation Israel inflicted on Lebanon—truly no one seems to care.

We are in the Ten Days of Repentance, between New Year (Rosh Hashanah) and the Day of Atonement (Yom Kippur)—the most solemn extended moment in the Jewish calendar, a time of soul-searching and repentance. Each morning pious Jews recite the lyrical pleas for forgiveness, *slichot*. There is all too much that needs to be forgiven. So today has been chosen for a protest visit to Hebron: the Children of Abraham—a peace group founded two years ago to work in this city, to protect Palestinian civilians from the depredations of the settlers—is bringing a busload of activists to demonstrate. We are carrying signs inscribed with passages from classical Jewish texts, mostly verses from the Bible and the prayer book about confessing our sins and the pressing need for a true turning of the heart, *tshuvah*. The Hebron settlers, among the most ruthless in the occupied territories, won't like these inscriptions.

But there is a good chance we'll never make it that far. Even before we get on the bus in Jerusalem, we hear that the army has declared all of Hebron a closed military zone—in our honor. This is their usual tactic; they will be waiting for us. We will have to try to sneak into the city from some secondary road, probably through what is known as H1—that part of the city that is under Palestinian control. Entering H1 is a crime for Israelis, and there is an excellent chance that some or all of us will be arrested by the army or the border police as soon as we reenter Israeli-controlled Hebron (H2). Eran, briefing us before departure, says: "Anyone who isn't eager to be arrested should leave now, without any hard feelings."

I had forgotten, I think, how harsh it is, this business of working for peace; how close one is, at any moment, to violence or danger, to prolonged discomfort and the temporary loss of freedom. It all comes back to me like a sudden blow. Hagit, a new face, takes the microphone to add a few words about the experience of being arrested. She is casual, nonchalant: "It is a ritual," she says, "that they like to go through. One just has to wait until it's over. Usually it goes no further; usually there are no indictments." She is high-spirited and confident; she seems even to enjoy the repeated cat-and-mouse game with the soldiers. This, too, I had forgotten—the amazing, straightforward courage of these young people, committed to making peace, prepared to take the risks.

But then I think to myself: Don't idealize. No heroics, please. We don't need any more heroes; they are always a huge nuisance. Sometimes they're positively dangerous—I remember them well from the (first) war in Lebanon. The great beauty of the young people gathered for today's demonstration lies in their sweet ordinariness. We're not so special. Probably everyone here has come, as I have come, for all sorts of wildly obscure, oblique reasons. Out of loyalty to one another, to friends; nothing is worse than the shame of letting them down. Out of a certain insouciant taste for adventure, for something outside the usual routine. Out of anger—the rage at having been lied to by our government for years and years, at having been made silently complicit in *their* crimes. Out of the need to put oneself to the test. And then—last on the list—out of some kind of inchoate, stubborn moral sense, after all, projected on to the shadow-play screen of politics.

I ask myself if I would mind getting arrested. No, not really. Under current conditions, it might even be something of an honor. I've been through it before. So, as my grandmother would have said, let them arrest me—*abi gesundt*, "as long as we're healthy." Suddenly happy at heart, I climb into the bus.

On the way to the first roadblock, there is time to talk things through with Amiel. "Look at the essential lesson of the war," I say. "If there were rational people in the Israeli establishment, in the army command or the intelligence community, they would surely come to the conclusion that our best chance is to cut a deal, as quickly as possible, with whatever moderate forces exist on the 'other side'; failing that, there will be destruction here on a scale that we can't sustain." He agrees but, to my surprise, offers an optimistic reading of the situation. "The optimal condition for forward movement is when both sides think they have (more or less) won the last war—like now." That was what happened after the Yom Kippur War, thirty-three years ago, when the old leadership was thrown out after massive public protest. "Yes," I say, "but today's grassroots protesters are already fading away." "Then, too, it took some time." I have never heard him so full of hope—and this after he has just described to me how the peace movement has shrunk over the last months, how overworked and exhausted the activists are. "There is," he says, "an amazing level of activity, but very few activists left in the field." "It sounds," I say, "like the Buddhist notion that suffering is real, though there is no sufferer."

We pass the roadblock at al-Khadr. The second one, farther south, is more formidable, but the soldiers make no attempt to stop us. Roadblock number three, close to Hebron, is another matter. It's clear we have no chance of getting by; Ezra, who has gone ahead, calls to say we will have to take an alternative route. So the bus zigzags through the hills, along smaller roads that hug the villages. Soon, however, we notice that we have "guests"—a police escort in unmarked cars. They are on to us, and they are ready.

Our only option is to abandon the bus and make our way on foot to a bus stop just inside H1, where we can, with luck, catch Palestinian buses or taxis. We slow down to let the police car pass us on the road; then the bus stops, and we rush outside. We clamber up a small footpath to a long, dusty road leading into Hebron. These are good moments; I am glad to rediscover the peculiar, heady freedom that comes from walking over the hills, under the noses of the soldiers, toward a goal that makes sense to me. We have a few minutes of grace as we wait, praying a bus will come quickly. Instead soldiers turn up, a large contingent. They have found us. They block the road on all sides. We are stuck.

Hebron recedes. We wind our way back to our bus, drive a few kilometers, disembark again on the main north-south highway, Road Number 60. Here we will make our stand. We gather up our signs and start marching north toward the huge settlement of Qiryat Arba', the Jewish suburb of Hebron. The signs are more eloquent than usual. Mine says: *Lema'an nechdal mi-'osheq yadeinu*, "So that we may end the oppression wrought by our own hands"—one of those haunting phrases from the prayer book for Yom Kippur. Others read: "Now is the time for *tshuvah*, the turning of the heart." "Let us repent: re-open the Shuhada Road" (the main street of Hebron, closed by settlers to Palestinians). Somewhat mysteriously: "Go not up, for the Lord is not among you" (Numbers 14:42; this one was Hillel's doing, and he will have to explain). Or, in a different mode: "Who killed Nibin Jamjum?" She was a young Palestinian girl who happened to be standing in the doorway of her house in July 2002, when a contingent of armed settlers walked by; one of them shot her dead, just for the fun of it. In itself, that is nothing so unusual. But in this case, there was not even a minimal effort to find the killer; the police failed to open a file and refused to investigate.

An impressive convoy of police and border police pulls up beside us; rapidly they push us to the edge of the road. Where, exactly, are we? Nowhere. Anywhere. So why protest here? But in a way, that is the point. Any spot, randomly chosen on the highway south to Hebron, has the same explosive horror, the same surreal conflation of ancient villages and their vineyards and olive groves, new housing units for settlers with their guns and watchtowers and barbed wire, drab army jeeps, border police, the regular ("blue") police, a donkey or two, or maybe a camel, religious Jews (mostly settlers) driving by in their skullcaps and *tzitzit* fringes, a maze of signposts pointing helplessly into the labyrinth of fences within fences, stolen fields, pieces of the old Palestine looped awkwardly inside the ugly urban sprawl of expanding Israel.... Also, of course, there will be the same eerie intensity of light and taste, the same sense of a world soaked in old wisps of words. So we might as well stand here. Our signs are in Hebrew, but we quickly convert a few into Arabic for the sake of the Palestinians who wander past. Let them know that someone cares.

After a while the police allow us to shift our operation to a larger intersection farther up the highway, just outside the village of Beit ʿAnun. Standing there in the afternoon sun, we chant a few slogans in Hebrew and Arabic: *"naʿam liʾs-salam, la liʾ l-ihtilal"*: "Yes to Peace, No to Occupation." "One, two, three, four, now is the time for *te-shu-vah*." *"Bi-khalil wa-bi-lachish, al-banat bidha taʿish"*: "In Hebron and in Lachish, young girls just want to live." Most beautiful of all—someone's spontaneous flash of inspired rhyme—*"mi-khalil li-Bilʿin / mesarvim lihyot oyevim"*: "From Hebron to Bilʿin / we refuse to be enemies!" And so on. Does anyone hear us? Some settlers roll down the windows of their cars to spit at us. I'm glad if we have irritated them, even for a moment. An elegant Palestinian gentleman stares, a little incredulous, at this odd confabulation of Israeli peace activists standing outside his home; then he breaks into a smile and, with great dignity, waves his fingers at us with the V-sign. A tall, thin Palestinian woman, completely draped in black, walks slowly past, listening intently; then she says in a melodious whisper, *"Naʿam liʾs-salam"*: "Yes to Peace."

Before we leave, Hillel speaks for a few minutes, directing his words more, I think, to the dozens of policemen and soldiers sent here to contain us. Hillel had a good classical education in Jewish texts. He also speaks a perfect Arabic. In the old days, he would wander from village to village in the territories, welcomed into many homes. He knows every corner of Palestine, and as he warms to his theme, all the old passion breaks through. "It is not by chance that we have come here today, in the Ten Days of Repentance. These are days of accounting and looking into one's heart. The people of Israel are, we believe, in a bad way; a bad *moral* way. We couldn't stay at home under these conditions. We came to Hebron because Hebron is the epitome of everything that is wrong with the Jews—a place of terrible violence, of robbery, of profound arrogance and contempt for other human beings. These sins are so severe that they come close to undermining the right of the people of Israel to live in the Land of Israel. It is not that we think that we are much better than the settlers in Hebron; but we want them to think again about the path that they have chosen. We hope for a change of heart.

"There is this sign that we are holding: 'Go not up, for the Lord is not among you.' It comes from the Torah reading of Shelach, from the book of Numbers, which tells of the twelve men Moses sent to spy out the Land of Israel. They also passed through Hebron. When they came back to the Israelites in the desert, ten of the spies 'spread an evil report of the land,' saying that it is a land 'that eateth up the inhabitants thereof.' But two of the spies, Joshua the son of Nun and Caleb the son of Jephunneh, said, 'The land which we passed through to spy it out, is an exceeding good land, a land which floweth with milk and honey.' And these two spoke the truth. For truly this is a good, good land, a beautiful land. Then some of the Israelites tried to go up to the land, although Moses warned them: 'Go not up, for the Lord is not among you.' But they disregarded his words, and they were killed by the Canaanites and the Amalekites.

"That is how it is. If God is not in your midst, then it is not possible to go up. And God is not in the midst of those who murder and those who steal. We know what it is that God wants of us—it is not so difficult to know; he has told us: 'Do justice, love mercy, and walk humbly with your God' (Micah 6:8). That is what we must do, and it means we have to stop stealing. It makes no difference if it is the home or field of one man that is stolen, or the lands and homes of an entire village or of a city like Hebron. We cannot pray on Yom Kippur unless we stop the theft."

I would so much like to believe that at least one of the soldiers or the policemen has heard him and is beginning the slow process of changing his mind.

We leave, a little happy, a little miserable—we didn't reach Hebron. On the way back, I think to myself: This is how it will be. Not forever, but for now, and into the foreseeable future. For now, the settlers will remain in place; for now, the greed, the hate, the killing of innocents with impunity—all this will continue against the constant background screech of the self-righteous. Policemen will do their duty. Soldiers will follow orders, no matter how wrong or foolish these orders may be. Perhaps there will be another needless war. And in the midst of it all, there will be the lonely few, on both sides, who refuse to be enemies, who will take any risk for the other's sake and for the sake of peace.

Glossary

Al-Haram al-Sharif. The sacred enclosure including the Dome of the Rock and the Al-Aqsa Mosque on the ancient Temple Mount in Jerusalem.

Bagatz. Hebrew acronym for the Israeli High Court of Justice; short for an appeal submitted to this court or a ruling by it.

Bat Shalom. Israeli feminist grassroots organization of Jewish and Palestinian Israeli women working together for a genuine peace in the Middle East. In 1994 Bat Shalom joined with a Palestinian organization, the Jerusalem Center for Women, to form the Jerusalem Link.

Brit Shalom. A movement founded in 1925 by Jewish intellectuals and scholars in Palestine (including Shmuel Hugo Bergman, Ernst Simon, and Gershom Scholem) working toward Arab-Jewish dialogue and coexistence. The name is taken from Ezekiel 32:25.

B'Tselem. Israeli Information Center for Human Rights in the Occupied Territories (founded 1989). The name, literally "in the image," derives from Genesis 9:6: "For in His image did God make man."

CPT. Christian Peacemaker Team, an organization of pacifist volunteers serving in Hebron and the South Hebron Hills to protect Palestinian civilians from settler violence (recently, the CPT is also active in Iraq).

dunam. A unit of land measure = 1,000 square meters.

Gemara. Aramaic commentary on the Mishnah or the codified oral law; together, Mishnah and Gemara constitute the Talmud.

Green Line. The pre-1967 boundaries of Israel and the Palestinian territories of the West Bank and Gaza.

Gush Shalom. "Peace Bloc," founded by Uri Avnery in 1993.

Haaretz. Major Israeli daily newspaper.

HaKampus Lo Shotek. "The Campus Will Not Be Silent." Organization of students and faculty at Hebrew University and Tel Aviv University working for peace.

HaMoked. Literally, "Focal Point": the Center for the Defence of the Individual, a Jerusalem-based human rights organization concentrating on discrimination and abuse in the occupied territories.

ICAHD. The Israeli Committee Against House Demolitions, a non-violent, direct-action organization formed to resist Israel's destruction of Palestinian homes in the Occupied Territories and Jerusalem and to assist Palestinian victims of Israeli policy (incorporated July 2004).

'Id al-Adha. The Muslim holiday of sacrifice, also known as 'Id al-Qurbān, beginning on the tenth day of the month Dhu al-Hijja and continuing for four days; the holiday marks the culmination of the *hajj* or pilgrimage to Mecca.

keffiyeh. Checkered head scarf worn by Arab males.

Ketziot. A large military prison in the far south of the country.

khirbeh. In Arabic, literally "ruin"; small pastoralist settlements in the South Hebron Hills.

Machsom Watch. Founded in January 2001 by Ronnee Jaeger, Adi Kuntsman, and Yehudit Keshet, this organization of women volunteers monitors the behavior of Israeli soldiers and officials toward Palestinian civilians at the dozens of army checkpoints in the occupied territories.

Minchah. The afternoon prayer.

miri. "State" land under the Ottoman-period agrarian system; land not registered in the name of private owners.

Moledet. Right-wing Israeli party, founded in 1988 by Rehavam Ze'evi, advocating physical "transfer"—i.e., expulsion—of all Palestinians from territory west of the Jordan River. (Following Zeevi's killing, the leadership of the party was assumed by Beni Elon.)

Motzei Shabbat. Saturday night, after the ending of the Shabbat day of rest.

Mukhabbarat. Arabic for Shin Bet, the General Security Service.

Netivot Shalom. Also called Oz Veshalom, a Zionist peace movement founded in 1975 to foster tolerance, pluralism, and justice in accordance with traditional Jewish values.

New Profile. Organization of Israeli feminist men and women dedicated to the "civilization of Israeli society," fundamental human rights, and the struggle against the occupation of Palestinian territory.

Rabbis for Human Rights. Founded in 1988, this organization of 130 rabbis has been remarkably effective in protecting Palestinian farmers from threats by settlers to everyday agricultural tasks such as planting and harvesting; in rebuilding Palestinian houses destroyed by Israel; in replanting trees (over 10,000) in devastated Palestine areas; and in human rights and educational work within Israel.

refusenik. The common Hebrew term for soldiers refusing to serve in the Israeli army on grounds of conscience.

Russian Compound (Arabic: Moskubiyya). Jerusalem police headquarters, situated in downtown Jerusalem in buildings erected in the late nineteenth century to house Russian pilgrims.

Sayyeret Matkal. General Staff Reconnaissance, a prestigious commando unit in the Israeli army.

shahid. Arabic "martyr"; the usual term for those who have been killed, also for those who kill themselves as suicide bombers, in the struggle against Israel.

Shavuot. The spring harvest festival of Pentecost.

Shin Bet. General Security Service or Israel Security Service, responsible for internal security matters.

Shulchan Aruch. Codification of Jewish law by Joseph Caro (sixteenth century).

Yesh Gvul. "There Is a Limit"; a movement, founded during the Lebanon War in 1982, of soldiers refusing to serve in the Israeli army for reasons of conscience.

za'atar. A mixture of wild thyme, sesame, and salt.

Select Dramatis Personae

Amiel, Latinist at the Hebrew University
Amnon, teacher, Jerusalem
Anat, psychologist, Jerusalem
Aviad, journalist, Jerusalem
Catherine, scholar of English literature, Jerusalem and Beersheva
Ezra, activist at the center of the struggle in South Hebron, Jerusalem
Gadi, historian, Tel Aviv University
Galit, folklorist, Hebrew University
Hani, activist, Isawiyya
Irit, film archivist, Jerusalem
Janet, Peace Now activist, Jerusalem
Leena, lawyer and scholar, NYU
Louise, scholar of cultural studies and English literature, Hebrew University
Lucia, ICAHD activist
Manal, lawyer, Jerusalem
Maya, student of comparative literature and German, University of California, Berkeley
Muhammad Abu Hummus, activist, Isawiyya
Natasha, photographer, Jerusalem
Navid, essayist, journalist, scholar, Cologne
Neve, political scientist, Ben-Gurion University, Beersheva
Raanan, filmmaker, Jerusalem

Salomke, psychologist, Jerusalem
Yasmin, linguistic and translator, Tel Aviv
Yigal, Sanskritist, Tel Aviv University
Yuri, Sinologist, Hebrew University